Photo and Video Editing for SENIORS

Studio Visual Steps

Photo and Video Editing for SENIORS

Create fantastic movie and photo projects

www.visualsteps.com

This book has been written using the Visual Steps™ method.
Cover design by Studio Willemien Haagsma bNO

© 2011 Visual Steps
Edited by Mara Kok, Jolanda Ligthart and Rilana Groot
Translated by Chris Hollingsworth, *1ˢᵗ Resources* and Irene Venditti, *i-write* translation services.

First printing: April 2011
ISBN 978 90 5905 167 6

Resources used: Some of the computer terms and definitions seen here in this book have been taken from descriptions found online at the Windows Help and Support website.

Do you have a suggestion or would you like to ask a question?
E-mail: info@visualsteps.com

Would you like more information?
www.visualsteps.com

Website for this book:
www.visualsteps.com/officeseniors
You can also register your book here.

Register your book
By registering your book, you will be kept aware of any important changes that are necessary to you as a user of the book. You can also take advantage of our periodic newsletter informing you of our product releases, company news, tips & tricks, special offers, free guides, etc.

Table of Contents

Appendices

Foreword

Dear readers,

Nowadays, there is a wide variety of programs available to edit photos. One of the most user-friendly is *Windows Live Photo Gallery.* This book covers the most essential features in this program. You can create beautiful pictures in minutes with just a few mouse-clicks. You can arrange your pictures in any order you want and add tags to them. You can also share your photos with others, by making an online photo album, a slide show, or a movie, complete with spoken commentary and sound. You can even use the program to import your photos directly from you digital camera to your computer.

Along with *Windows Live Photo Gallery*, the second program featured in this book is *Windows Live Movie Maker*. This is a free program that allows you to create professional-looking movies with your own video clips and photos. We will explain step by step how to install the program to your computer, and how to use it to create, edit and finalize your movies. Among other things, you can add special effects, transitions, sound and captions to your movie. To be able to show the movie to other people, you will learn how to prepare it and send it by e-mail, burn it to a DVD or upload it to *YouTube*. Finally, we will discuss how to import your videos and photos from a digital video camera, photo camera or a mobile phone.

We hope you have lots of fun with this book!

Emma Schipper and Henk Mol
Studio Visual Steps

P.S. Feel free to send us your comments and suggestions regarding this book. The e-mail address is: info@visualsteps.com

Visual Steps Newsletter

All Visual Steps books follow the same methodology: clear and concise step-by-step instructions with screen shots to demonstrate each task. A complete list of all our books can be found on our website **www.visualsteps.com** You can also sign up to receive our **free Visual Steps Newsletter**.

In this Newsletter you will receive periodic information by e-mail regarding:
- the latest titles and previously released books;
- special offers, supplemental chapters, tips and free informative booklets.
Also, our Newsletter subscribers may download any of the documents listed on the web pages **www.visualsteps.com/info_downloads** and **www.visualsteps.com/tips**
When you subscribe to our Newsletter you can be assured that we will never use your e-mail address for any purpose other than sending you the information as previously described. We will not share this address with any third-party. Each Newsletter also contains a one-click link to unsubscribe.

Introduction to Visual Steps™

The Visual Steps handbooks and manuals are the best instructional materials available for learning how to work with computers and computer programs. Nowhere else will you find better support for getting to know the computer, the Internet, *Windows* or related software.

Properties of the Visual Steps books:
- **Comprehensible contents**
  Addresses the needs of the beginner or intermediate computer user for a manual written in simple, straight-forward English.
- **Clear structure**
  Precise, easy to follow instructions. The material is broken down into small enough segments to allow for easy absorption.
- **Screen shots of every step**
  Quickly compare what you see on your own computer screen with the screen shots in the book. Pointers and tips guide you when new windows are opened so you always know what to do next.
- **Get started right away**
  All you have to do is switch on your computer, place the book next to your keyboard, and begin at once.

In short, I believe these manuals will be excellent guides for you.

dr. H. van der Meij

Faculty of Applied Education, Department of Instruction Technology, University of Twente, the Netherlands

Register Your Book

When you can register your book, you will be kept informed of any important changes that are necessary to you as a user of the book. You can also take advantage of our periodic Newsletter informing you of our product releases, company news, tips & tricks, special offers, etc.

What You Will Need

In order to work through this book, you will need a number of things on your computer:

Your computer should run the English version of **Windows 7** or **Windows Vista** (including *ServicePack 1*). You can check which version you have by starting up your computer and viewing the opening screen. The screen shots in this book have been made on a *Windows 7* computer. If you are working on a *Windows Vista* computer, you may see slightly different windows when compared to the *Windows* screen shots shown in this book. However, this will not affect the operations that are explained in this book.

The programs **Windows Live Photo Gallery**, **Windows Live Movie Maker** and **Windows Live Mail**. In *Chapter 1 Download and Install the Windows Live Essentials programs* you will learn how to download and install the programs that you will need onto your computer.

A printer is recommended. If you do not have a printer, you can just skip the print exercises.

You do not really need to have all the other equipment, such as a digital photo camera or a scanner. In this book you will learn how to use the program by using the practice photos. You can download these from the website that goes with this book.

To burn your movie to DVD, you will need a DVD burner and at least one writable DVD.

How to Use This Book

This book has been written using the Visual Steps™ method. You can work through this book independently at your own pace.

In this Visual Steps™ book, you will see various icons. This is what they mean:

Techniques
These icons indicate an action to be carried out:

 The mouse icon means you should do something with the mouse.

 The keyboard icon means you should type something on the keyboard.

 The hand icon means you should do something else, for example insert a CD-ROM in the computer. It is also used to remind you of something you have learned before.

In addition to these icons, in some areas of this book *extra assistance* is provided to help you successfully work through each chapter.

Help
These icons indicate that extra help is available:

 The arrow icon warns you about something.

 The bandage icon will help you if something has gone wrong.

1 Have you forgotten how to do something? The number next to the footsteps tells you where to look it up at the end of the book in the appendix *How Do I Do That Again?*

In separate boxes you will find tips or additional, background information.

Extra information
Information boxes are denoted by these icons:

 The book icon gives you extra background information that you can read at your convenience. This extra information is not necessary for working through the book.

 The light bulb icon indicates an extra tip for using the program.

Prior Computer Experience

If you want to use this book, you will need some basic computer skills. If you do not have these skills, it is a good idea to read one of the following books first:

 **Windows 7 for SENIORS**
Studio Visual Steps
ISBN 978 90 5905 126 3

 **Windows Vista for SENIORS**
Studio Visual Steps
ISBN 978 90 5905 274 1

Test Your Knowledge

Have you finished reading this book? Then test your knowledge with a test. Visit the website: **www.ccforseniors.com**

This multiple-choice test will tell you how good your knowledge is of the *Office* applications covered in this book. If you pass the test, you will receive your free *Computer Certificate* by e-mail.

Website

On the website that accompanies this book, **www.visualsteps.com/photovideoediting**, you will find practice files and further information. This website will also keep you informed of any errata, recent updates or other changes you need to be aware of, as a user of the book.
Don't forget to visit our website **www.visualsteps.com** from time to time to read about new books and other useful information such as handy computer tips, frequently asked questions and informative booklets.

For Teachers

This book is designed as a self-study guide. It is also well suited for use in a group or a classroom setting. For this purpose, we offer a free teacher's manual containing information about how to prepare for the course (including didactic teaching methods) and testing materials. You can download this teacher's manual (PDF file) from the website which accompanies this book: **www.visualsteps.com/ photovideoediting**

The Screen Shots

The screen shots in this book were made on a computer running *Windows 7 Ultimate* edition. The screen shots used in this book indicate which button, folder, file or hyperlink you need to click on your computer screen. In the instruction text (in **bold** letters) you will see a small image of the item you need to click. The black line will point you to the right place on your screen.
The small screen shots that are printed in this book are not meant to be completely legible all the time. This is not necessary, as you will see these images on your own computer screen in real size and fully legible.

Here you see an example of an instruction text and a screen shot. The black line indicates where to find this item on your own computer screen:

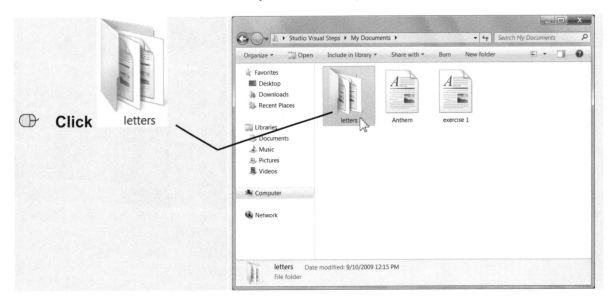

Sometimes the screen shot shows only a portion of a window. Here is an example:

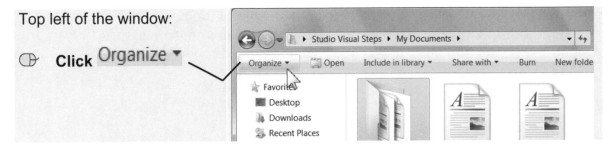

It really will **not be necessary** for you to read all the information in the screen shots in this book. Always use the screen shots in combination with the image you see on your own computer screen.

1. Download and Install the Required Windows Live Essentials Programs

You can download the *Photo Gallery*, *Movie Maker* and *Windows Live Mail* programs from the Internet for free. These programs are *Windows Live Essentials* programs. In this chapter we will explain how to download the programs.

You can use the *Photo Gallery* program to view, edit and manage your photos. For example, you can present your pictures in a slide show. You can also add labels or captions to your photos, which will help you find them more quickly.

The *Movie Maker* program offers you the possibility to make a movie out of your own movie clips and photos. You will be able to create an attractive movie by adding animated transitions, special effects, text and music to your images.

Photo Gallery and *Movie Maker* also contain options for sharing your videos and photos with others. You can do this with e-mail or by uploading the files to the Internet.

The *Windows Live Mail* program can be used to send e-mail messages. It is not necessary to download and install *Windows Live Mail*. If you do not want to use the program, you can skip some of the sections in *Chapter 5 Printing and Mailing Photos*.

You will also learn how to download the practice files to the hard disk of your computer.

In this chapter you will learn how to:

- download and install the required programs;
- download the practice files.

 Please note:

If you have already installed *Windows Live Photo Gallery*, *Movie* Maker or *Mail* to your computer, you may just want to glance through this chapter.

1.1 Downloading and Installing Programs

To download *Windows Live Photo Gallery, Movie Maker* and *Mail*, you will need to visit the *Windows Live Essentials* website. First, you open *Internet Explorer*.

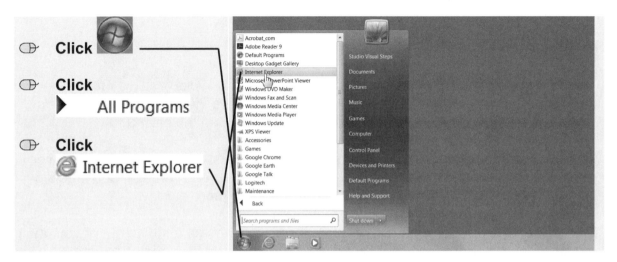

☞ **Click**

☞ **Click**

▶   All Programs

☞ **Click**

    🌐 Internet Explorer

💡 Tip

Open Internet Explorer from the taskbar or desktop

If the *Internet Explorer* icon is located on your taskbar, just click the icon . If the

Internet Explorer icon is on your desktop, double-click the icon Internet Explorer .

The screen shots in this book have been created with *Internet Explorer 9*. If you are using version 8, your windows will look somewhat different. This will not affect the operations handled here.

☞ **Open the web page download.live.com**
👣3

☞ **Click**

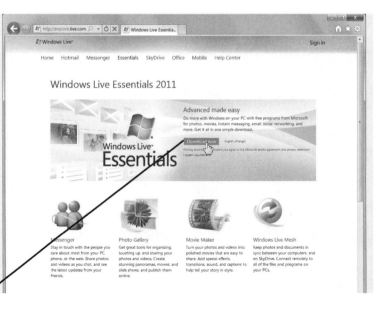

In *Internet Explorer 9* a small pop-up window will appear at the bottom of your screen:

In *Internet Explorer 8* you will see a small window.

You can run the program:

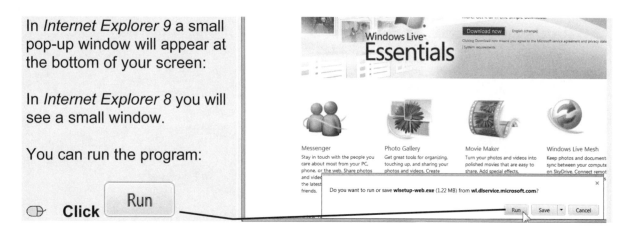

$\oplus$ **Click** Run

Your screen may turn dark and you will be asked for permission to continue:

$\oplus$ **If necessary, click** Yes **or** Continue

$\oplus$ **Click**
  ➔ Choose the programs y

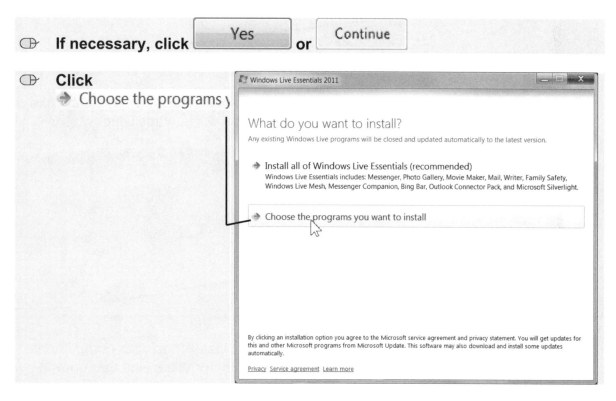

Now you will see the *Windows Live Essentials* installation window. Here you can select the programs you want to install. *Photo Gallery* and *Movie Maker* can only be installed together, not as separate programs.

➥**Please note:**

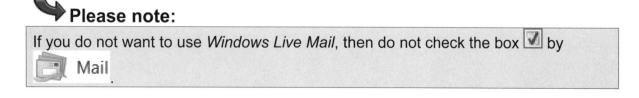

If you do not want to use *Windows Live Mail*, then do not check the box ☑ by

Mail.

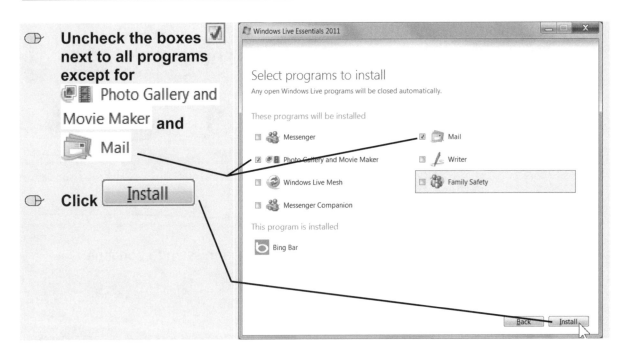

Windows Live Photo Gallery, *Movie Maker* and *Mail* will be installed. This may take a little while. After the programs have been installed, you will see this window:

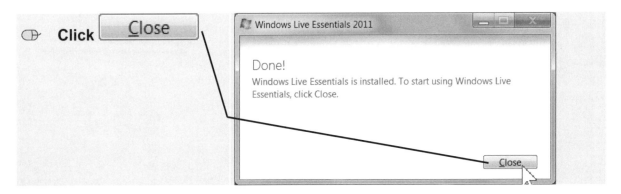

Now *Photo Gallery*, *Movie Maker* and *Mail* have been installed to your computer. In the next few sections you will learn how to download the practice files that go with this book.

1.2 Download the Practice Files for Photo Gallery

As you work through this book, you will need to use the practice files to perform the exercises as described. It is a good idea to download these practice files before you begin. Here is how to do that:

☞ **Open the www.visualsteps.com/photovideoediting web page** ✌³

Now you will see the website that accompanies this book. On the *Practice files* page you can download the practice files:

⟶ **Click** **Practice files**

Now you will see the compressed folder that contains the practice files. You are going to copy this folder to the *(My) Pictures* folder:

⟶ **Right-click**
[Practice files Photo Editing]

You will see this menu:

⟶ **Click** Save target as...

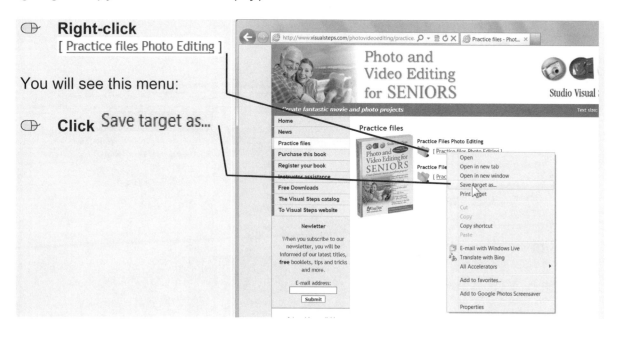

⊕ By 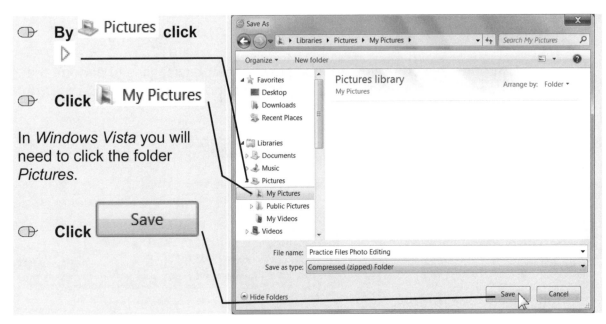 Pictures **click**
    ▷

⊕ **Click** 📁 My Pictures

In *Windows Vista* you will
need to click the folder
Pictures.

⊕ **Click** Save

Once the file has finished
downloading, in *Internet
Explorer 9* you will see a bar
at the bottom of the window:

In *Internet Explorer 8* you will
see a window.

⊕ **Click** Open folder

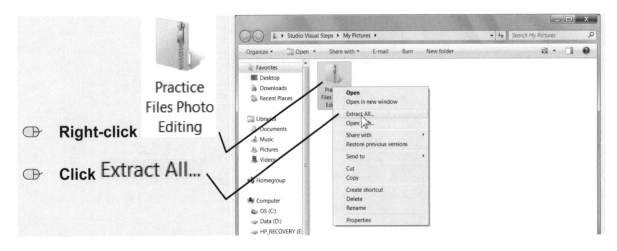

⊕ **Right-click** Practice
                   Files Photo
                   Editing

⊕ **Click** Extract All...

You are going to extract the files:

☞ **If necessary, uncheck the box ☑ next to** Show extracted files when c

☞ **Click** Extract

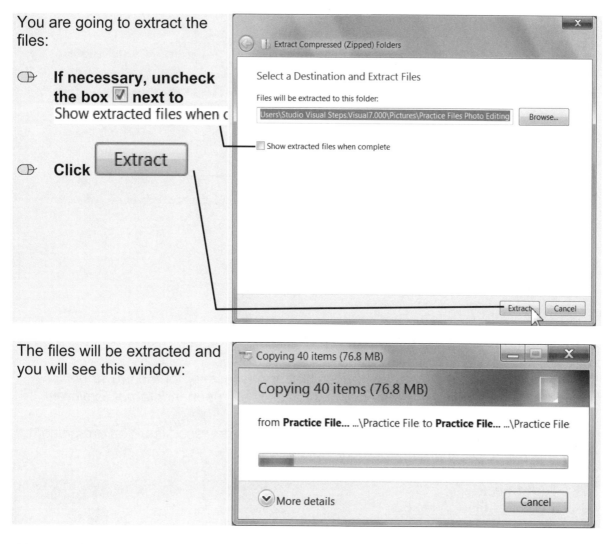

The files will be extracted and you will see this window:

Now the folder with the practice files has been saved in the (*My*) *Pictures* folder:

You can delete the compressed folder:

Practice Files Photo Editing

☞ **Right-click**

☞ **Click** Delete

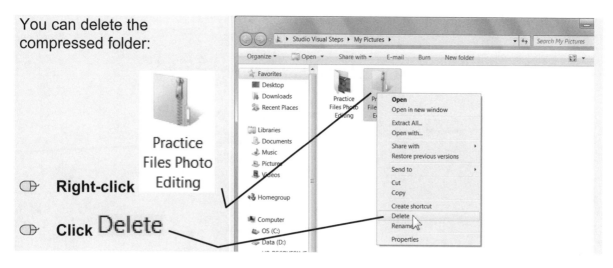

Now you will see the *Delete Folder* window:

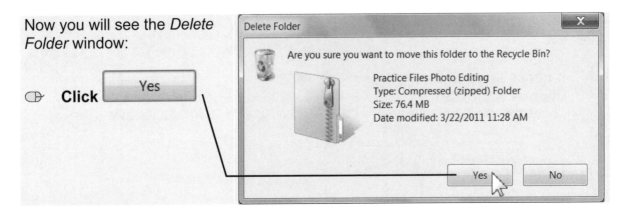

👆 **Click** Yes

The compressed folder has been deleted:

☞ **Close the folder window** 𝄞²

1.3 Download the Practice Files for Movie Maker

You can also download the practice files that are necessary for the *Movie Maker* chapters. The web page with the download files is still open in *Internet Explorer*.

You will see the compressed folder that contains the practice files. You are going to copy this folder to the (*My*) *Documents* folder:

👆 **Right-click**
     [Practice Files Video Edit

You will see this menu:

👆 **Click** Save target as...

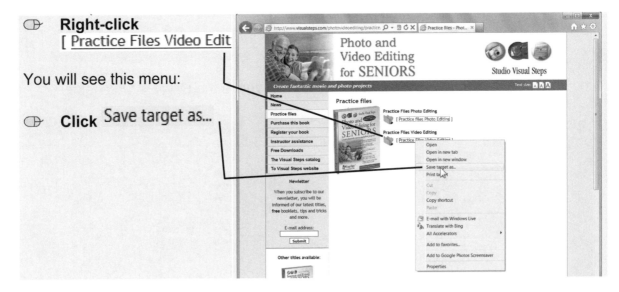

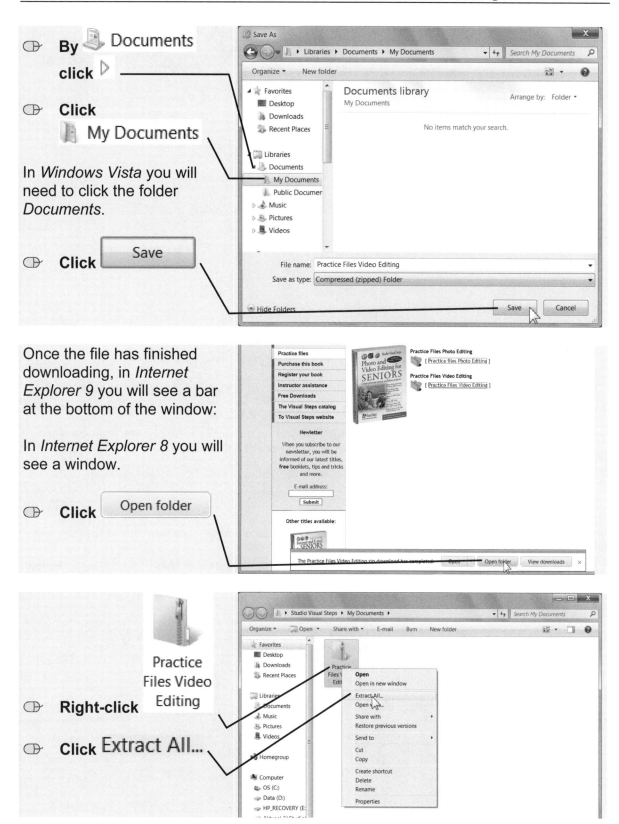

By 📄 Documents
click ▷

Click
🚪 My Documents

In *Windows Vista* you will
need to click the folder
Documents.

Click Save

Once the file has finished
downloading, in *Internet
Explorer 9* you will see a bar
at the bottom of the window:

In *Internet Explorer 8* you will
see a window.

Click Open folder

Practice
Files Video
Editing

Right-click

Click Extract All...

Extract the files:

☞ **If necessary, uncheck the box** ☑ **next to** Show extracted files when

☞ **Click** Extract

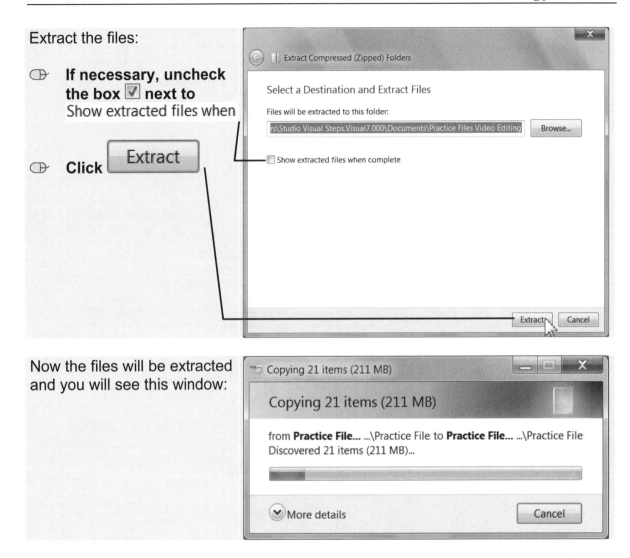

Now the files will be extracted and you will see this window:

The folder containing the practice files has been saved in the (*My*) *Documents* folder:

You can delete the compressed folder:

Practice Files Video Editing

☞ **Right-click**

☞ **Click** Delete

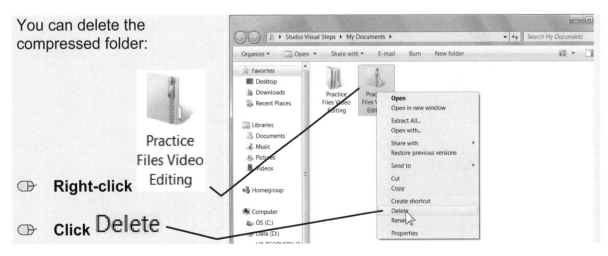

The *Delete Folder* window appears:

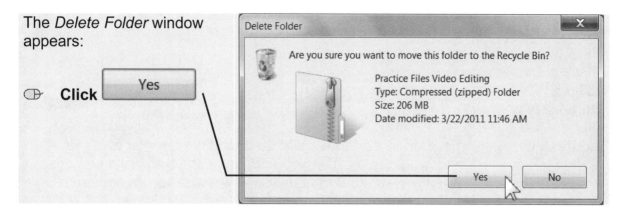

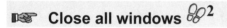 **Click** Yes

The compressed folder has been deleted:

☞ **Close all windows** 𝒮𝒫²

1.4 Background Information

Dictionary	
Address bar	The address bar appears at the top of the *Internet Explorer* window. It displays the web address of the web page you are currently viewing. By entering a new web address and pressing the Enter key, you can open the relevant web page.
Desktop	The desktop is the main screen area that you see after you turn on your computer and log on to *Windows*. When you open programs or folders, they appear on the desktop.
Download	Copying a file from another computer, or from the Internet to your own computer.
Install	Storing a program to your computer's hard drive. All files will be copied to the correct folder and the program will be added to the program list.
Internet Explorer	A program you can use to surf the Internet and view websites.
Movie Maker	With *Windows Live Movie Maker* you can create a movie of your photos and videos. You can save the movie to your computer or publish it online.
Photo Gallery	With *Windows Live Photo Gallery* you can manage, edit, and share your photos. You can also use *Photo Gallery* to import photos from an external device, such as a digital camera.
Taskbar	The taskbar contains the Start button as well as other buttons for each opened program or window. The default location for the taskbar is at the bottom of your screen.
Windows Live Essentials	A collection of programs that you can download from the Internet for free, such as *Windows Live Photo Gallery*.

Source: Windows Help and Support

System requirements for Windows Live Movie Maker

These are the minimum requirements for *Windows Live Movie Maker*:

- **Operating system**: *Windows 7* or *Windows Vista*.
- **Memory**: 1 GB RAM (for HD video, 2 GB RAM or more is recommended).
- **Processor**: 2.4 GHz (single processor) or faster (a dual core processor with two or more cores is recommended if you want to edit HD video).
- **Internet browser**: *Internet Explorer 8* (or higher), *Mozilla Firefox 3.0.1* (or higher), or *Safari 3.1* (or higher).
- **Internet connection**
- **Video card**: a video card that supports *Microsoft DirectX 9.0c* (or higher), and *Pixel Shader 2.0* (or higher).

  Use the *Microsoft DirectX* diagnostic tool to determine which *DirectX* version is supported by your video card. Open the *DirectX* diagnostic tool by clicking the **Start button**, typing **dxdiag** in the **Search box** and then clicking **dxdiag.exe** in the **Programs** list.

  After a quick test you will see your *DirectX* version:

DirectX Diagnostic Tool	▭ ▢ **X**

System | Display | Sound 1 | Sound 2 | Input

This tool reports detailed information about the DirectX components and drivers installed on your system.

If you know what area is causing the problem, click the appropriate tab above. Otherwise, you can use the "Next Page" button below to visit each page in sequence.

System Information

Current Date/Time:	Tuesday, March 22, 2011, 11:54:21 AM
Computer Name:	VISUAL7
Operating System:	Windows 7 Ultimate 32-bit (6.1, Build 7600)
Language:	English (Regional Setting: English)
System Manufacturer:	Hewlett-Packard
System Model:	HP Pavilion dv9000 (RP622EA#ABH)
BIOS:	Ver 1.00PARTTBLw
Processor:	Intel(R) Core(TM)2 CPU T5500 @ 1.66GHz (2 CPUs), ~1.7GHz
Memory:	2048MB RAM
Page file:	1347MB used, 2744MB available
DirectX Version:	DirectX 11

☑ Check for WHQL digital signatures

DxDiag 6.01.7600.16385 32-bit Unicode Copyright © 1998-2006 Microsoft Corporation. All rights reserved.

| Help | Next Page | Save All Information... | Exit |

- **Video memory: 256 MB or more is recommended for HD video.**
- **Additional programs**: *Windows Live Photo Gallery*.

Please note: *Windows Live Movie Maker* is not available for *Windows XP* and previous *Windows* editions.

Source: Windows Live Movie Maker Help

Video cards

Without a video card (also called a graphics accelerator card) you would not be able to see anything on your computer's screen.

If you want to use a video editing program, you will need a high quality video card. Using an inferior video card will mean that video editing will take up more time. This is how you recognize a high quality video card: by its large memory, its speed and its relatively high price.

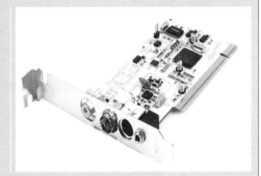

A fast video card will have lots of computing power and be able to quickly display the images on screen. Slower, inexpensive video cards are also able to render sufficient images per second to generate a clear picture. But the extensive features of a high quality video card will enable you to display much larger and sharper images on your screen. For example, a slow video card will clearly display a movie on a 4 x 4 inch screen. But if you want to play the movie full screen, the image will blur. A high quality video card will let you play a movie full screen and retain a sharp and clear image.

The card's memory size plays an important part regarding the speed of these computations.

Some video cards contain a useful extra feature, called a TV Out connection. This TV Out connector lets you display computer images on your TV screen. Another component is a Video In connection, also available on various video cards. This connection enables you to retrieve (capture) video images from a video recorder or television set.

If you want to use your computer for video editing, a high quality video card is essential. It is not necessary to buy the newest and most expensive video card, but it is a good idea to buy a middle class card. The computer systems you buy as a complete package (at various retail outlets) usually do not contain a high quality video card. Often a much cheaper card is installed, or an onboard video card, integrated on the motherboard. Make sure you pay attention to this when you are going to buy your computer: you can always have the cheaper card replaced by a more expensive one, or by a separate one.

1.5 Tips

 Tip

Remove Windows Live Essentials programs
If a program no longer functions correctly, or if you do not want to use the program anymore, you can remove it. This is how you do that:

⏺ **Click** [Windows logo], **Control Panel**, **Uninstall a program**

You will see an uninstall programs window:

⏺ **Click**
🪟 Windows Live Essential

⏺ **Click**
Uninstall/Change

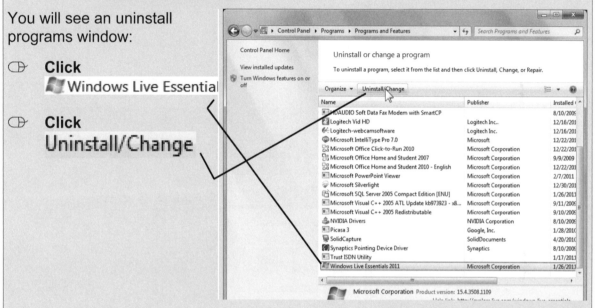

If you are using a *Windows Vista* computer, you screen will now turn dark. You will need to give permission to continue:

⏺ **If necessary, click** Continue

If you want to remove a program:

⏺ **Click**
➡ Remove one or more

You can also repair programs:

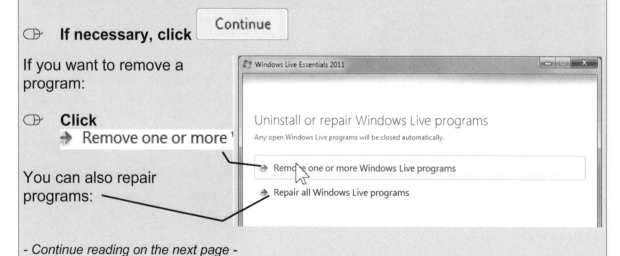

- Continue reading on the next page -

If you want to remove a program:

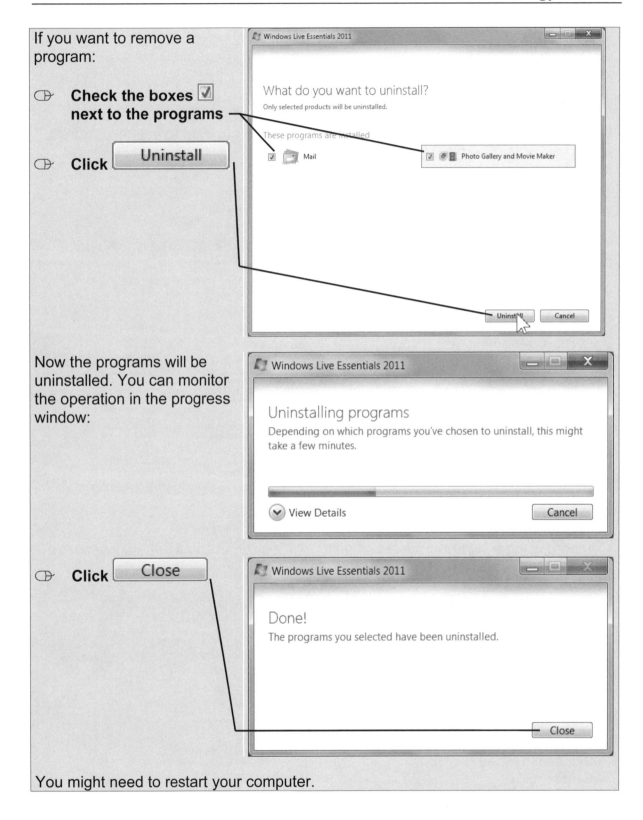

☞ **Check the boxes ☑ next to the programs**

☞ **Click** Uninstall

Now the programs will be uninstalled. You can monitor the operation in the progress window:

☞ **Click** Close

You might need to restart your computer.

2. Viewing Photos

Photo Gallery is a very suitable program for viewing your photo collection.
You can also organize your photos in various ways. If you are looking for a specific photo, the *Photo Gallery* search function can help you. If you would like to show your pictures to other people, you can display them in a slide show.

In this chapter you will learn how to:

- open *Photo Gallery*;
- arrange photos in different ways;
- scroll through the photos;
- search for photos;
- view a slide show.

 Please note:

To work through all the exercises in this chapter, you will need to download the relevant practice files from the website to the (My) *Pictures* folder on your computer. You can read how to do that in *Section 1.2 Download the Practice Files for Photo Gallery*.

2.1 Opening Photo Gallery

This is how you open *Photo Gallery*:

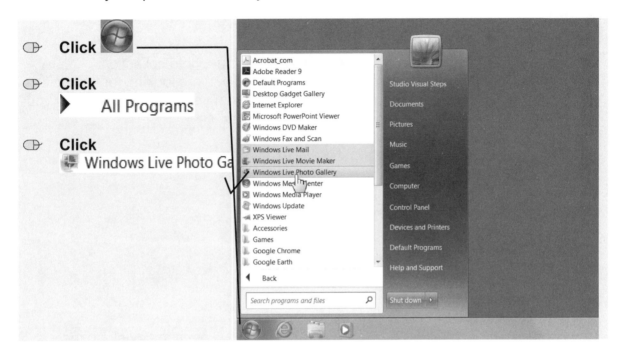

☞ **Click**

☞ **Click**
    ▶   All Programs

☞ **Click**
    Windows Live Photo Ga

You will be asked to accept the service agreement:

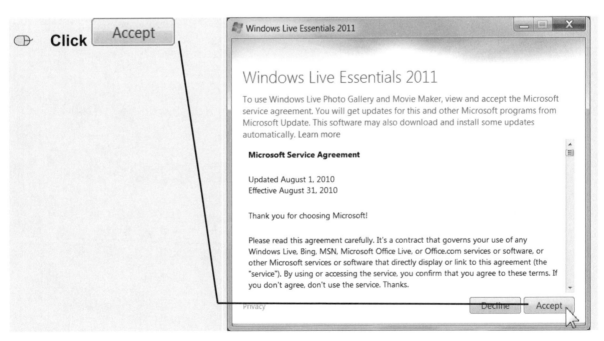

☞ **Click**   Accept

When you start *Photo Gallery* for the first time, you will be asked to sign in to *Windows Live*. If you just want to practice working with *Photo Gallery*, this is not necessary.

In *Chapter 5 Printing and Mailing Photos* you will find more information on the procedure for signing in to *Windows Live*.

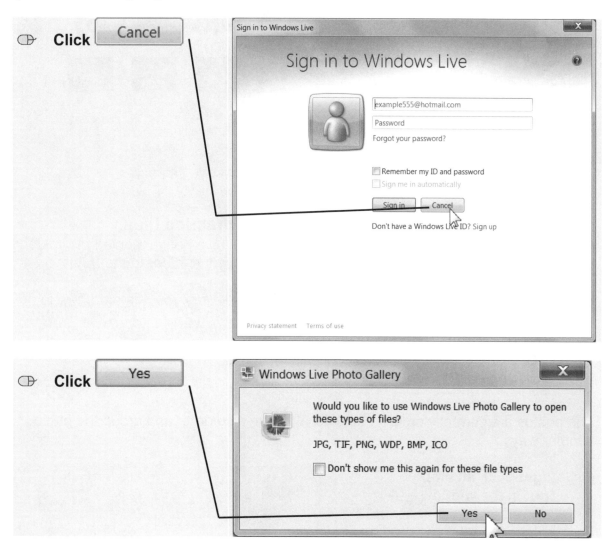

Please note:

If you are using *Windows 7*, the default setting shows you the contents of your *Pictures* library. A library is a collection of files of the same file type. These files may be stored in other folders and in different locations.

If you are using *Windows Vista*, you will just see the contents of both the *Pictures* and the *Public Pictures* folders.

To display just the practice files:

☞ **Click** My Pictures

In *Windows Vista* you will need to select *Pictures*.

☞ **Click**
🗁 Practice Files Photo

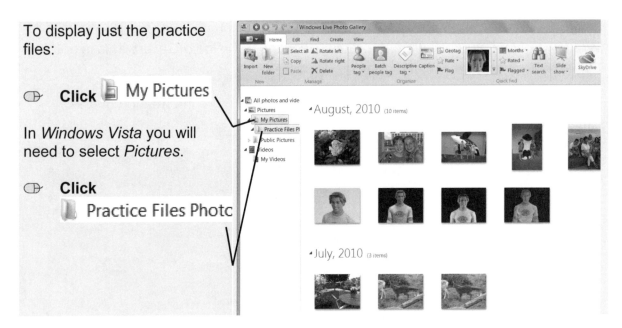

HELP! I do not see the folder with the practice files.

Is the *Practice Files* folder not there? Most likely, you have not yet copied this folder from the CD that goes with this book. You need to copy the folder to the (*My*) *Pictures* folder on your hard disk.
In *Section 1.2 Download the Practice Files for Photo Gallery* you can read how to do this.

2.2 Ordering Photos

The photos are currently ordered by date. You can also order and group the photos in other ways:

☞ **Right-click an empty spot in the window**

☞ **Click** Sort by

☞ **Click** File name

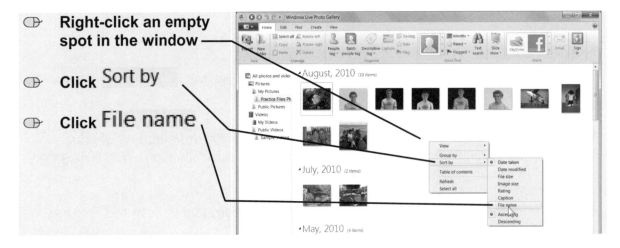

Now the photos have been ordered by their file name. But they are still grouped per month. You can disable this grouping like this.

☞ **Right-click an empty spot in the window**

☞ **Click** Group by

☞ **Click** None

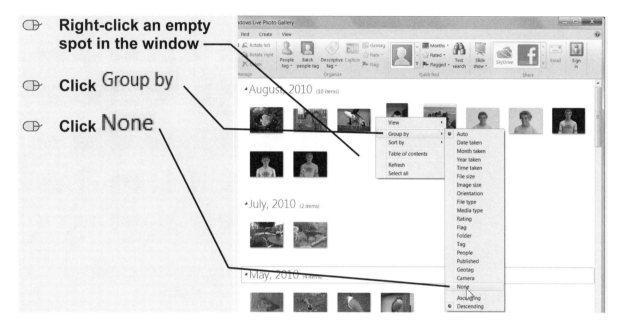

This way, you can arrange and group your photos any way you like. You can also display specific information for the photos, such as the file names:

☞ **Right-click an empty spot in the window**

☞ **Click** View

☞ **Click Thumbnails with file name**

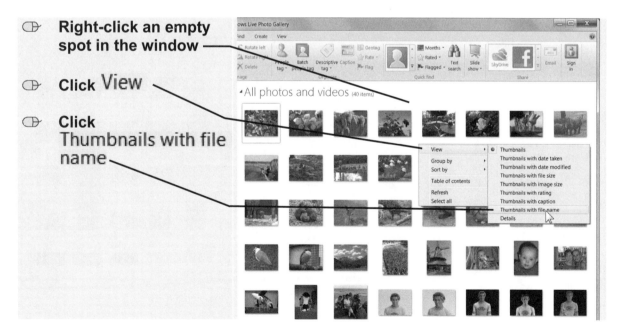

Now you will see all the file
names below the photos:

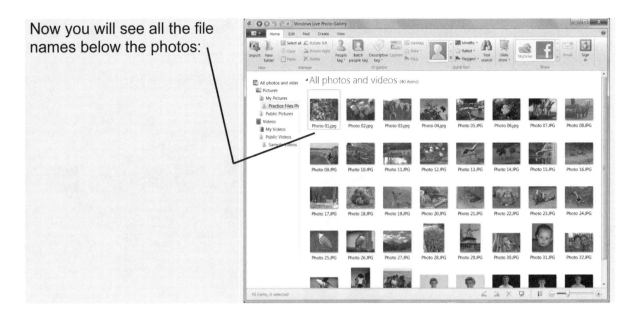

2.3 Scrolling Through the Photos

You can easily browse through your photos:

**Double-click the first
photo**

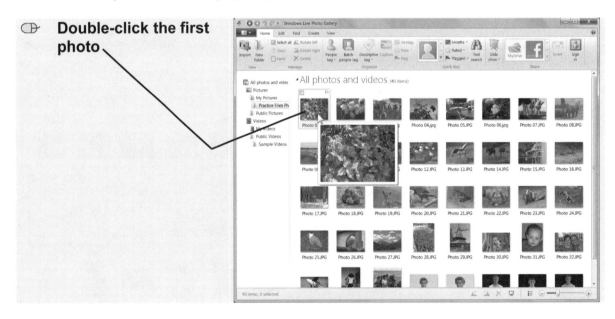

To skip to the next photo:

⊕ **Click**

☞ **View all the photos in the same way**

When you have returned to the first photo:

⊕ **Click** Close file

Now you will see an overview with thumbnail versions of all the photos:

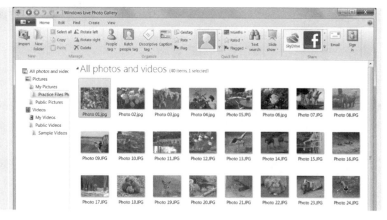

2.4 Searching For Photos

If you have a lot of photos stored on your computer, you may have a hard time trying to find a particular photo. *Photo Gallery* has various useful options that will help you quickly retrieve the photo you want. You can search for photos, for example, by their creation date. You can choose the day, month or year when the photo was made. You can practice doing this by searching for a photo that was shot in October 2008.

☞ **Click the** Find **tab**

☞ **Click** Months ▾

☞ **By** 2008 **click** Oct

Now you will only see the photos that were created in October 2008:

To display all the photos in the *Practice Files Photo editing* folder:

☞ **Click** Practice Files Photo e

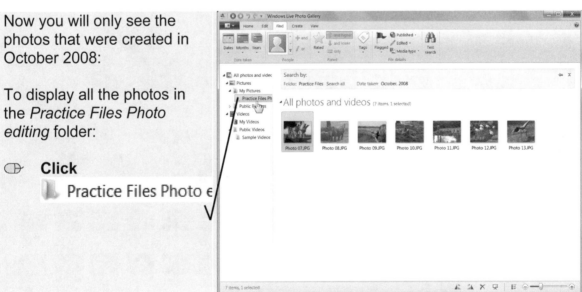

You can also search for photos by their file name (or part of the name):

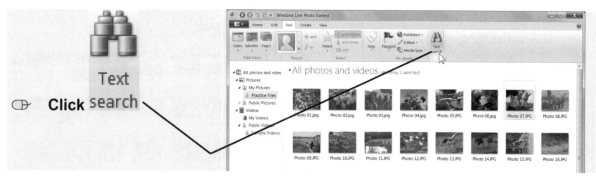

Click search

Type: 35

Now you will see the photo with the file name *Photo 35*:

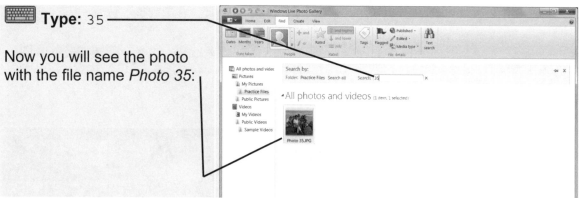

There are many other ways to find photos. Another useful method is to search through the labels that you may have added to your photos. In the next chapter you can read more about this method.

2.5 Viewing a Slide Show

You can view your photos, or show them to others, in an attractive manner by displaying them in a slide show:

To display all the photos in the *Practice Files Photo editing* folder:

Click

Practice Files Photo e

⬚ **Drag the scroll bar upwards**

⬚ **Click the first photo**

⬚ **Click** 🖳

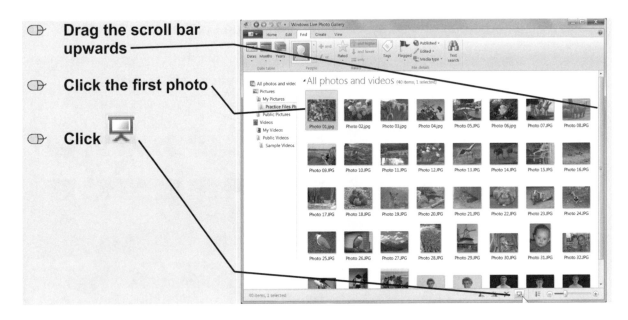

You will see a slide show:

⬚ **Move the mouse pointer**

You can pause the slide show:

⬚ **Click** ⏸

You can move to the next picture:

⬚ **Click** ▶

To close the slide show:

☞ **Click**
Back to Photo Gallery

To close *Photo Gallery*:

☞ **Click** **X**

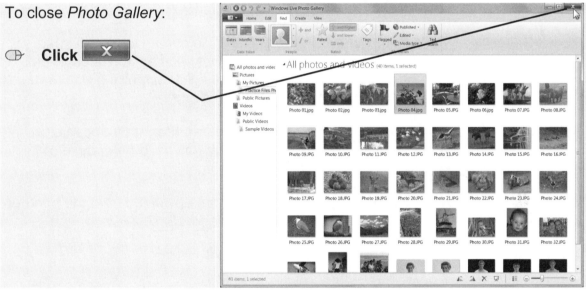

In this chapter you have learned how to open *Photo Gallery* and how to use some of the various methods for arranging and displaying your photos. You have also learned how to find a particular photo.

2.6 Background Information

Dictionary	
Folder	A folder is a container for your computer files.
Library	In some ways, a library is similar to a folder. However, unlike a folder, a library does not contain the actual files but only has references to these files. A library gathers and displays files that are stored in several locations on the computer. This way, you can easily find, organize and manage files of the same file type, such as pictures. Available in *Windows 7*.
Photo Gallery	With *Windows Live Photo Gallery* you can arrange, edit, and share photos. You can also use *Photo Gallery* to import photos from an external device, such as a digital camera, a USB stick, or an external hard drive.
Screensaver	A screen saver is a moving picture or pattern that appears on your computer screen when you haven't used the mouse or keyboard for a specified period of time.
Windows Live Essentials	A collection of programs that you can download from the Internet for free, for instance, *Windows Live Photo Gallery*.

Source: Windows Help and Support, Windows Live Essentials help pages

File types
Windows Live Photo Gallery supports the following file types:
JPEG/JPG, TIF/TIFF, GIF, BMP, PNG, and WDP.
Please note: Some of these file types cannot be edited in *Photo Gallery*. In the background information section of *Chapter 4 Editing Photos* you can read more about this topic.

Photo editing processes

Photo editing consists of three separate processes. First, the photos need to be imported to your computer. Next, the photo is edited with a photo editing program. After the editing is done, the photo can be used for a variety of different purposes. For example, it can be stored and exported to an external device or medium.

In this diagram you will see a number of options:

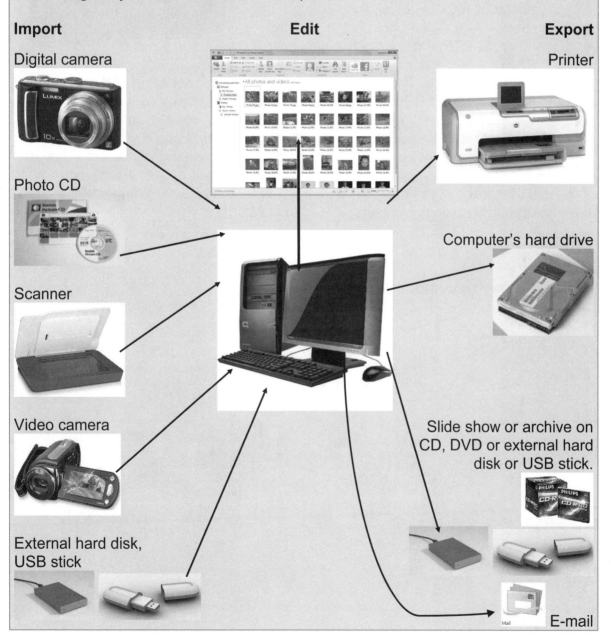

What is digital photography?

Digital photography is a method of shooting photos by using a light-sensitive microchip, storing these photos electronically and then displaying them.

In fact, a digital camera is very similar to an 'old fashioned' photo camera; only the roll of film has been replaced by a CCD, a chip that registers the image in pixels. The digital photo is then stored on a memory card. Most cameras use special memory cards to this end.

The sharpness of a photo is determined by the degree of resolution of the CCD. In other words: the more pixels, the clearer the photo. That is why we use the megapixel dimension for digital cameras. One megapixel equals a million pixels. One of the most remarkable differences between traditional and digital cameras is the way in which the photo is taken. You will not find a lot of digital cameras that still use a regular viewfinder, which you can press against your eye. Instead, you need to use the LCD screen at the back of the camera to take a picture. You will notice that the photographer holds the camera at a distance from his eyes.

A digital camera's components

Shutter release:

On/off switch:

Flash:

Sensor:

Lens:

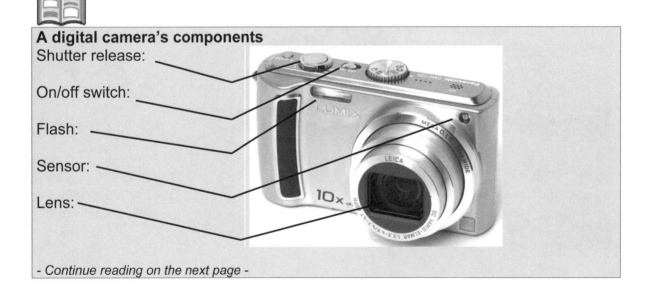

- Continue reading on the next page -

There is a lot of difference between cameras, regarding the number of options available and the manner in which the buttons are placed. Some cameras only have a few settings, which can usually be accessed from the back of the camera on the LDC screen.

Select recording mode:

Microphone:

Zoom buttons:

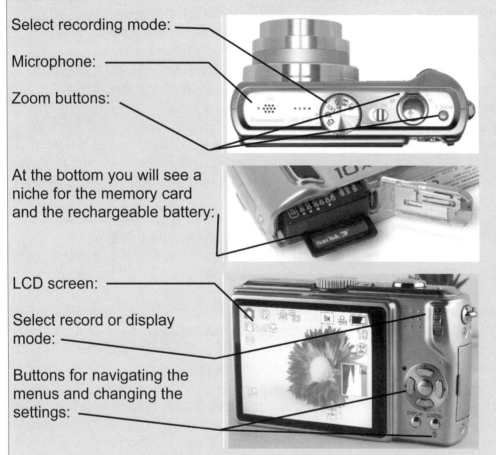

At the bottom you will see a niche for the memory card and the rechargeable battery:

LCD screen:

Select record or display mode:

Buttons for navigating the menus and changing the settings:

Apart from this, most cameras have a connector for a USB cable that can be used to connect the camera to a computer. This is how you import your photos. You can also read the data directly from the memory card with a card reader.

Buying a digital camera
If you want to buy a digital camera, pay attention to the following things:

- **The resolution:** If you intend to enlarge and print your photos, you will need a high resolution camera. If you only want to use your photos for a website, a camera with a lower resolution will suffice.

- **The memory:** A camera with only internal memory is not very flexible to use. If you buy a camera that uses memory cards, you can expand the memory by buying (extra) memory cards with a larger capacity.

- **The viewfinder:** The best option is to look for a combination of the 'old fashioned' viewfinder with an LCD screen. Particularly if you want to take pictures at the beach, in the snow, or in the dark. In those situations, the image on an LCD screen is often difficult to see. By using a viewfinder you can see your object more clearly.

- **The power consumption:** It is recommended to choose a camera with rechargeable batteries or a battery that can be loaded outside the camera. Otherwise, you will never be able to recharge the battery and take pictures simultaneously. In this way, you can always have a set of spare batteries on hand.

- **The zoom range:** Most digital compact cameras do not have exchangeable lenses, like digital reflex cameras often do. So you will not be able to use a more powerful lens to zoom in and get a clearer picture of your object. But digital cameras often have built-in zoom lenses that can magnify objects, by a factor of three to twelve (or more).

- **Optical or digital zoom:** There exist two kinds of zoom: the optical and the digital zoom. The digital zoom enlarges the image electronically, as it were. In this case, the photo will become less clear. The digital zoom will reduce the file size and also the required memory space. Photos made with the digital zoom are usually of poorer quality than photos made with the optical zoom or not zoomed at all.

- The optical zoom works the same way as the zoom lens on your regular camera. This zoom method ensures optimum quality, even after blowing up the picture. This is because an optical zoom adjusts the image angle. The camera will use the full resolution, regardless of the zoom distance. In this way, the photo quality remains the same. That is the reason that a camera with an optical zoom function is recommended.

- **Ease of use:** Some cameras have so many options; you may never need to use them all. Also, some cameras are easier to use than others. When you go to buy a camera, make sure you get some good advice about the options available and how the camera operates. You will soon know if the camera meets your needs.

Pixels, bitmap, resolution and color depth

Each computer image (a drawing, illustration or photo) is composed of a number of dots or tiny squares. These dots are called *pixels*. A photo is actually a kind of grid consisting of a large number of dots. This type of a drawing or illustration is also called a *bitmap* (a chart of points). You will sometimes see this term in *Windows*. Photos are also composed as bitmaps:

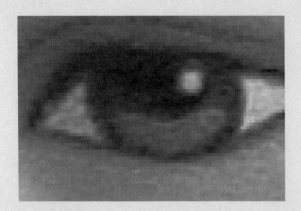

The quality of a photo depends on the number of pixels it uses. If a photo consists of a large number of pixels, the image will be clearer and sharper. If there are fewer pixels, the photo will become blurry or fuzzy. The number of pixels per inch is also called the resolution.

Apart from that, the quality of a photo is also determined by the number of colors that are used. Each pixel can be a different color. The more different colors are used, the more information the photo can contain. That is called the color depth. The more colors, the more realistic the photo will appear. Currently, 16 million colors is the standard number of colors for a regular computer. But professional photographers and graphic designers use many more colors.

Megapixels

Often, the resolution is expressed in *megapixels*. The number of megapixels is usually printed on the camera:

One megapixel equals 1 million pixels. So, a resolution of 800 x 600 pixels equals 0.4 megapixels. The 14.1 megapixels of the camera in this picture will result in photos with a maximum resolution of 4320 x 3240 pixels.

2.7 Tips

🔅 Tip

Zooming in and zooming out
If you think your photos are too small, you can zoom in.

☞ **Drag the slider** **to the right**

To zoom out, drag the slider to the left again.

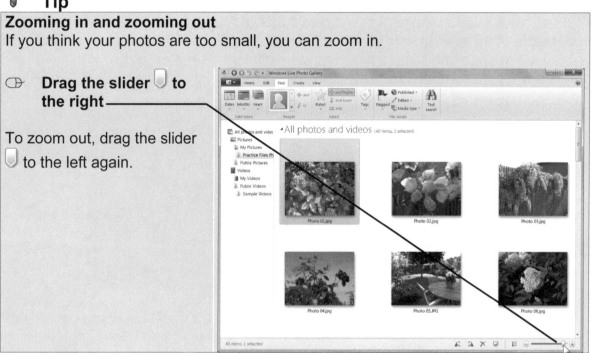

🔅 Tip

Photo as desktop background
In *Photo Gallery* you can select a photo and use it as a desktop background.

☞ **Click the desired photo**

☞ **Click the** Create **tab**

☞ **Click** Set as desktop

Now the photo will be set as a background for your desktop.

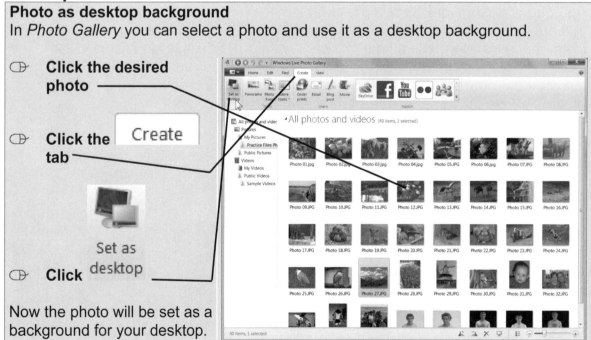

Tip

Delete photos

While you are scrolling through the photos, you can easily delete the ones you no longer want.

Please note: Take caution before you delete a photo. The photo will be deleted not only from *Photo Gallery*, but also from your computer's hard drive! (It will first be moved to the recycle bin, but if you empty it, the deletion is permanent).

Click ✗

Click [Yes]

💡 Tip

Photos as a screen saver
If you do not use your computer for a while, you may see an animated picture on your screen. This is also called a screen saver. In *Photo Gallery* you can select your own photos to act as a screen saver.

☞ **Click**

☞ **Click**

 Screen saver setting

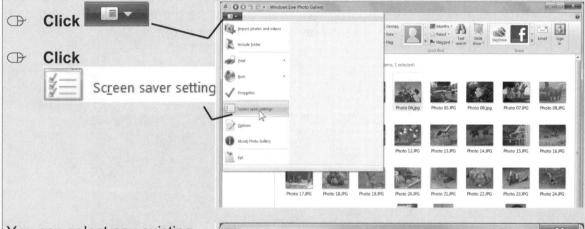

You can select any existing folder that contains pictures for the screen saver:

☞ **Click** Settings...

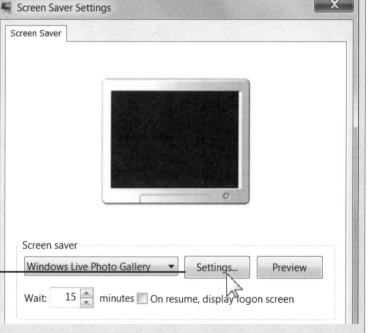

- *Continue reading on the next page -*

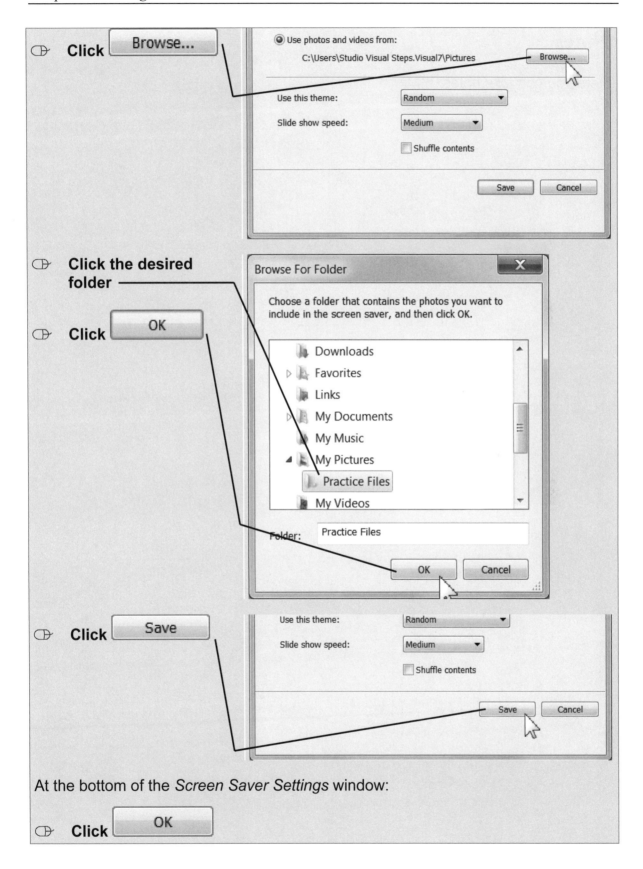

Click **Browse...**

Use photos and videos from:
C:\Users\Studio Visual Steps.Visual7\Pictures   Browse...

Use this theme: Random
Slide show speed: Medium
☐ Shuffle contents

Save   Cancel

Click the desired folder

Click OK

Browse For Folder

Choose a folder that contains the photos you want to include in the screen saver, and then click OK.

- Downloads
- ▷ Favorites
- Links
- ▷ My Documents
- My Music
- ◢ My Pictures
  - Practice Files
- My Videos

Folder: Practice Files

OK   Cancel

Click Save

Use this theme: Random
Slide show speed: Medium
☐ Shuffle contents

Save   Cancel

At the bottom of the *Screen Saver Settings* window:

Click OK

Notes

Here you can take notes.

3. Arranging Photos

In the previous chapter you learned how to view your photos in various ways. In this chapter you will learn how to arrange your photos. You can arrange your photos by storing them in different folders. You can also add various tags to the photos, so you will be able to find them quickly and easily. Think of tags as a kind of label.

One way of tagging your photos is by adding the names of the people represented in the photo. You can add the names of the people you see in the photo separately. In *Photo Gallery* this is called 'tagging people'.

In this chapter you will learn how to:

- arrange photos into folders;
- add the name of a person as a tag;
- add other types of tags to photos;
- find tagged photos.

 Please note:

To work through all the exercises in this chapter, you will need to download the relevant practice files from the website to the (My) *Pictures* folder on your computer. You can read how to do that in *Section 1.2 Download the Practice Files for Photo Gallery*.

3.1 Arranging Photos in Folders

Do you have a lot of photos stored on your computer? Making different folders will help you organize the photos and you will be able to find them quicker. You can do this of course, by using *Windows Explorer*, but you can also create folders directly in *Photo Gallery* and move your photos to these folders. These folders will be displayed in *Windows Explorer* as well.

☞ **Start *Photo Gallery* 🐾¹**

The *Practice Files* folder has already been selected. In this folder you are going to create a new folder:

☞ **Click** New folder

⌨ **Type:** birds

⌨ **Press** Enter ↵

☞ **Click** Photo 24.JPG

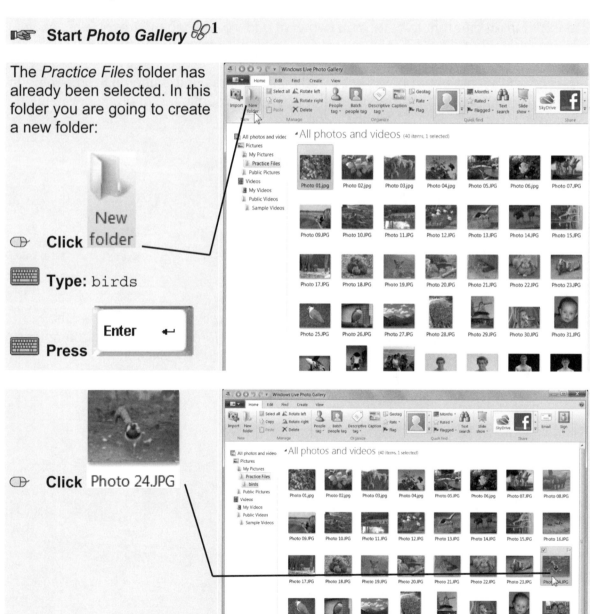

⬚ **Check the box ☑ by**

Photo 25.JPG

⬚ **Check the box ☑ by**

Photo 26.JPG

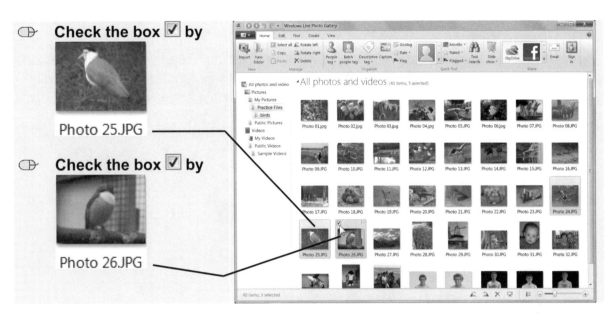

💡 **Tip**

Select multiple photos at once
There is another way of selecting multiple photos at the same time:

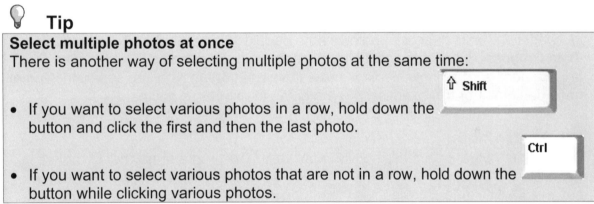

- If you want to select various photos in a row, hold down the **⇧ Shift** button and click the first and then the last photo.

- If you want to select various photos that are not in a row, hold down the **Ctrl** button while clicking various photos.

⬚ **Point the mouse pointer to one of the photos, for example**

Photo 25.JPG

⬚ **Drag the photo to the 📁 birds folder**

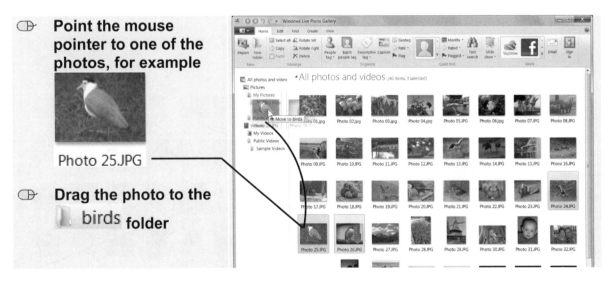

Now the photos have been moved to the *birds* folder.

Please note:

You will still see the photos. That is because the *Practice Files* folder is still selected. In this view, *Photo Gallery* displays all the photos in the *Practice Files* folder. The *birds* folder is a subfolder inside the *Practice Files* folder.

☞ **Click** birds

Now you will see only the photos in the *birds* folder:

3.2 Adding Tags to Persons

Do you want to keep track of all the people who are portrayed in your photos, or do you want to be able to select photos by the people who are in them? *Photo Gallery* offers the possibility of adding individual's names to your photos. This is called 'tagging people'. If a photo displays more than one person, you can separately tag all these persons. For this exercise you are going to use Ken's photos.

 Please note:

The order of operations in this section may vary. The program may not be able to recognize the photos all at once. Even if you have used *Photo Gallery* before, you may see slightly different windows than the examples in this book. Or the order of operations may differ from the way they are described.

☞ **Click**
   Practice Files Photo edit

☞ **Drag the scroll bar downwards**

☞ **Click** Photo 36.jpg

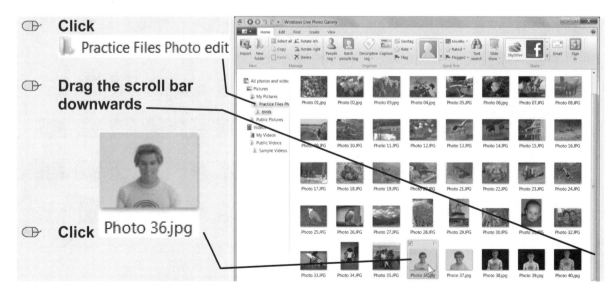

Click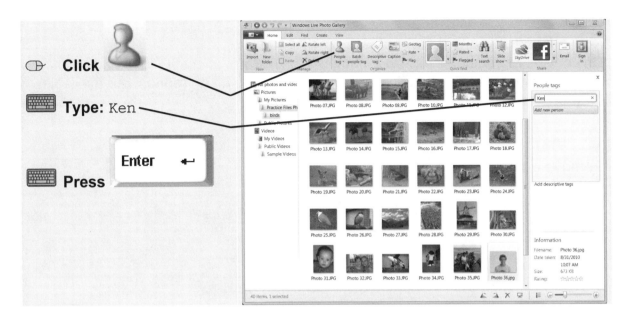

Type: Ken

Press

Photo Gallery contains a special *Batch people tag* function that will give you a number of suggestions for tagging people. This enables you to tag a large number of photos at once. The more you use the people tag function, the more accurate the suggestions will be. Here is how to use it:

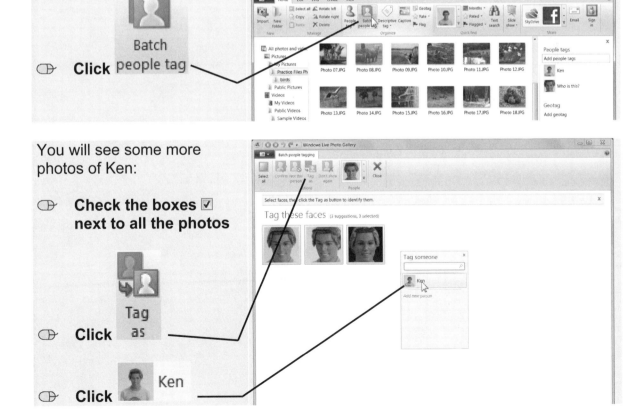

Click Batch people tag

You will see some more photos of Ken:

Check the boxes ☑ next to all the photos

Click Tag as

Click Ken

HELP! I see a different set of photos.

Do you see more photos, or fewer photos? This will not affect the following operations. Just carry out the instructions with the photos of Ken that are available on your screen.

Tip

Remove a tag
This is how you remove a tag:

⊕ **Position the mouse pointer on** Ken

⊕ **By** Ken **click** ▾

⊕ **Click Remove tag**

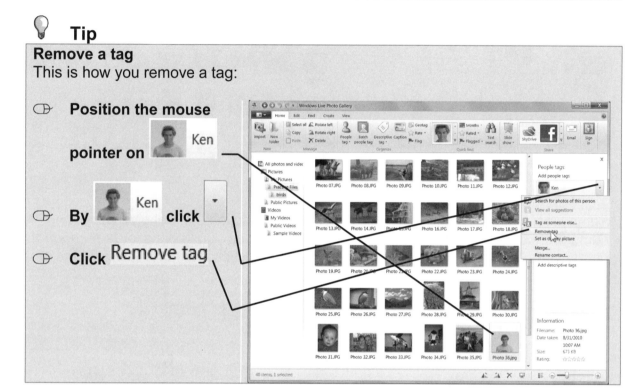

⊕ **Click Tag them**

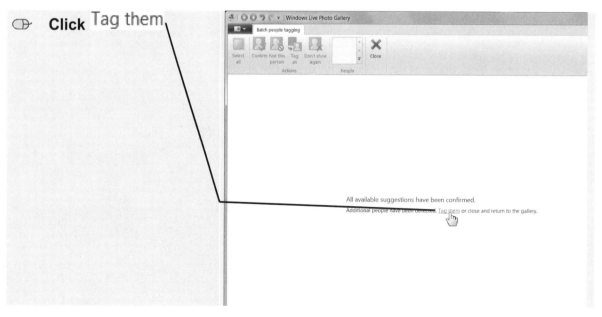

You will see the other
suggestions:

☞ **Check the boxes ☑️
next to the other
photos of Ken**

☞ **Click** Tag as

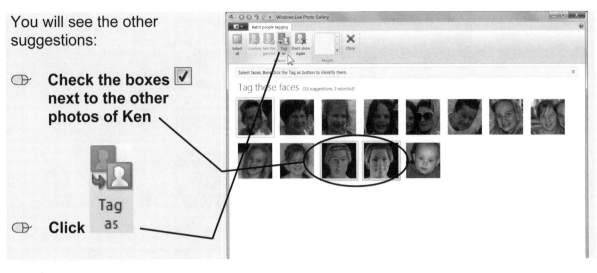

☞ **Click** Ken

☞ **Click** Close

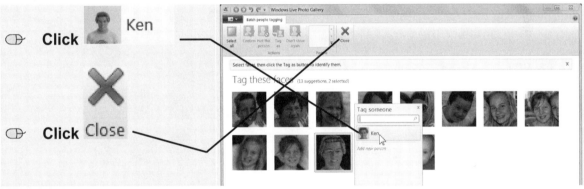

☞ **Drag the scroll bar
downwards**

☞ **Click** Photo 37.jpg

Now you will see that the tag
has been added to all of
Ken's photos:

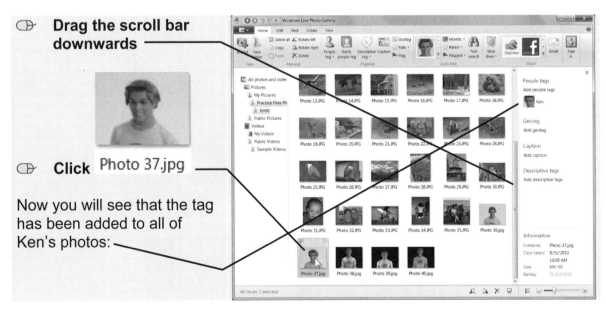

You can add separate tags to different people in your photos.

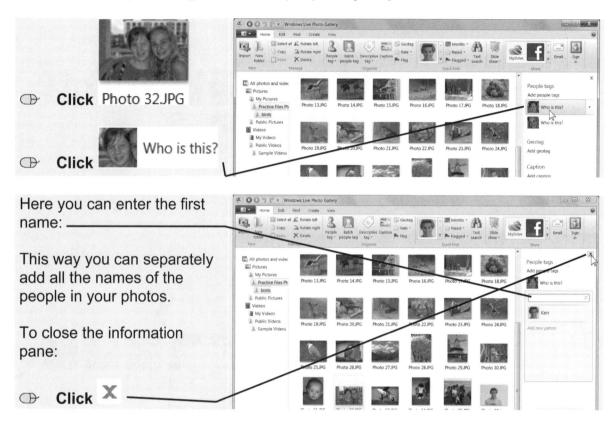

☞ **Click** Photo 32.JPG

☞ **Click** Who is this?

Here you can enter the first name: ⎯⎯⎯⎯

This way you can separately add all the names of the people in your photos.

To close the information pane:

☞ **Click** **X**

💡 **Tip**

Select people yourself
Sometimes *Photo Gallery* does not distinguish accurately between one face and another in a photo. In that case, you can select the faces and tag them yourself.

☞ **Double-click the photo**

☞ **Click** Add people tags

The pointer will turn into ➕:

☞ **Drag a rectangle around a person's face**

Now you can enter the name: In this way you can tag each person in the photo.

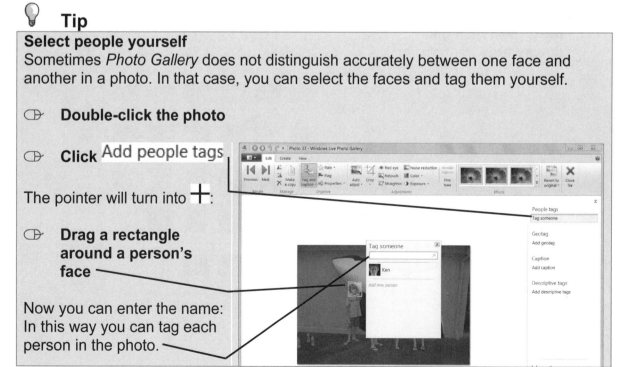

3.3 Add Other Types of Tags to Photos

You can also add other types of tags to your photos beside the people tags. For instance, you can add a review by assigning a number of stars to the picture. You can also add a marker, a descriptive tag or a so-called geotag (location) to your photos.

Here is how to add descriptive tags to some of the photos.

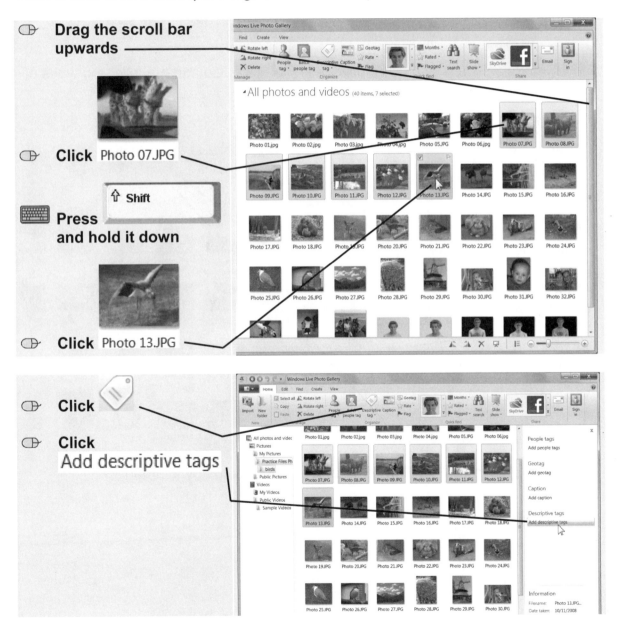

Type: Zoo

Press Enter ↵

Click X

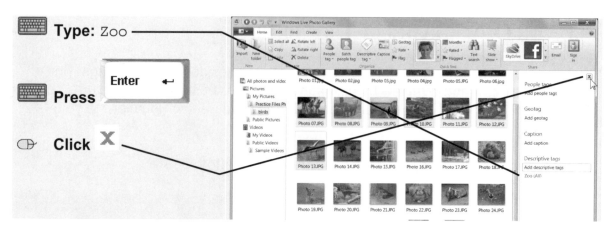

Along with people tags and descriptive tags, you can also add the following types of tags to your photos:

A caption with a brief description of the photo:

A geotag, this sets the location of where the photo was taken:

A rating, this can indicate the quality or importance of the photo. You can assign a number of stars ranging from 0 to 5:

A flag, a way of marking a photo. The flag can denote anything you want:

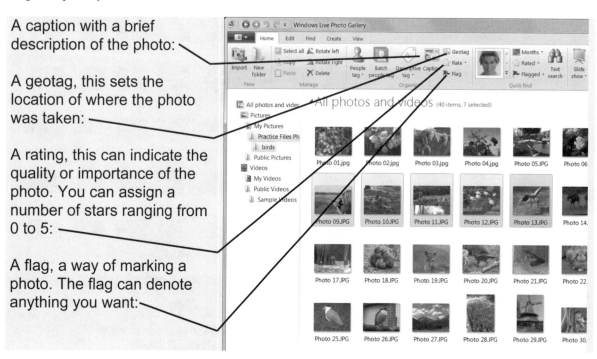

In the next section you will learn how to search for photos by their tags.

3.4 Finding Tagged Photos

Now you are going to search for the photos of Ken, by using the tag you added previously:

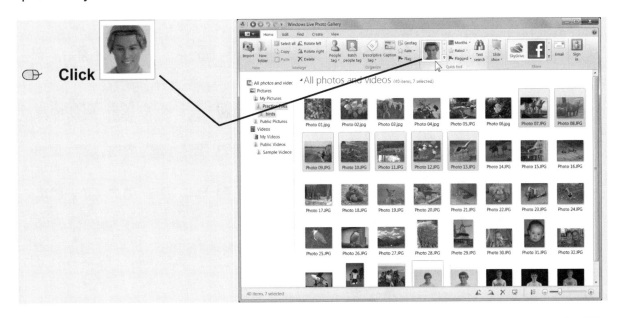

☞ **Click**

Now you will see all the photos of Ken:

Tip

Searching tags for multiple persons
If you have added tags for more than one person, you can find them in the following way:

    ▢ **By the tags click** ▼

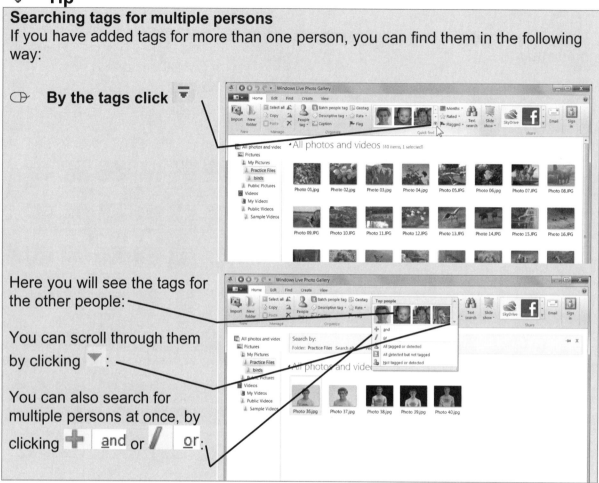

Here you will see the tags for the other people:

You can scroll through them by clicking ▼ :

You can also search for multiple persons at once, by clicking ➕ and or / or :

Now you are going to look for photos with the descriptive tag *Zoo*.

To display all the practice photos:

    ▢ **Click** ✖

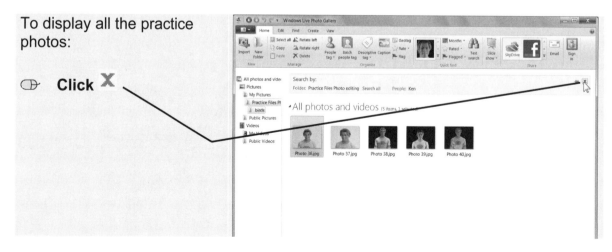

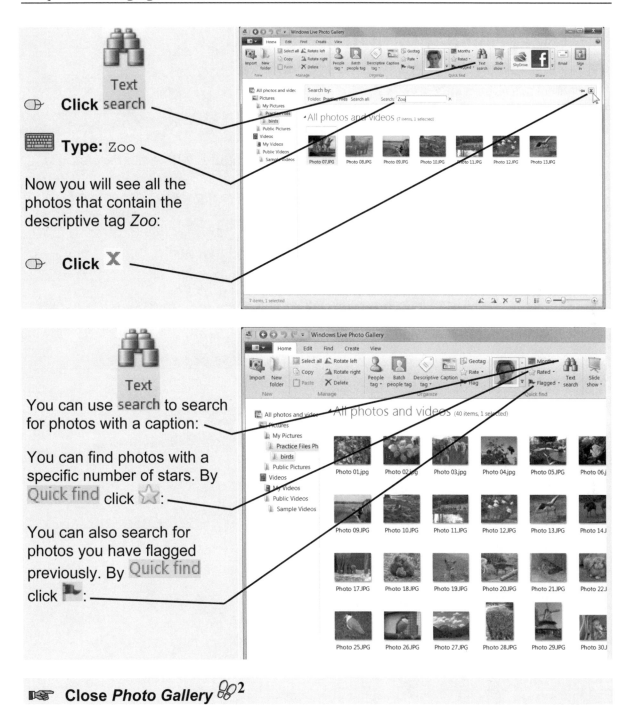

Text

☞ **Click** search

⌨ **Type:** Zoo

Now you will see all the photos that contain the descriptive tag *Zoo*:

☞ **Click** X

Text

You can use search to search for photos with a caption:

You can find photos with a specific number of stars. By Quick find click ☆:

You can also search for photos you have flagged previously. By Quick find click ⚑:

☞ **Close** *Photo Gallery* ⚙²

In this chapter you have learned how to arrange photos in folders. You have also learned how to add tags to your photos and how to search for photos by the tags that have been attached to them.

3.5 Background Information

Dictionary	
Folder	A folder is a container on your computer where files are stored.
Tag	In *Photo Gallery* you can add *people tags* and *descriptive tags* to photos.
Tagging	Tagging means adding a label (tag) to a photo, or to a person in a photo.
Windows Explorer	A *Windows* program that enables you to manage your folders and files.

Source: Windows Live Essentials help pages, Windows Help and Support

4. Editing Photos

Photo Gallery offers various options for simple photo editing. For instance, you can remove red eye, adjust the exposure, rotate or crop a photo. You can also let *Photo Gallery* enhance your photos automatically.

In this chapter you will learn how to:

- rotate photos;
- crop photos;
- remove red eyes;
- enhance photos automatically;
- straighten photos;
- adjust the exposure;
- use additional options for photo editing.

➥ Please note:

To work through all the exercises in this chapter, you will need to download the relevant practice files from the website to the (My) *Pictures* folder on your computer. You can read how to do that in *Section 1.2 Download the Practice Files for Photo Gallery*.

4.1 Rotate Photos

If you shoot your photos in the vertical direction they may not display properly in *Photo Gallery*. They may be turned sideways. This can be for a variety of reasons. You may have an older camera which does not record the orientation information into the photo itself. This problem is easily corrected, however.

 Please note:

The following procedures will be done in the editing window. That is the view you see when you double-click a photo. You can also perform the same actions in the main window. This is how to select the photo you want to rotate:

☞ **Click the photo**

☞ **Click the** 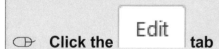 **tab**

☞ **Start** *Photo Gallery* ✂¹

Open the photo in the editing window:

☞ **Double-click**

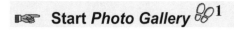

Photo 15.JPG

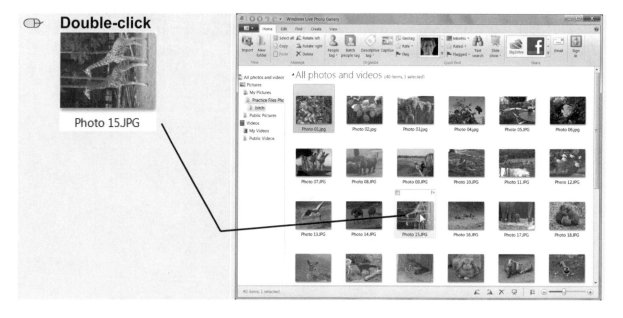

Rotate the photo clockwise a quarter turn:

⊕ **Click** ◢◣

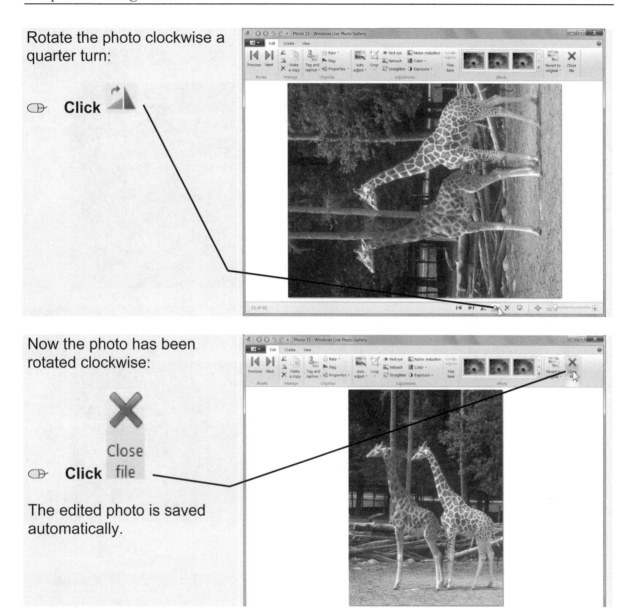

Now the photo has been rotated clockwise:

✕

Close
file

⊕ **Click** file

The edited photo is saved automatically.

4.2 Crop Photos

One of the benefits of digital photography is the possibility of cropping the photo in a later stage:

☞ **Open the photo** Photo 16.JPG **in the editing window** ✂¹²

☞ **Click** [crop icon]

Photo Gallery will propose a cut-out of the photo:

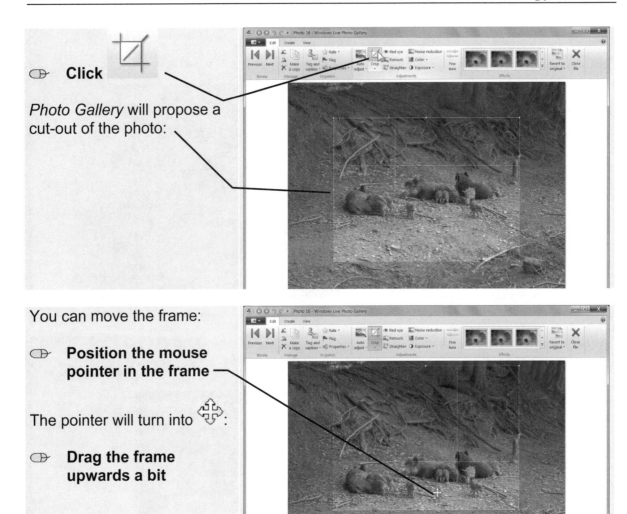

You can move the frame:

☞ **Position the mouse pointer in the frame**

The pointer will turn into ✥:

☞ **Drag the frame upwards a bit**

You can modify the size of the frame:

☞ **Position the mouse pointer on the rectangle ☐ at the bottom right**

The pointer will turn into ⬉:

If you do not position the mouse pointer on one of the corner handles, the pointer will look like this ⬌.

☞ **Drag the frame to a smaller dimension**

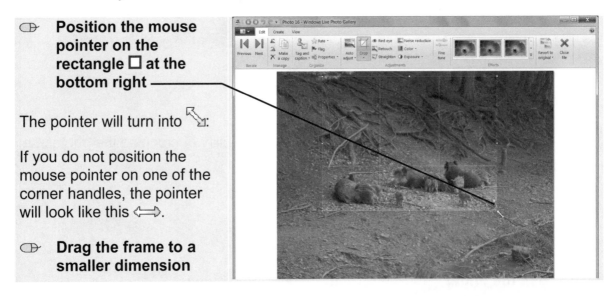

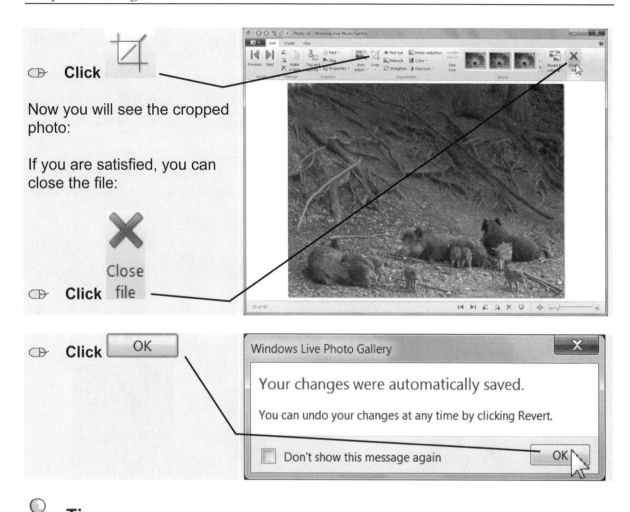

Click

Now you will see the cropped photo:

If you are satisfied, you can close the file:

Click Close file

Click OK

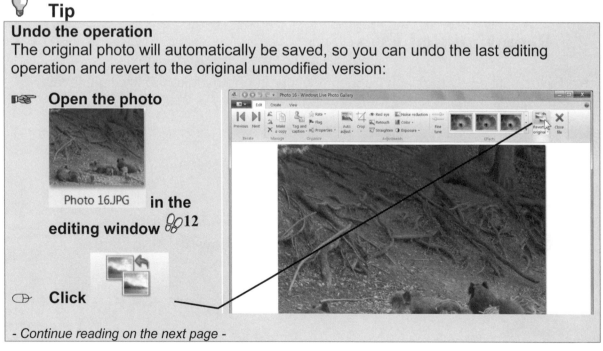

Windows Live Photo Gallery

Your changes were automatically saved.

You can undo your changes at any time by clicking Revert.

☐ Don't show this message again   OK

💡 Tip

Undo the operation
The original photo will automatically be saved, so you can undo the last editing operation and revert to the original unmodified version:

☞ **Open the photo**

Photo 16.JPG **in the editing window** ✂12

Click

- Continue reading on the next page -

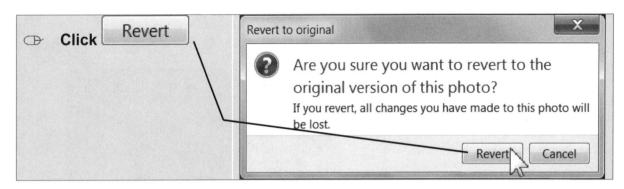

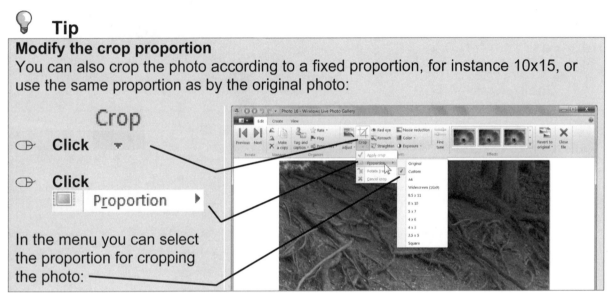

4.3 Removing Red Eyes

Red eyes caused by the flash frequently occur in photos taken at low light levels. *Photo Gallery* contains a tool for removing these red eyes.

☞ **Open the photo** Photo 31.JPG **in the editing window** 𝒪𝒪**12**

- Click 👁 Red eye

- **Drag a rectangle around the eye**

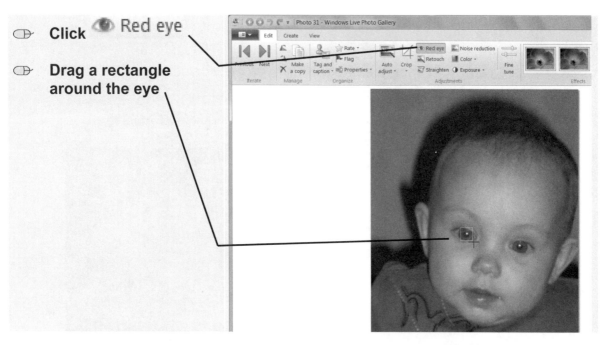

The red eye has been fixed:

☞ **Fix the other red eye in the same way**

- **Click** Close file

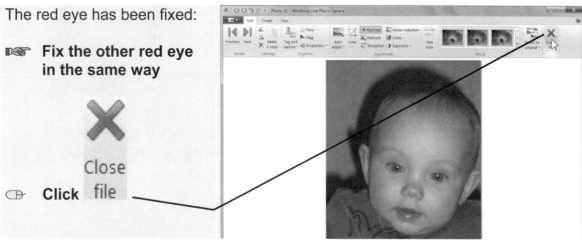

If you do not want to see this window again:

- **Check the box ☑ next to**
  Don't show this message ag

- **Click** OK

Windows Live Photo Gallery

Your changes were automatically saved.

You can undo your changes at any time by clicking Revert.

☑ Don't show this message again   OK

💡 **Tip**

Zooming in while fixing red eyes
It can be useful to zoom in on the photo, while you are correcting the red eyes:

☞ **Position the mouse pointer on 🔍 and move to the right**

Do you want to move the photo a bit? Then press

Alt

and hold it down. The

pointer will turn into ✋ and you will be able to move the photo.

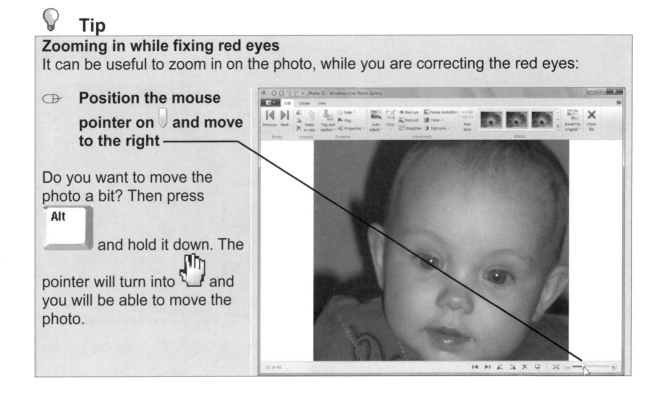

4.4 Adjust Photos Automatically

Photo Gallery contains a very useful function to quickly modify a single photo or a group of photos at once, called the *Auto adjust* function. Here is how to apply it:

☞ **Open the photo** Photo 08.JPG **in the editing window** 🐾**12**

This photo is rather blurred and would benefit by some correction. For this, you are going to use the *Auto adjust* option:

☞ **Click**

The color and the exposure of the photo have greatly improved:

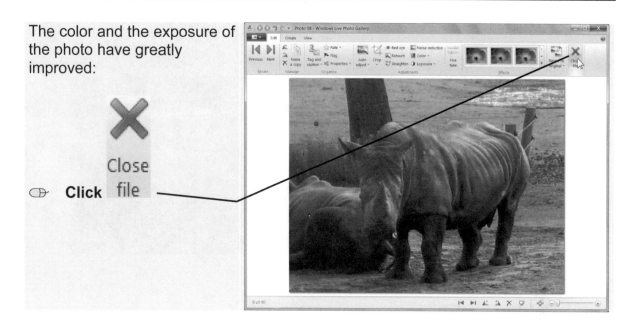

☞ **Click** Close file

4.5 Retouching

Photo Gallery contains more options for editing your photos. For example, you can remove a smudge from a photo. In *Photo Gallery* this is called *retouching* a photo.

☞ **Open the photo** Photo 02.jpg **in the editing window** ⓒⓒ 12

☞ **Click** Retouch

☞ **Drag a rectangle around the little stain on the leaf**

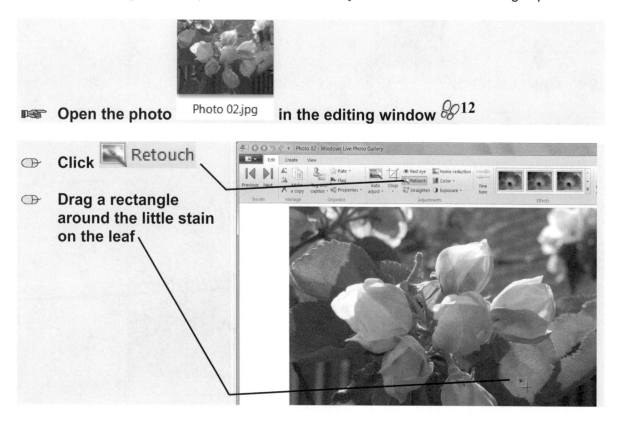

Now the stain had gone:

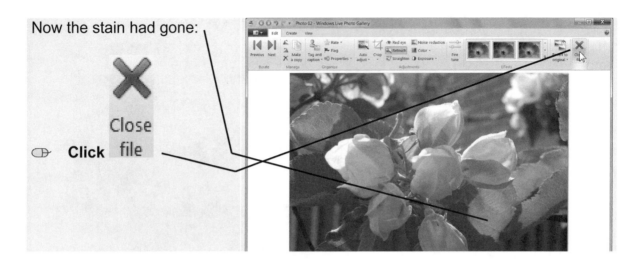

☞ **Click** Close file

4.6 Straightening

In some pictures, the object is sometimes skewed. The photo may look more pleasing if this is corrected. You can use the *Straighten* option to do this:

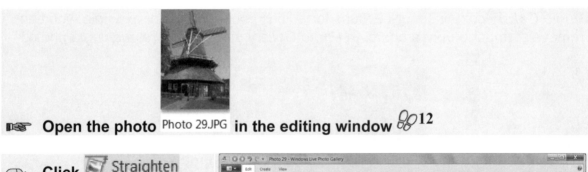

🖙 **Open the photo** Photo 29.JPG **in the editing window** ✂️12

☞ **Click** 📐 Straighten

You will see that the windmill has been straightened:

☞ **Click** Close file

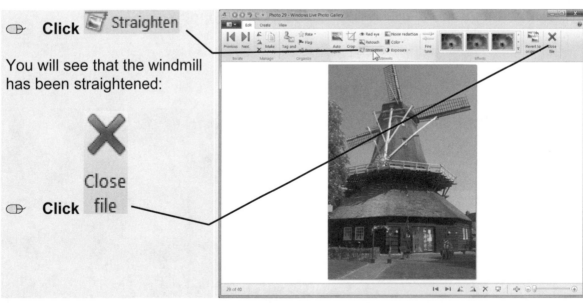

4.7 Adjust the Exposure

You can let *Photo Gallery* lighten up photos that are too dark.

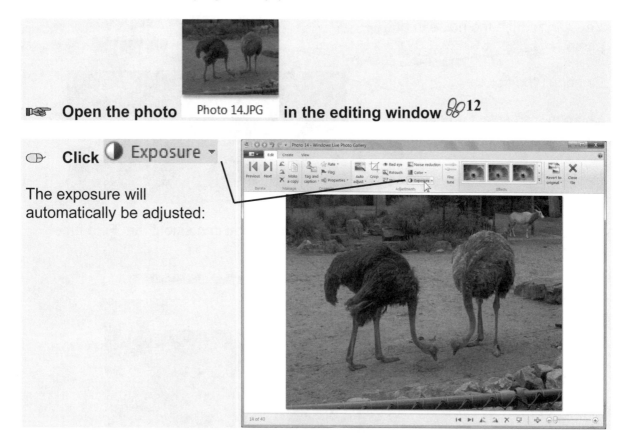

☞ **Open the photo**   Photo 14.JPG   **in the editing window** 👣¹²

The exposure will automatically be adjusted:

💡 **Tip**

Select your own type of exposure
Instead of letting the exposure be adjusted automatically, you can also choose a degree of exposure yourself:

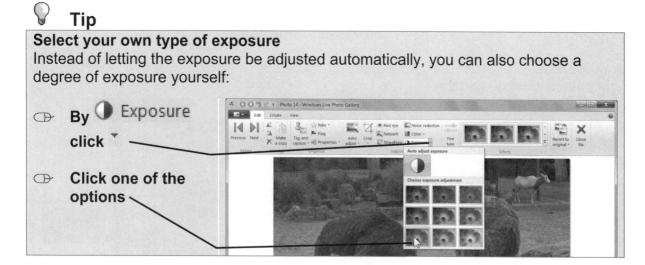

☞ **By ◑ Exposure**

click ▾

☞ **Click one of the options**

4.8 Additional Editing Options

Photo Gallery contains several other options for editing your photos:

You can reduce the noise in a photo:

Or adjust the colors:

You can also select an effect, for instance, black and white:

If you want to influence the adjustments a bit more, you can select the 'Fine tune' option.

☞ **Click** Fine tune

Select one of the editing options:

☞ **Click** Adjust exposure

You can edit the photo manually, by dragging the sliders ▯:

To close the fine tune window:

☞ **Click** ✖

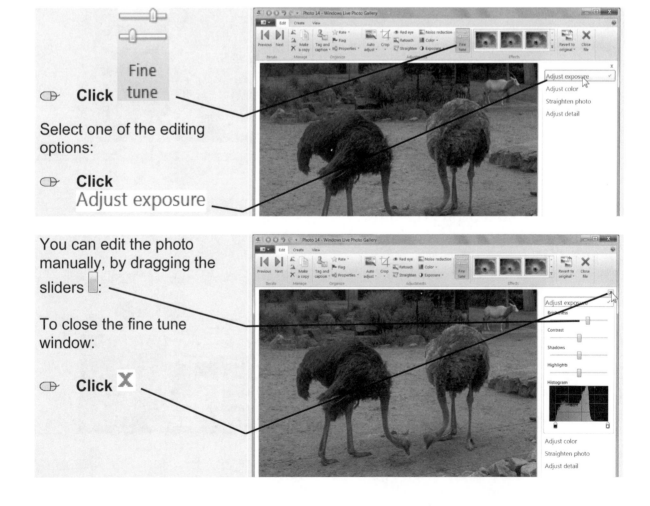

☞ **Close** *Photo Gallery* 👣²

In this chapter we have discussed various options for editing photos in *Photo Gallery*. You can try all these editing options on your own. You can always use the *Revert* option to revert back to the original photo.

4.9 Background Information

Dictionary	
Retouch	Editing a photo to remove small flaws.
Zoom in	View details in a photo up close.

Source: Help for Windows Live, Wikipedia

Why some photos cannot be edited

Sometime you will not be able to edit a photo in *Photo Gallery*, or change the file properties (such as tags, classifications or titles). If this occurs, you may see a message that tells you the file cannot be edited.

If you see such a message, you will probably not be able to edit the photo because of the following reasons:

- *The photo file is a read-only file*: If a photo is saved as a read-only file, you will not be able to edit the photo, or change the file properties. You can solve this problem by changing the read-only setting. In the *Tips* at the back of this chapter you can read how to do this.

- *The photo has been stored to a read-only location*: For example, if your photos have been saved to a CD, DVD or an external media player, you will not be able to edit them, or change the file properties. You can solve this problem by copying the photos you want to edit to a folder on your computer.

- *The photo has been saved in a file format that is not supported by the program*: In *Photo Gallery*, some file formats, such as BMP, PNG, RAW, or GIF cannot be edited. If you want to edit a photo that has been saved in one of these formats, you can open the photo in *Paint* first and then save it in a file format that is supported, for example JPG.

4.10 Tips

💡 Tip

Change the settings for Auto adjust

By default, the color and exposure of the photo will be adjusted and the photo will be straightened, if necessary. But you can change these settings:

☞ **Click** Auto adjust ▾

☞ **Click** Settings...

Here you can select the adjustments for the *Auto adjust* function: ————

Also, you can determine the quality of the picture. A higher quality means the file will become larger: ————

In the bottom of the window:

☞ **Click** OK

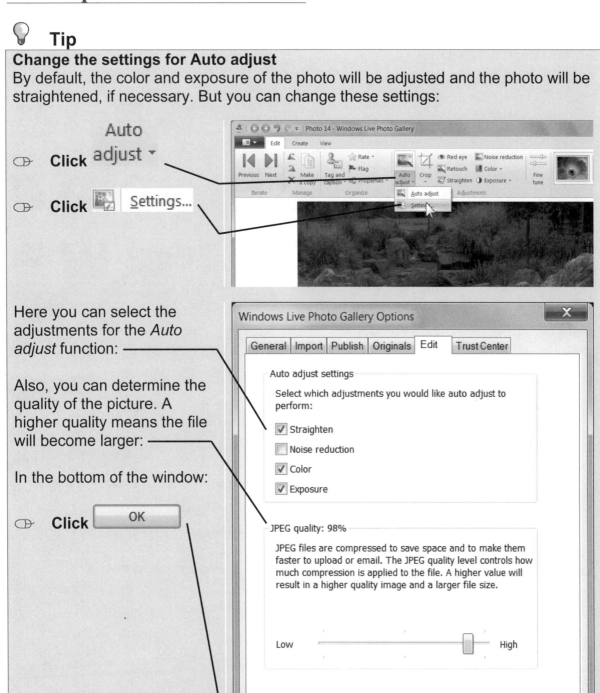

Tip

Disable read-only
If a photo file has a read-only property, you cannot edit it in *Photo Gallery*. This is how to disable this property:

☞ **Right-click the photo**

☞ **Click** Properties

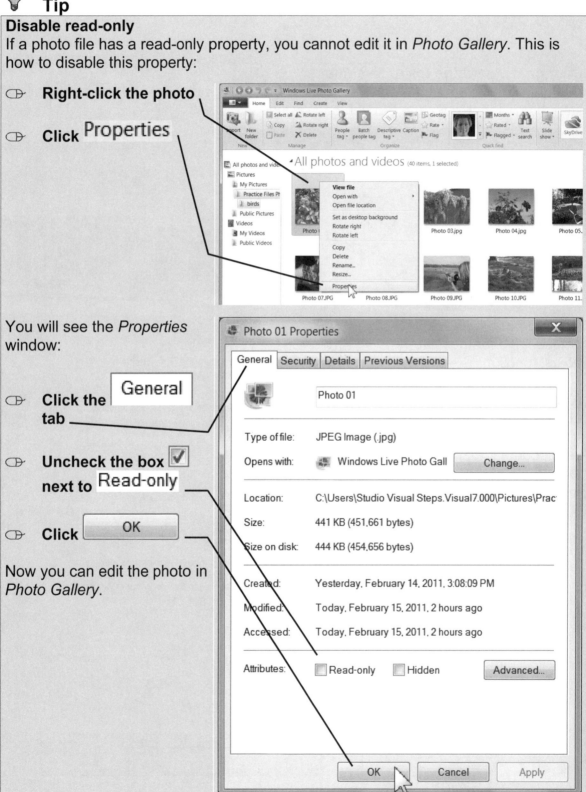

You will see the *Properties* window:

☞ **Click the** General **tab**

☞ **Uncheck the box** ☑ **next to** Read-only

☞ **Click** OK

Now you can edit the photo in *Photo Gallery*.

5. Printing and E-mailing Photos

In *Chapter 2 Viewing Photos* you learned how to use *Photo Gallery* to view photos on your computer as a slide show. Perhaps you would like to print some of these photos or even frame them. *Photo Gallery* provides the option of printing photos in a variety of different sizes. You can use *Photo Gallery* to send your photos by e-mail, directly from the program. You can also send the photos as attachments to an e-mail message but then you need to make sure the files are not too large.

If you have a *Windows Live ID* and use *Windows Live Mail*, you can send a 'photo message'. A smaller version of the picture will be sent to the recipients, but at the same time the original version will be stored on the Internet, in a secure location. Recipients can download the original version with a single mouse-click. In this way you can send more than one photo at a time without the worry of overloading someone's inbox.

In this chapter you will learn how to add an e-mail account. In *Windows Live Mail* you can manage multiple e-mail accounts in one place, such as *Hotmail* accounts. Then you will learn how to create a photo message and how to send attachments with an e-mail message.

If you already have a *Windows Live ID* and/or you are already using *Windows Live Mail*, you can skip the first two sections. If you do not want to create a *Windows Live ID,* and/or you do not want to install *Windows Live Mail*, you can go directly to *section 5.4 Sending Photos as an Attachment*.

In this chapter you will learn how to:

- print photos;
- add an e-mail account to *Windows Live Mail*;
- send a photo message;
- send photos as an attachment to an e-mail message.

 Please note:

To work through all the exercises in this chapter, you will need to download the relevant practice files from the website to the (My) *Pictures* folder on your computer. You can read how to do that in *Section 1.2 Download the Practice Files for Photo Gallery*.

5.1 Printing Photos

☞ **Start** *Photo Gallery* ✂¹

First you are going to select the photos you want to print:

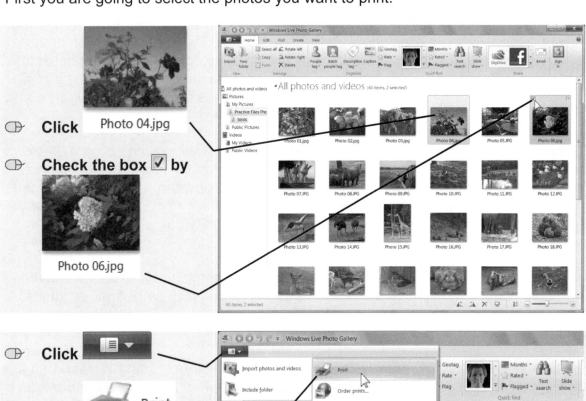

☞ **Click** Photo 04.jpg

☞ **Check the box** ☑ **by**

Photo 06.jpg

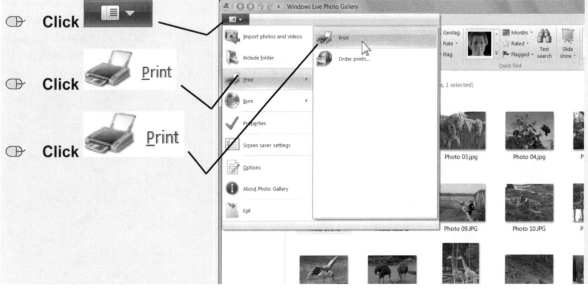

☞ **Click**

☞ **Click** Print

☞ **Click** Print

In this window you can change various print settings. The number of options available may be different than the ones shown here; this depends on the printer you use.

You will see your default printer: ———
If you want to select a different printer, click 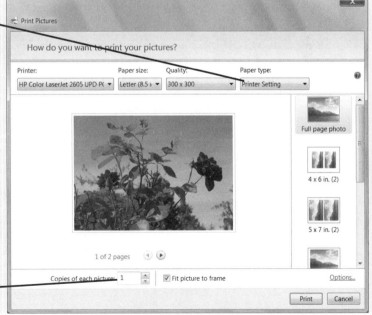 and select the printer.

Here you can select the paper size: ———
The default paper size is Letter (8,5). You do not need to change this for this exercise.

Depending on your printer, you can select the print quality: ———

You may also be able to select the paper type: ———
This might be important if you are using photo paper, for example. If you want to use regular printer paper, you do not need to change these settings.

Here you can select the number of copies you want to print: ———

Tip

Fit the image to the frame
The actual dimensions of digital photos do not always correspond to the default print sizes. That is why you may often see a white border when you want to frame your picture in a standard-sized photo frame.

If you want to print a photo in the exact frame size (for instance 4 x 6 inch) you need to check the box ☑ next to Fit picture to frame.

Photo Gallery will enlarge the image, so the photo will be printed in the same size you have chosen.

Please note: due to this adjustment, a portion of the photo may be outside the printable area. As a result, the border of the photo may not be printed.

Now you are going to print the photos in the 3.5 x 5 inch size.

☞ **Drag the scroll bar downwards**

☞ **Click** 3.5 x 5 in. (4)

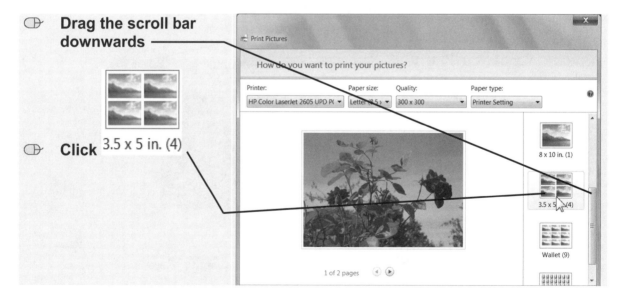

In the preview you will see that there is still space for two more photos:

This is how you print the photos twice:

⊕ **By**
Copies of each picture:
click ▲

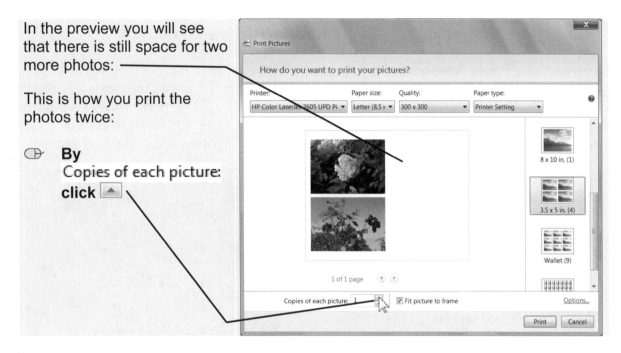

☞ **Check if your printer has been turned on**

If you want to print the photos:

⊕ **Click** Print

If you do not want to print the photos:

⊕ **Click** Cancel

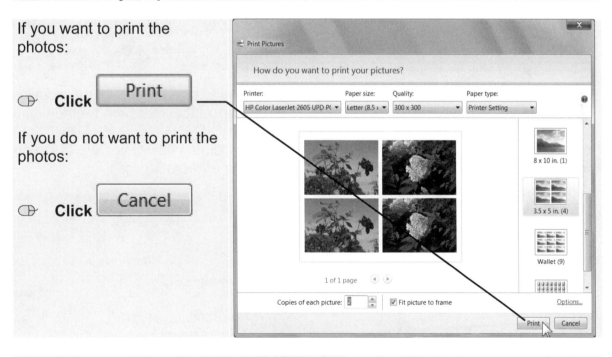

☞ **Close** *Windows Live Photo Gallery* ♐²

5.2 Add an E-mail Account in Windows Live Mail

You can use *Photo Gallery* to send photos by e-mail. If you use *Windows Live Mail* and have a *Windows Live ID* you can also send photos in a photo message. If you do not have a *Windows Live ID,* you can read *Appendix C. Create a Windows Live ID* and learn how to obtain one. In *Windows Live Mail* you can add multiple e-mail accounts, such as a *Hotmail* account, among others. To open *Windows Live Mail*:

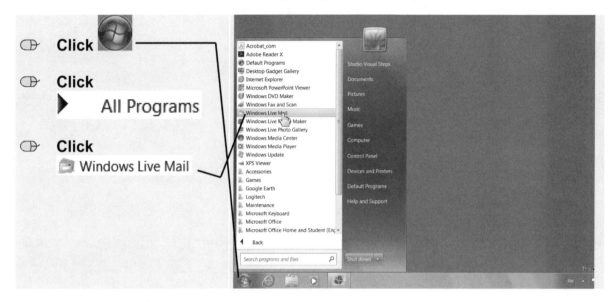

When you open *Windows Live Mail*, you may be asked to sign in with your *Windows Live ID*. If you do not yet have an account, you can cancel this message for the time being. Now you will learn how to set multiple accounts.
If you have already set a *Windows Live ID* for your account, you will be able to log on right away. You can continue with *section 5.3 Sending a Photo Message*.

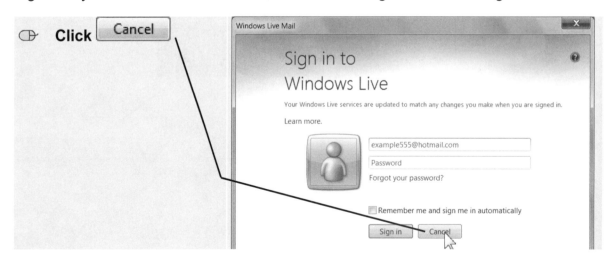

HELP! I see a different window.

Do you see the second window on this page? Then continue on from that window.

Now you are going to add an e-mail account, so you will be able to receive and send e-mail messages:

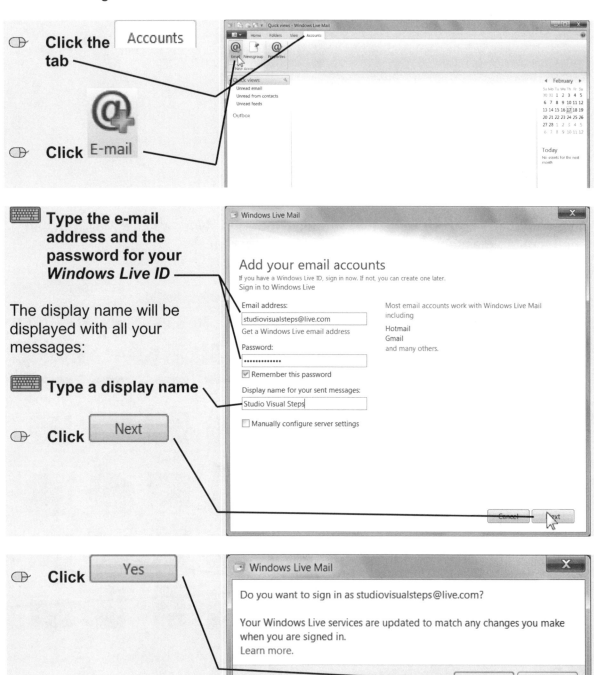

➦ **Click the** Accounts **tab**

➦ **Click** E-mail

⌨ **Type the e-mail address and the password for your** *Windows Live ID*

The display name will be displayed with all your messages:

⌨ **Type a display name**

➦ **Click** Next

➦ **Click** Yes

If you want, you can add
another e-mail account:
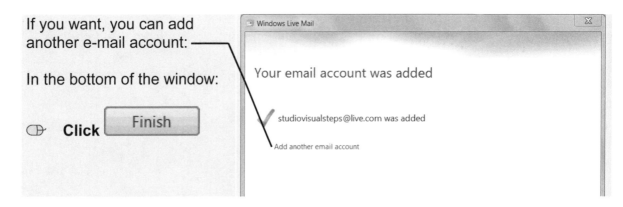
In the bottom of the window:

👉 **Click** Finish

Now your e-mail account has been added.

5.3 Sending a Photo Message

If you have a *Windows Live ID* and you have installed *Windows Live Mail*, you can
send a photo message from the *Photo Gallery* program.

👉 **Start** *Photo Gallery* ✌¹

Now that the photos are
selected, you can create the
photo message:

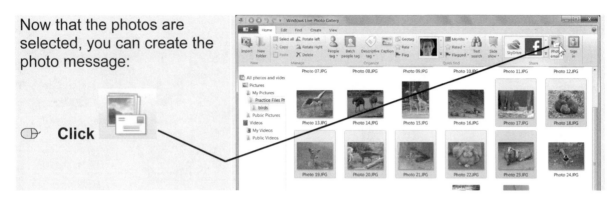

Click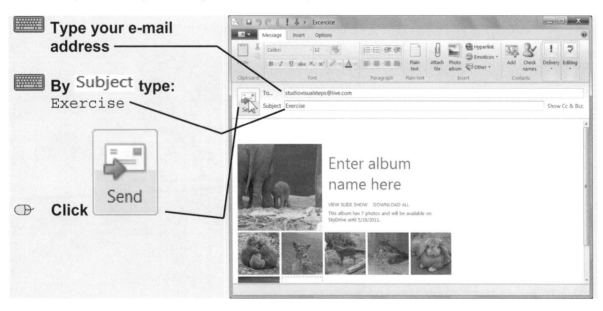

You may need to sign in first with your *Windows Live ID*, if you want to send a photo
message.

Type the e-mail
address and password
for your *Windows Live
ID*

Click Sign in

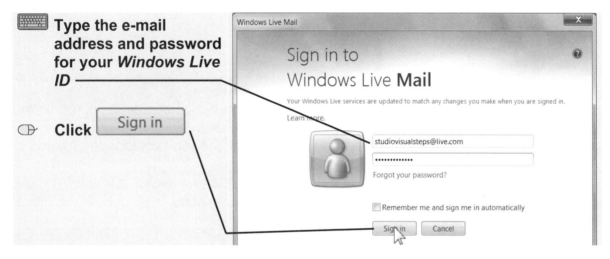

You can practice by sending the photos to your own e-mail address:

Type your e-mail
address

By Subject type:
Exercise

Click Send

Please note:

Sending a photo message
may take a while. You will
probably see this window:

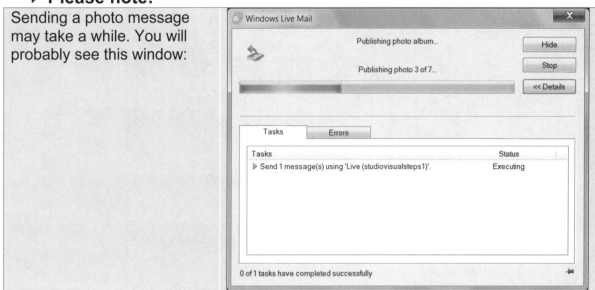

The recipient, in this case yourself, will now receive an e-mail containing compressed
versions of the photos. Simultaneously, the original versions will be saved on the
Internet, in a secure location. The e-mail message will tell you how long the photos
will be available.

Take a look now at the e-mail message in *Windows Live Mail*:

☞ **Double-click the e-mail
message**

| ✉ | **Exercise** | 11 |
| | Studio Visual Steps | |

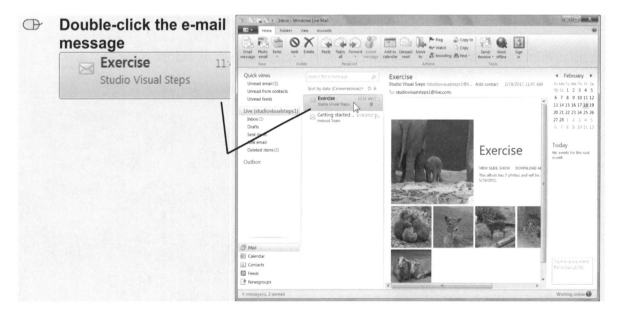

Click
VIEW SLIDE SHOW

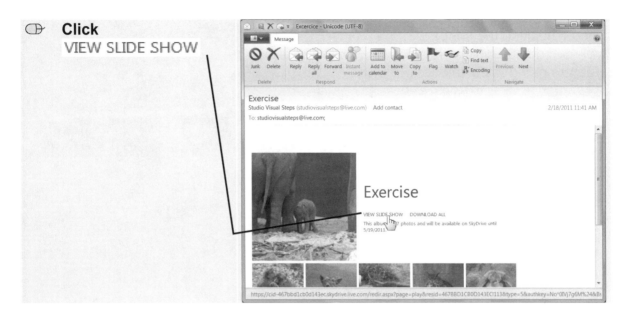

You can also download the pictures and save them to your computer.

➡ **Please note:**

The recipient must be signed in with a *Windows Live ID* if he or she wants to download the photos.

In this example you are going to download all the photos:

 Click Download

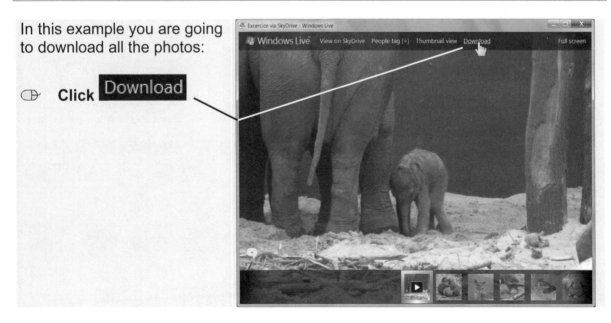

If you have not signed in yet with your *Windows Live ID*, you may be asked to sign in:

☞ **If necessary, sign in with your *Windows Live ID* 👣4**

By unchecking the boxes ☑
you can decide which photos
you are going to download:

👉 **Click** Download

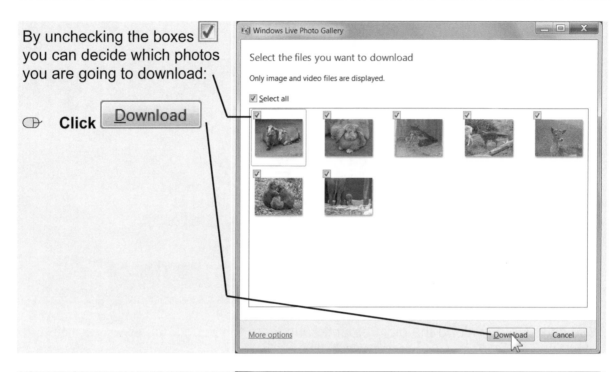

During the downloading
process you will see this
window:

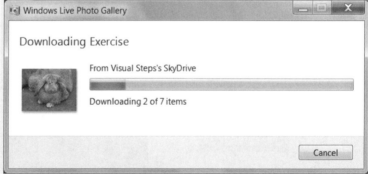

The photos have been stored
in the *Downloaded/Exercise*
folder:

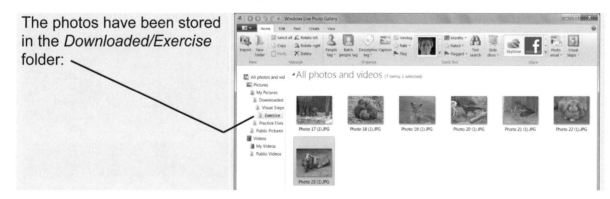

👉 **Close the slide show window** 👣²

👉 **Close the e-mail window** 👣²

5.4 Sending Photos As Attachment

Photo Gallery also allows you to send photos as an attachment to an e-mail message. This does not require a *Windows Live ID*.

If you have not yet opened *Photo Gallery*:

☞ **Start *Photo Gallery*** ✏¹

If you have not yet selected the photos:

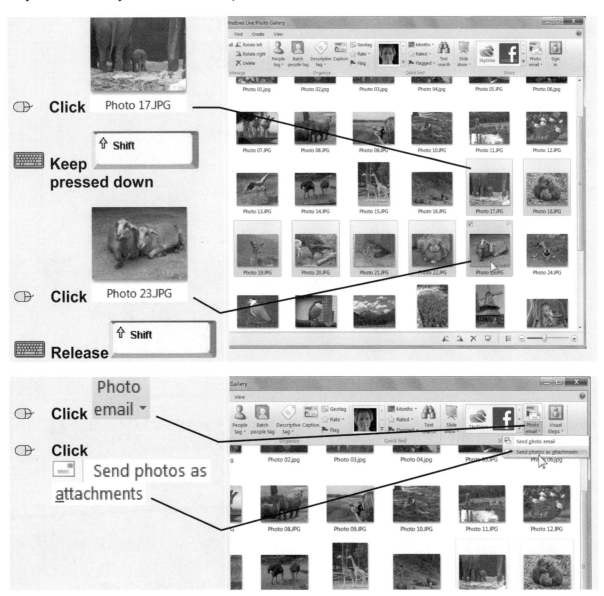

HELP! I do not see Photo email ▾ .

If you have not installed *Windows Live Mail* and have not added an e-mail account, you will not see Photo email ▾ in *Photo Gallery*. You will see E-mail instead.

In that case you need to click E-mail .

If the attachment is too large to send by mail, you can reduce the size of the images:

Here you can see the size of the attachment: ——

⬚ **Click**

Medium: 1024 x 768

⬚ **Click**
Smaller: 640 x 480

⬚ **Click** Attach

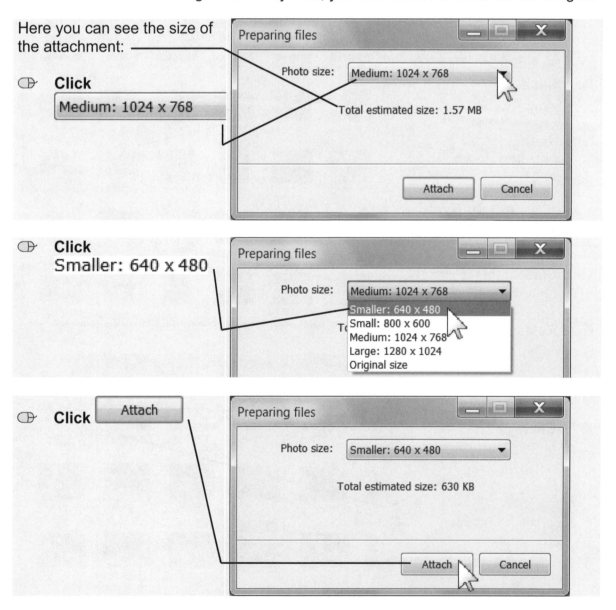

A new e-mail message will be
opened automatically.
The photos have been added
to the message as an
attachment:

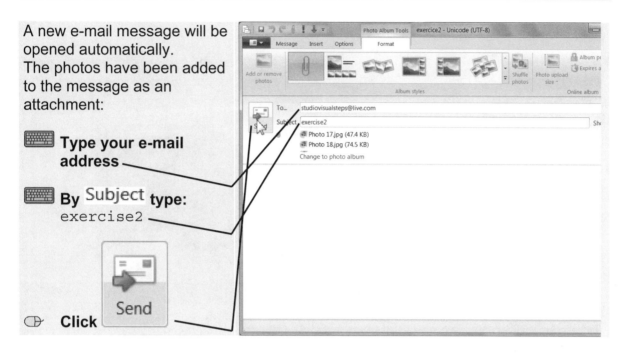

⌨ **Type your e-mail
address**

⌨ **By** Subject **type:**
exercise2

🖰 **Click** Send

Now the photos have been sent to your own e-mail address. You can take a look at
this message:

☞ **If necessary, open your e-mail program**

🖰 **Double-click the e-mail message**

You can view the photos and
save them on your computer.
The method for saving the
photos will vary, depending
on the e-mail program you
use.

If you are using *Windows Live
Mail*, you can save the photos
in the following way:

🖰 **Double-click the photo**

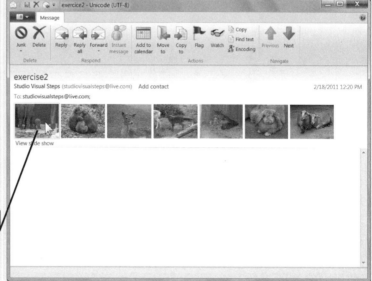

You will see the photo in *Windows Live Photo Gallery*:

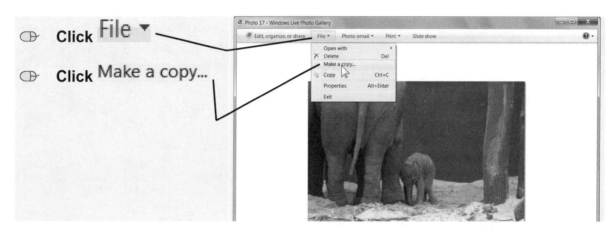

⊕ Click **File** ▼

⊕ Click **Make a copy...**

You will see the *Make a copy* window:

If you want, you can select a different folder, or change the file name: ———————

⊕ Click [Save]

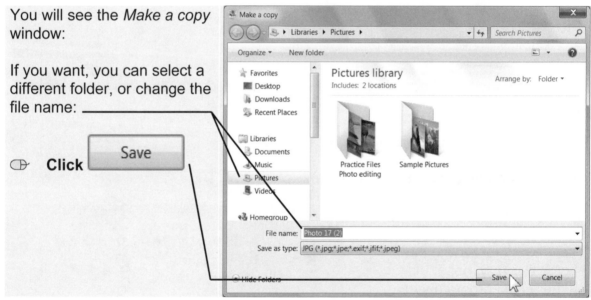

☞ **Close all windows** 👣²

In this chapter you have learned how to create and send a photo message. Photo messages can be very useful, because it gives you a way of sending a lot of pictures at once and they take up a lot less space in the inbox of the recipient's e-mail program. The recipient can decide whether he wants to download the photos to his computer, or not. The photos will be stored (temporarily) in a safe location on the Internet. In order to do this though, you will need to have *Windows Live Mail* and a *Windows Live ID*.

You can also send photos as an attachment to an e-mail message, but then you will be restricted by the maximum size allowed for sending photos by e-mail.

5.5 Background Information

Dictionary	
Download	Copying a file from another computer or from the Internet to your own computer.
E-mail account	An account consists of information given to you by your Internet provider or by *Windows Live ID*. With this information you will be able to send and receive e-mail messages.
Hotmail	Free online e-mail service provided by *Windows Live*.
Internet Explorer	A program you can use to surf the Internet and view websites.
Photo message	An e-mail message that includes compressed pictures, whereby the original photos are stored at a secure location on the Internet. The recipient can view and download the original photos from within the e-mail message.
Pixels	A dot on a computer screen or in a digital image. All of these dots put together create an image. Anything you see on your screen consists of multiple pixels.
Resolution	The number of available pixels of your monitor. A higher resolution will provide a higher quality image. In a digital camera the resolution indicates the number of pixels of the light-sensitive chip.
Windows Live ID	An account that enables you to use all *Windows Live* products. If you have en e-mail address that ends in *hotmail.com* or *live.com*, you will automatically have a *Windows Live ID*.
Windows Live Mail	The latest *Windows* e-mail program. The program is part of *Windows Live Essentials* and can be downloaded from the Internet for free.

Source: Windows Live Essentials Help pages, Windows Help and Support

Resolution and print size

The more dots (pixels) a photo contains, the larger the photo size you will be able to print while retaining a high quality (300 DPI).

In the table below you will see the connection between the resolution and the maximum print size:

Resolution	Pixels	Print size (width x height)
VGA (Webcam)	640 x 480	2.1 x 1.6 in
1,3 megapixels	1280 x 960	4.3 x 3.2 in
2 megapixels	1600 x 1200	5.3 x 4 in
3,3 megapixels	2048 x 1536	6.8 x 5.1 in
4 megapixels	2288 x 1712	7.6 x 5.7 in
5 megapixels	2560 x 1920	8.5 x 6.4 in
6 megapixels	2816 x 2112	9.4 x 7 in

In this table you can see that if you want to enlarge a photo and print it in the standard 8 x 10 in size, your photo will have to consist of more than six megapixels. As most modern digital compact cameras use a resolution of ten megapixels, or more, that should not be a problem.

Quick overview of printer types

For printing at home, there are three main printer types capable of professional quality output from digital originals.

Inkjet

The most popular printer type for printing photos. An inkjet printer will spray very small drops of ink on to the paper, through a series of spraying nozzles. Modern inkjet printers with photo quality can handle resolutions up to 2880 DPI. This will result in very sharply defined, pattern-free photos. Furthermore, many inkjet printers can use six different colors of ink, which will enhance the smoothness of color transitions in the print even further.

- Continue reading on the next page -

Dye-sublimation

In this system a carefully-controlled heating element transfers small, variable-size dots of pigment from a three or four-color ribbon to the paper. Successive panels will be printed, first in yellow, then in magenta, cyan and finally an extra overcoating layer. Paper and film are available in a single package, suited to a particular print size, for example, 8 x 10 inches.

The dye-sublimation system is a half-tone procedure, comparable to that of a traditional photo. Dye-sub prints are known for their smooth color transitions in particular. They do not form a pattern and are not easily recognized, even with a magnifying glass. This means a dye-sublimation print can barely be distinguished from a conventional photo. The overcoating layer which is applied as a final layer will make the print extra solid. The layer will protect the colors from the influence of ultraviolet light, which is the main cause of discoloration. Furthermore, damage and tears are prevented. The protective layer will also render the photo washable and virtually unaffected by fingerprints. These printers are also called Dye-Sub printers.

Fujifilm PG-series

Fujifilm PG350 and PG4000-II printers use a special dye-transfer process; the resulting prints have a look and feel that closely mimics traditional photographic color prints with excellent sharpness. Both PG series printers include a calibration system that enables them to produce consistent output.
Source: www.microsoft.com

How does an inkjet printer work?

An inkjet printer is also called a bubble jet printer. This type of printer has a print head that moves across the paper horizontally. The print emerges line by line. With every passing, the print head will spray tiny dots of ink on the paper. The amount of ink that is sprayed each time, equals the size of one millionth of a drop of water.

- Continue reading on the next page -

Because the ink is sprayed, there is no direct contact between the print head and the paper. That is why an inkjet printer does his job quite silently. Modern inkjet printers are all color printers. But you can choose an option for printing only in black and white.

Inkjet printers use ink cartridges in different colors (for example, cyan, magenta, yellow, and black) with which all other colors can be created by mixing. Special photo printers sometimes contain six, eight, or even ten separate color cartridges. The special ink used by this kind of photo printer resists the UV light better, according to the manufacturers. This means the colors will last longer.

An inkjet printer's print is made up of countless tiny drops of ink. The smaller the drops, the higher the resolution, and the sharper the picture. This is expressed in *Dots Per Inch*.

Dimensions for the clarity of pictures are 300, 600, and 1200 Dots Per Inch (DPI), or even more for special photo printers (2880 DPI). Because the spraying technique is often built-in in the ink cartridge, an empty cartridge nearly always means you will need to replace the spraying element as well. That is one of the reasons why inkjet cartridges are so expensive. But an inkjet printer is practically maintenance-free, that is one of its advantages.

Special photo printer

Inkjet paper

For daily use, for instance for printing a letter, you can use the regular 24 lb paper you can buy at the office supplies store. You can buy different types of paper for laser printers, inkjet printers and copiers. The inkjet printer paper is often a bit more expensive, but also less coarse. This will prevent the ink from spreading. Because of this you will get somewhat better results than with ordinary copy paper. But photos require a different kind of paper.

You can buy special photo paper for printing photos. This paper is extra white and very fine-grained. It is also called *Brilliant White Paper*.

The most expensive kind is the so-called *Glossy Paper*, called this way because of its shiny surface. If you use this paper, your print will resemble a regular photo.
This paper is also called
High Resolution or *720 DPI Paper*.

You can also buy photo paper in the well-known 8 x 10 inch size. Usually such a package contains twenty or twenty five sheets. But it is also sold on perforated letter-size sheets which will let you print two 8 x 10 photos per sheet.

Photo paper is not only sold by printer manufacturers, but also by paper manufacturers and other retail outlets. You are not obliged to buy the same brand of paper as your printer brand. But sometimes special kinds of paper are optimized for specific types of printers. This is especially relevant to the print resolution and the amount of ink that is used. Although a different brand of paper may also produce more than adequate results with your printer.

Special types of paper

There are even more ways of printing your photos. What about printing your own photo on a label?

You can buy label paper that is suitable for printing photos. You can get photo labels on letter-sized paper, so you can print your photo in any size you want and then cut out the label.

Smaller photo labels are also available in various sizes.

You can also print your photo on special paper which can transfer the image onto cloth, such as a T-shirt. This paper is called *Iron Transfer Paper.* It contains a special layer which will transfer the ink to the fabric when the paper is heated by flat-iron. The photo needs to be mirrored on the paper, when printed. That is necessary to transfer the photo to the T-shirt in the correct way. If you print the photo the wrong way round, the photo will be transferred to the T-shirt as a mirror image.

Transfer paper is sold in small packages, containing just a few sheets. A sheet has the standard legal paper size. After you have printed the paper, you will need to do quite a lot of finishing. First you need to cut out the image or the photo. Then you need to place the paper on the cloth, upside down, and heat it with the flat iron. The package usually contains detailed instructions for use.

5.6 Tips

 Tip

Contact sheets
Photo Gallery provides the option of printing *contact sheets.* This can be very handy. The sheet will contain 35 thumbnail views of your photos. Below the photos you can see the file names. Here is how to print a contact sheet of the practice photos:

To select all the photos:

👈 **Click** ☐ **or** ☐ **Select all**

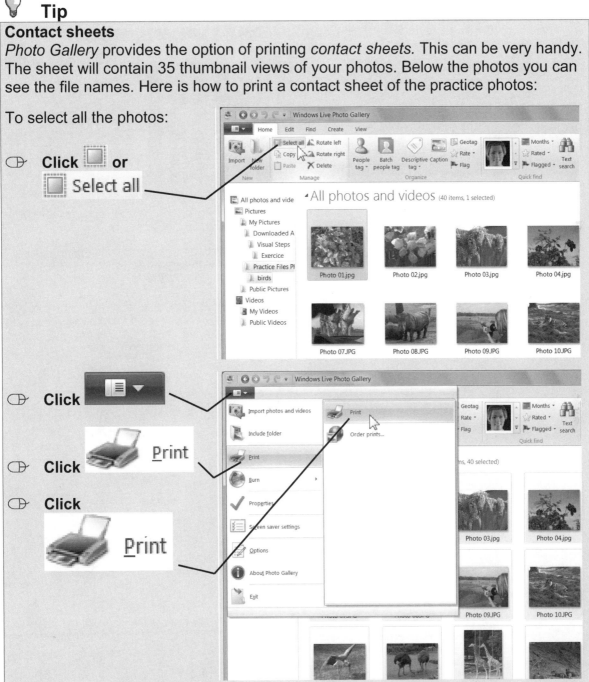

👈 **Click**

👈 **Click** 🖨 **Print**

👈 **Click** 🖨 **Print**

- Continue reading on the next page -

☞ **Drag the scroll bar downwards**

☞ **Click** Contact sheet (35)

You can see that a second page is needed, if you want to include all of the photos:

☞ **Click** Print

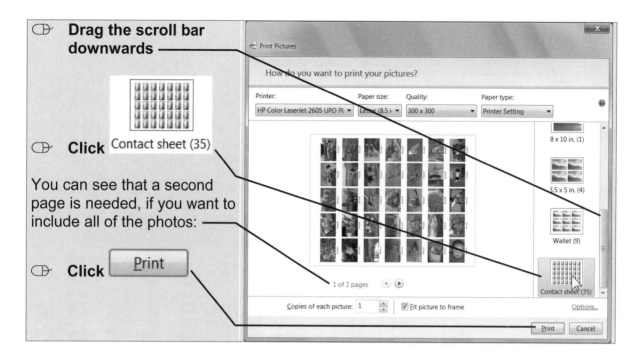

6. Burning Photos to a CD or DVD

There can be several reasons for wanting to store your photos on a CD or DVD. For example, you may want the certainty of knowing that you have a backup copy of all your important pictures.

Or perhaps you want to bring some recent pictures from a vacation or family event along with you and show them to others. You can view the photos on another computer, or you can create a video DVD that can be played on a DVD player or Blu-ray player connected to a television set. In that case you can create a slide show, select a style for the transitions between the photos and even add music.

In this chapter we will first explain how to burn photos to a CD or DVD. Later we will go over all of the steps needed to create a video DVD.

In this chapter you will learn how to:

- burn photos to a CD or DVD;
- create a video DVD.

 Please note:

To work through all the exercises in this chapter, you will need to download the relevant practice files from the website to the (My) *Pictures* folder on your computer. You can read how to do that in *Section 1.2 Download the Practice Files for Photo Gallery*.

 Please note:

If you want to burn photos to a CD or DVD, you will need to have a CD or DVD burner and a recordable CD or DVD disk. At the time of this writing, the *Photo Gallery* program did not yet have an option for burning photos to a Blu-ray disk.

 Tip

Rewritable CDs and DVDs
Use rewritable CDs and DVDs. This type of disk is more expensive than regular CDs and DVDs. But you can delete data from these disks and thereby use them more than once; you can add data to these disks over and over again. You will recognize these CDs and DVDs by the letters *RW* on the label.

6.1 Burning Photos to CD or DVD

You can burn your photos to a CD or DVD. A DVD has far more storage capacity than a CD.

☞ **Start** *Photo Gallery* 🐾¹

First you will need to select the photos you want to burn to the CD or DVD:

☞ **Click the first photo**

⌨ **Keep** ⇧ **Shift** **pressed down**

☞ **Drag the scroll bar downwards**

☞ **Click the last photo**

⌨ **Release** ⇧ **Shift**

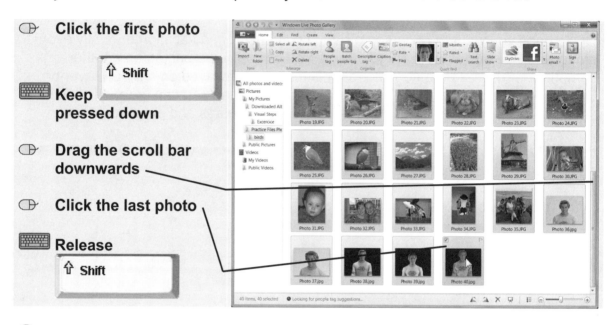

💡 **Tip**

Select all photos
You can easily select all the photos at once:

☞ **Click the** Edit **tab**

☞ **Click** ☐ **Select all**

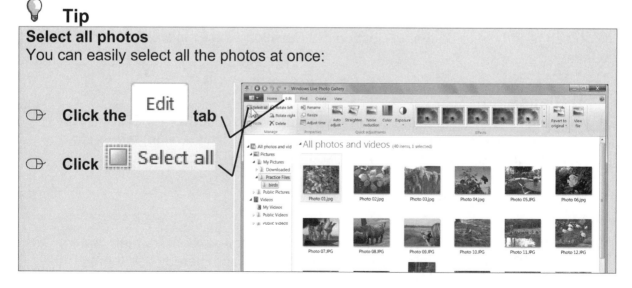

Click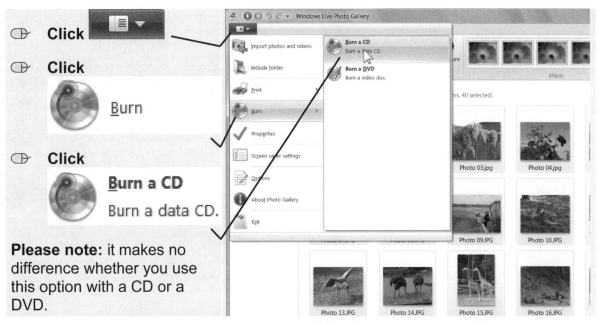

Click

Burn

Click

Burn a CD

Burn a data CD.

Please note: it makes no difference whether you use this option with a CD or a DVD.

Now you can insert a blank CD or DVD into your burner:

☞ **Insert a blank CD or DVD disk into your CD/DVD burner**

⌨ **Type:** Practice photos

You will see two options regarding the use of your CD or DVD disk. You are going to select the first option with the Live File System formatting. If you select this option, you will be able to add more photos to the disk later on:

Click Next

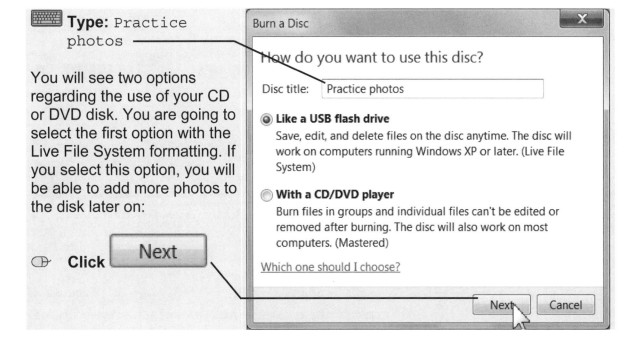

First, the CD or DVD will be formatted. Afterwards you will see the *AutoPlay* window. You can close this window:

⊕ **Click** ❌

Now you can start copying the photos to the CD or DVD:

⊕ **Click**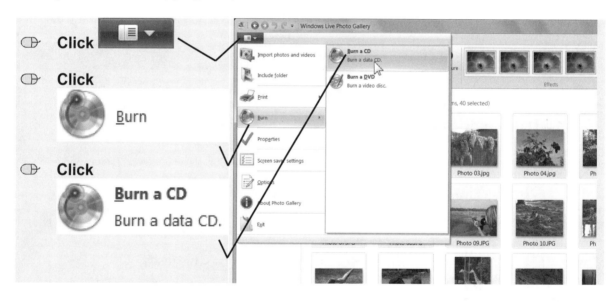

⊕ **Click** 🔘 Burn

⊕ **Click** 🔘 **Burn a CD**
Burn a data CD.

The photos will be copied.

You will see a progress window:

In *Windows Explorer* you can check if the photos have been properly burned to the CD or DVD:

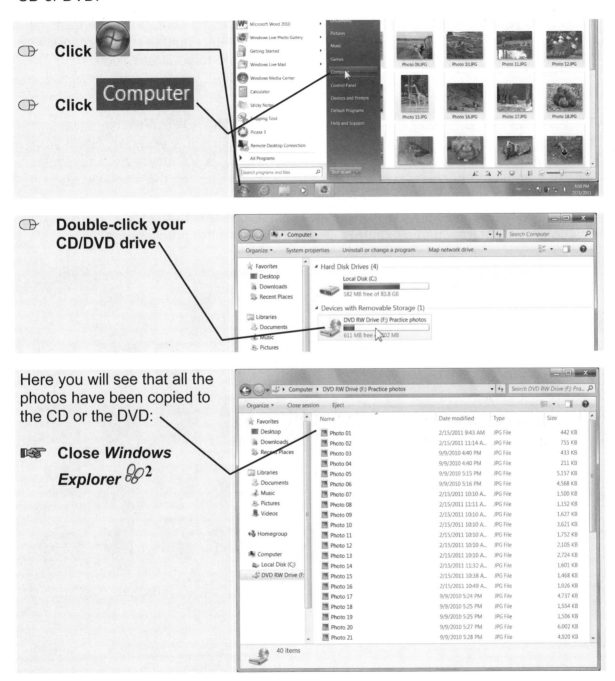

⊕ **Click**

⊕ **Click** Computer

⊕ **Double-click your CD/DVD drive**

Here you will see that all the photos have been copied to the CD or the DVD:

☞ **Close *Windows Explorer* 🐾2**

Now you can remove the CD/DVD disk from your burner. Since you selected the Live File System option in the *Burn a Disc* window, you will need to 'finalize' the disk first, before you can play it on other systems. This process may take a while.

☞ **Remove the CD/DVD from your burner**

6.2 Creating a Video DVD

You can create a DVD with a slide show of your photos. You can add slide transitions and background music. This so-called video DVD will also include a DVD menu. You can play it on a DVD player or Blu-ray player connected to your television.

🐦 Please note:

To create a video DVD you will need to have the *Windows DVD Maker* program installed. Most *Windows* editions will automatically include this program. But if your computer uses the *Windows Vista Home Basic* edition, or *Windows 7 Starter*, you will not be able to use this program. You can just read through the following section.

First you will need to select the photos you want to use for your video DVD. You can use your own photos. In this example, you will be using the practice photos:

Click Photo 07.JPG

⇧ **Shift**

Keep pressed down

Drag the scroll bar downwards

Click Photo 26.JPG

Release

⇧ Shift

☞ **Insert a blank DVD disk into the CD/DVD burner**

☞ **If necessary, close the *AutoPlay* window** 🦶²

The *Windows DVD Maker* program will start automatically.

You can change the order of the photos by clicking a photo and then using the ⬆ and ⬇ buttons:

You can add or remove photos by clicking ➕ Add items or ➖ Remove items.

☞ Click Options

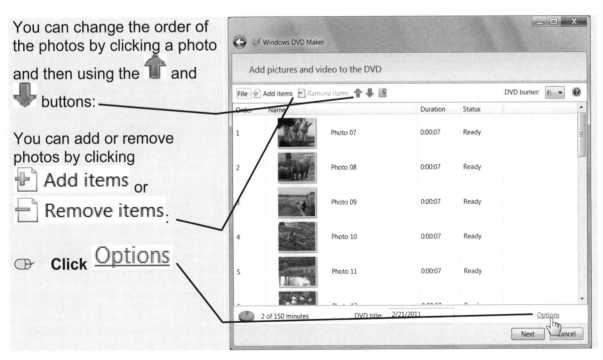

In the next window you can change a number of settings for your video DVD:

For example, you can adjust the aspect ratio: ─────

If you want to play the DVD on a North American player, you can leave the ⊙ NTSC option enabled: ─────

☞ **Click** [OK]

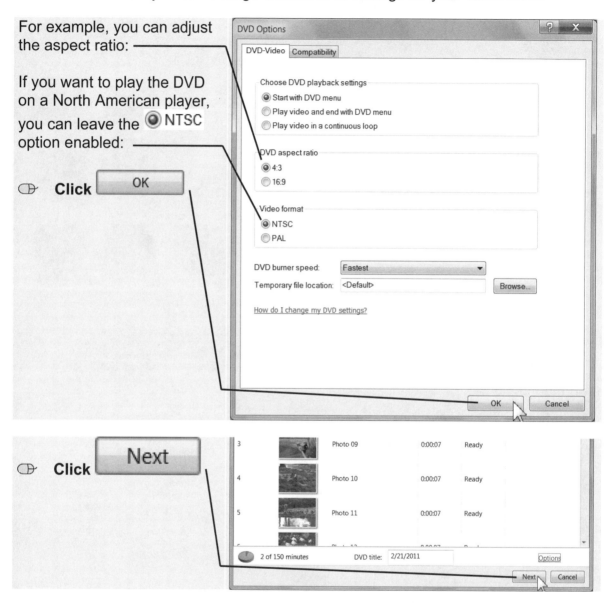

☞ **Click** [Next]

Now you can modify the slide show settings:

☞ **Click** 🖻 Slide show

You can add music to the slide show:

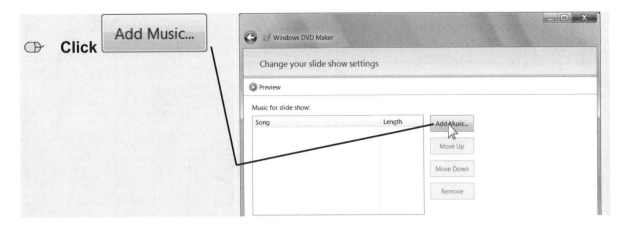

In this example we have used the sample music that is included in *Windows*, but you can choose your own music file if you want.

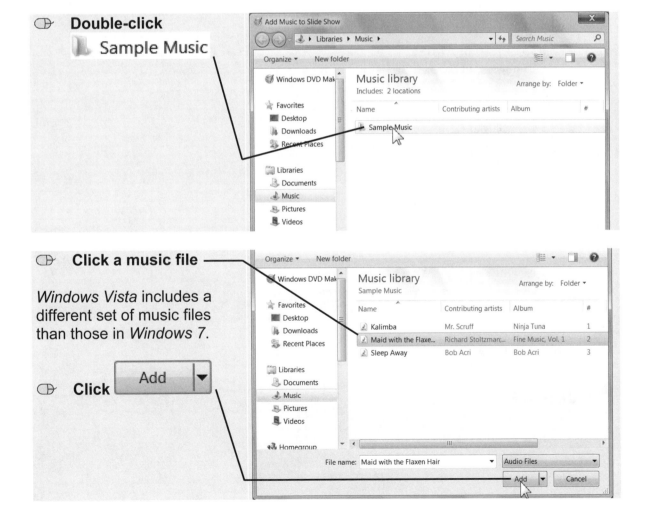

Here you can see how long the music and the slide show will take: ———

You can adjust the length of the slide show to match the length of the music:

☞ **Check the box ☑ next to**
Change slide show length
to match music length

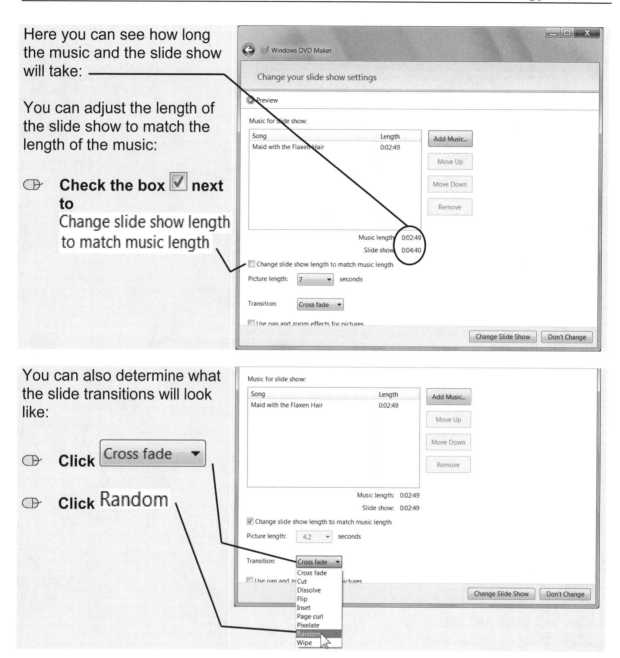

You can also determine what the slide transitions will look like:

☞ **Click** Cross fade ▼

☞ **Click** Random

Now you can take a look at the results:

☞ **Click ⊙ Preview**

☞ **Make sure your computer's sound system is turned on**

⊕ **Click** Play

You will see the slide show with its various transitions between from one photo and the next, and you will hear the background music.

⊕ **Click** OK

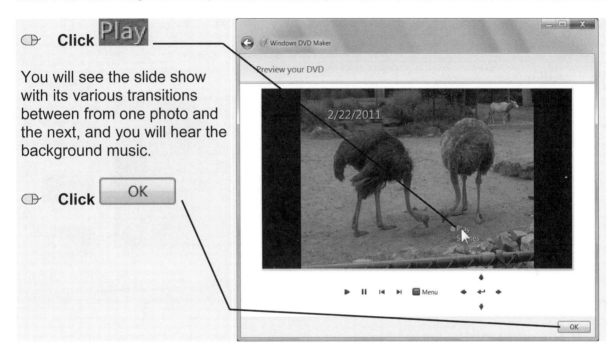

If you are satisfied with the slide show, you can apply the changes:

⊕ **Click**

Change Slide Show

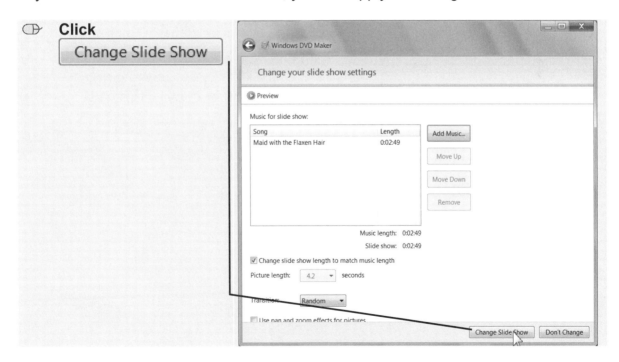

Now you can burn the DVD:

In the bottom of the window:

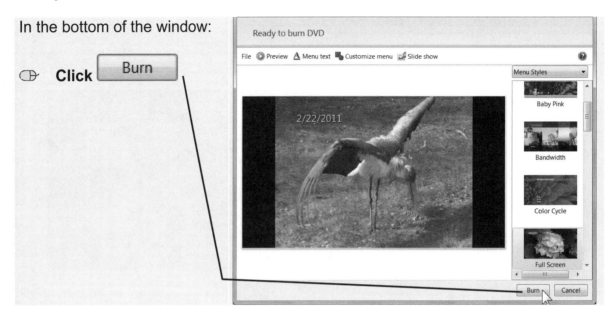

⊕ **Click** [Burn]

⤷ **Please note:**

The burning process may take a while.

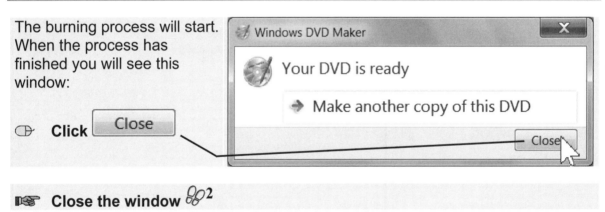

The burning process will start. When the process has finished you will see this window:

⊕ **Click** [Close]

 Close the window $\mathscr{O}^2$

You do not need to save the project:

⊕ **Click** [No]

☞ **Close** *Photo Gallery* $\mathscr{O}^2$

You can play the DVD on a DVD player or Blu-ray player connected to your television set. In this chapter you have learned how to burn photos to a CD or DVD. You have also learned how to create a video DVD with a slideshow of all your photos.

6.3 Background Information

Dictionary	
Backup	A spare copy of the data from your computer's hard drive.
Burn	Storing information on a CD or DVD.
External hard drive	Portable hard disk drive that can easily be connected to your computer.
Formatting	The process by which a storage medium, such as a CD or DVD is electronically prepared for use by a certain operating system. During this process an empty index is also created.
Live File System	A file format that can be used for creating CDs and DVDs. You can add files to disks that have been formatted with Live File System any time. And you will not need to copy (burn) all the files at once. This system is available on *Windows 7*, *Windows Vista* and *Windows XP* computers. Sometimes it may not be compatible with other devices.
USB stick	Type of memory that can be read and written through a USB port connection. Is also called memory stick.
Windows DVD Maker	Computer program that is routinely included on *Windows Vista* and *Windows 7* computers with the exception of *Windows Vista Home Basic* and *Windows 7 Starter*. The program can write data to a DVD and includes a DVD menu. You can play such a DVD on a DVD or Blu-ray player connected to your television.
Windows Explorer	A *Windows* program you can use for arranging and editing files and folders.

Source: Windows Help and Support, Wikipedia

DVD standards

At the moment there still exist two DVD standards: -r and –rw, and +r and +rw. Both types of DVDs are supported by different groups of manufacturers. *Pioneer* and *Apple* support DVD-r and DVD-rw. Dvd+r and +rw was developed by *Sony* and *Philips* and is quite common in Europe.

The advantage of -r and -rw is that these disks can be played on any DVD or Blu-ray player. Including the DVD player connected to your television set.
The disadvantage of +r and +rw is that some of the older players connected to your TV will not recognize this type of disk.

Some of the older DVD burners will be able to recognize only one of these two standard types. The current generation of DVD burners can recognize both types.

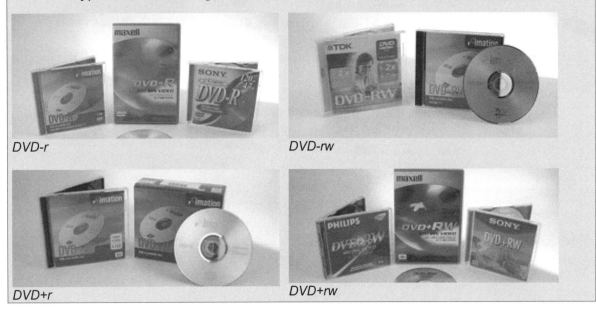

DVD-r

DVD-rw

DVD+r

DVD+rw

Single and dual layer DVD

A regular recordable DVD has a capacity of around 4.7 GB. But you can also get dual layer DVDs which have a capacity of approximately 8.5 GB. To use these disks you will need a special dual layer DVD burner. This burner is capable of burning the information onto the dual layer DVD in two separate layers.

Burners

When the first DVD burners were introduced they were extremely different from each other. Some burners were only capable of burning DVD 'minus' disks (-r and -rw), others could only handle DVD 'plus' disks (+r and +rw). The current generation of DVD burners can burn both types of disks.

If you own an older DVD burner, then check your manual for the type of disks it is capable of burning.

Usually the DVD burners' specifications can tell you which types of disks can be burned:

Modes supported:

• DVD-ROM, DVD-R, DVD-RW, DVD+R, DVD+RW, DVD-Video, CD-ROM, CD-ROM XA, CD-Audio, CD Extra, CD Text, CD-I Ready, CD-Bridge, Photo-CD, Video CD, Hybrid CD

The latest development in DVD burning is the Blu-ray burner. At the time this book was written, the *Photo Gallery* program did not have an option for burning to a Blu-ray burner.

The right combination

It is quite possible that the DVD burner in your computer will burn disks that cannot be played on your (older) DVD player connected to your TV.
The combination of DVD burner, the disk you use, and the player, determines whether you will be able to play the DVD:
• check which type of disk your DVD burner will burn;
• check which type of disk your DVD player will play;
• use the right type of disk.
Even if you have chosen the right combination, it may happen that your DVD player has problems playing your home-burned DVD on your TV. Try using a different brand of DVD disk, but use the same type of DVD. Or use a recordable (r) disk instead of a rewritable (rw) one.
Sometimes you will need to experiment a little. Fortunately there are a lot of new developments in this field. The manufacturers are trying to produce players that can play as many types of disks as possible.

Players

The first DVD players were very different from each other as well. Some players could only play DVD minus disks (-r and -rw). Others were only capable of playing DVD plus disks (+r and +rw). Some players experienced difficulties with the rw disks.

Next, players were introduced that could play not only DVDs but also MP3 CDs and CDs which contained JPG photo files. The current generation of DVD and Blu-ray players no longer distinguishes between the various DVD standards.

If you own an older DVD player, check the manual for the type of disk and the type of files this player is best suited to.

Sometimes you can find this information on the player itself:

In the manual, on the manufacturers' websites and on several comparison websites you can check a DVD player's specifications. Here you can see which types of DVDs and CDs this particular player can play:

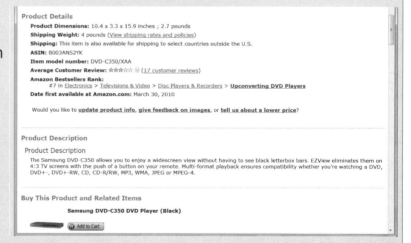

The Blu-ray and HD DVD players are the latest thing on the market.

A Blu-ray player (also called a BD player) can play Blu-ray disks as well as regular CDs or DVDs.

Types of CDs and DVDs
Here is a brief overview of the main characteristics:

Type	Properties	Capacity	Can be played on
CD-rom	Read-only.	650 MB	All computers and players (CD and DVD players).
DVD-rom	Read-only.	4.7 GB	All computers and players (DVD players).
CD-r	Recordable in multiple sessions. Data cannot be deleted.	700 MB up to 900 MB	After finalizing, compatible with most computers and players (CD and DVD players).
CD-rw	Rewritable in multiple sessions. Data can be deleted.	700 MB	Compatible with a lot of computers and players but not all of them. Especially older players will have issues.
DVD-r or DVD+r	Recordable in multiple sessions. Data cannot be deleted.	4.7 GB	After finalizing, compatible with most computers and players (DVD players).
DVD-rw or DVD+rw	Rewritable in multiple sessions. Data can be deleted.	4.7 GB	Compatible with a lot of computers and players but not all of them. Especially older players will have issues.
Dual layer DVD DVD DL	DVD with double storage capacity.	8.5 GB	Only suitable for the newest players. Not yet supported by all software programs.

Note:
- r stands for recordable. Data can be written to the disk, but not deleted. rw and re stand for rewritable. Data can be written to disk more than once and can also be deleted.

DVD prices and quality

Shortly after the introduction of DVD burners, the price level for DVD recordables and DVD rewritables was quite high. But as of this writing, the costs have gone down dramatically.

There still can be a huge price difference between the various brands. The cheapest DVD-r is the white or generic DVD-r. These are often DVDs that have not made it through the manufacturer's quality tests and are sold as generic disks without a specific brand name. The well-known brands are the most expensive.

Consumer's organizations and computer magazines regularly conduct tests as to the quality of various DVD-r brands. One of the most remarkable conclusions is that the most expensive brands are not necessarily the best.

The storage life of DVD-r and DVD-rw disks is also researched on a regular basis. Some brands cannot live up to the expectations because the data on their disks turns out to be illegible after a number of years. Because of this, it is recommended to use high quality, dependable disks for backups that need to be saved for many years. Check these kinds of tests for the current situation.

If you are using lots of DVD-r disks, it is worth your while to be on the lookout for bargains. But you can also save money by using DVD rewritables. As opposed to DVD recordables, you can write data to DVD rewritables over and over again. This can be useful if you often burn files you just want to save for short periods of time. But remember that DVD rewritables are more expensive than DVD recordables.

Dvd-rewritable

Dvd-recordable

7. Creating an Online Photo Album

A useful way of sharing photos with other people is by creating an online photo album. You can upload the photos to the Internet and determine who is allowed to view these photos.

If you want to let other people know you have a new photo album available, you can send them an e-mail message containing a link. The recipients will be able to view the photos and they can also download them to their own computer. Although in order to download photos, the recipient will need to have a *Windows Live ID*.

In this chapter we will first explain how to use *Photo Gallery* to create an online photo album. Next, we will explain how to send an e-mail link to others. Finally, we will show you how to modify your online photo album at a later stage.

In this chapter you will learn how to:

- create a photo album;
- send a link;
- modify the album.

 Please note:

To work through the exercises in this chapter, you will need to have a *Windows Live ID*. If you do not yet have a *Windows Live ID*, you can read how to obtain one in *Appendix C Create a Windows Live ID*.

 Please note:

To work through the exercises in this chapter, you can use your own photos. If you want to use the photos that go with this book, you will need to download the relevant practice files from the website to the (My) *Pictures* folder on your computer. You can read how to do that in *Section 1.2 Download the Practice Files for Photo Gallery*.

7.1 Creating an Online Photo Album

You can use *Photo Gallery* to create a photo album and publish it to *SkyDrive*. This is part of the *Windows Live Essentials* program and can be used as a place for storing files on the Internet. You can share files uploaded to *SkyDrive* with other people.

☞ **Start** *Photo Gallery* 𝒶1

First, you need to select the photos you want to include in your online photo album. If you want, you can use your own photos. In this example we will be using the practice photos that go with this book.

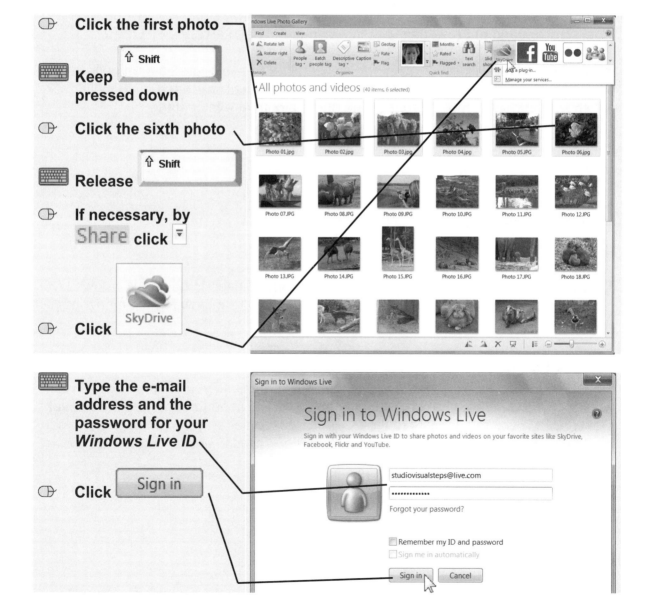

⊕ **Click the first photo**

⌨ **Keep pressed down** ⇧ Shift

⊕ **Click the sixth photo**

⌨ **Release** ⇧ Shift

⊕ **If necessary, by** Share **click** ▾

⊕ **Click** SkyDrive

⌨ **Type the e-mail address and the password for your** *Windows Live ID*

⊕ **Click** Sign in

Now you are going to enter a name for your photo album and determine who is allowed to view your photos:

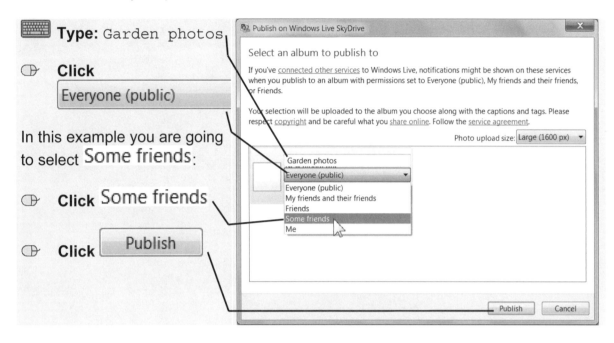

Type: Garden photos

☞ **Click**

Everyone (public)

In this example you are going to select Some friends:

☞ **Click** Some friends

☞ **Click** Publish

Now the files will be uploaded to *Windows Live SkyDrive*.

When the uploading process has finished, you will see this window:

☞ **Click** View online

Internet Explorer will be opened and you will see your online photo album. Now you can set the permissions for sharing the photo album:

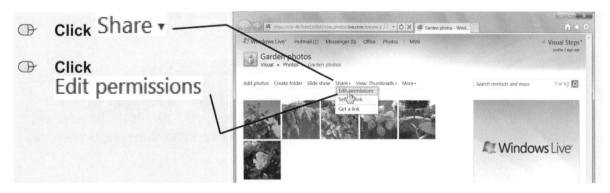

☞ **Click** Share ▾

☞ **Click** Edit permissions

You can allow new people to view your album by adding their e-mail address here. Each e-mail address needs to be separated by a comma or a blank space.

 Type one or more e-mail addresses

If you want to select addresses from your contact list, click
Select from your contact list.

☞ **Click** Save

💡 **Tip**

Allow others to add, edit and delete photos
When you grant permission to people initially, they are only allowed to view the photos. If you want them to be able to add, edit, and delete photos as well, you can change the settings:

☞ **Click** Can view photos

☞ **Click** Can add, edit details, and

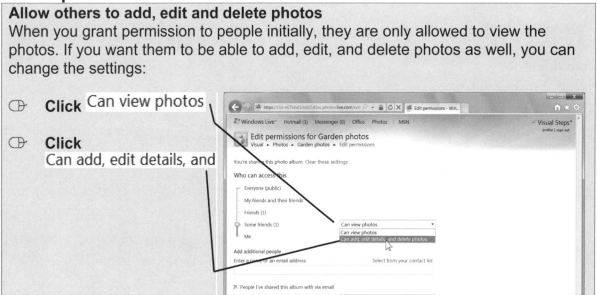

Now you have created an online photo album and you have determined who has permission to view these photos. In the following section, you can learn how to let other people know you have uploaded a new album by sending them an e-mail link.

7.2 Sending a Link

Once you are satisfied with your newly created online photo album, you can let others know about it by sending them an e-mail link. The recipient can follow this link to view the photos.

☞ **Click** Share ▾

☞ **Click** Send a link

You can practice by sending a link to your own e-mail address, so you can see what the e-mail message will look like:

⌨ **Type your e-mail address**

If you want to add more e-mail addresses, make sure they are separated by a comma or a blank space.

If you want to select addresses from your contact list, click To :

☞ **Click** Send

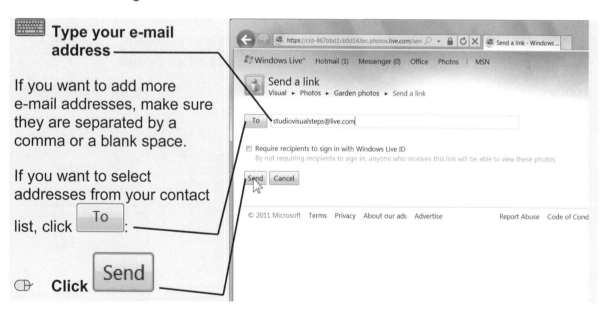

Tip

Sign in with Windows Live ID
Your e-mail's recipients do not need to sign in with a *Windows Live ID* in order to view the photos. But if you want them to sign in, you can require them to do so:

☞ **Check the box ☑ by**
Require recipients to sig

Now you can take a look at the e-mail message:

☞ **Click Hotmail (1)**

☞ **Click the e-mail message**

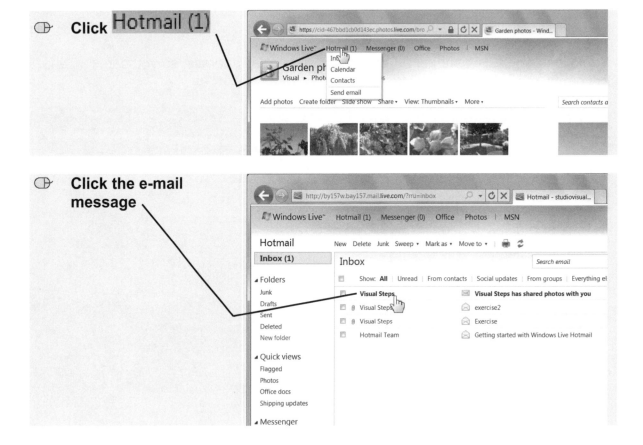

Click **View album**

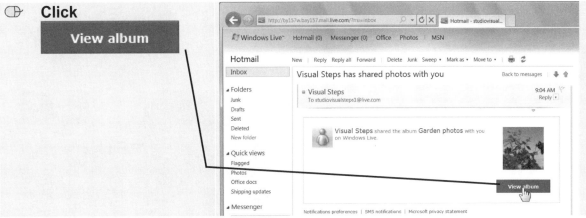

You will see a slide show with all of the pictures:

The recipient can leave a message by clicking :

If you have sent the e-mail link to someone who has a *Windows Live ID*, this person will be able to download the photos in the following way:

Move the mouse pointer across the photo

Click **View on SkyDrive**

The recipient will still need to sign in first with his or her *Windows Live ID*. Since you have already signed in, this does not apply.

The recipient can download the photo by clicking Download:

To view the other photos, click ►►, and then click the photo you want to view:

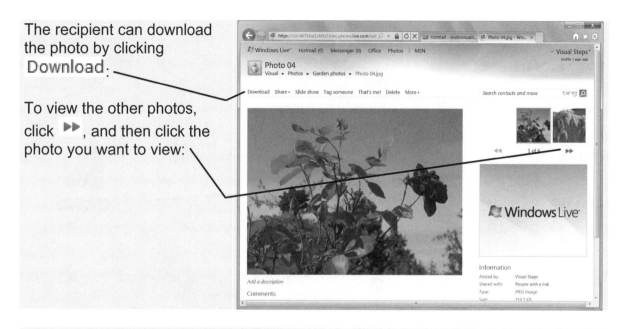

☞ **Close** *Internet Explorer* ℘²

7.3 Modifying the Album

Now you have successfully uploaded a photo album to *Windows Live SkyDrive*. If you ever need to make changes to the album, you can do so whenever you want. You start by doing the following:

☞ **Open the home.live.com web page** ℘³

If you are already signed in:

⊕ **Click** Continue

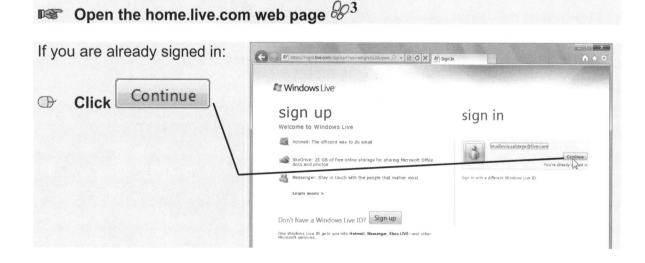

If you are no longer signed in:

☞ **Sign in now with your *Windows Live ID*** 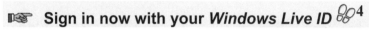⁴

⊕ **Click** Photos

⊕ **Double-click the photo album**

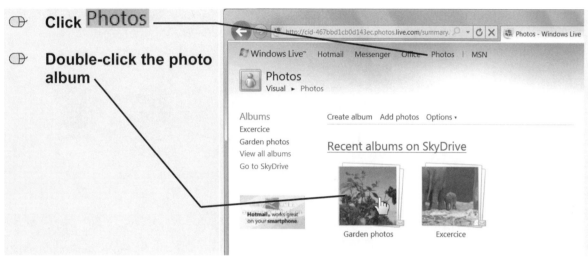

For example, you may wish to add one or more new photos:

⊕ **Click** Add photos

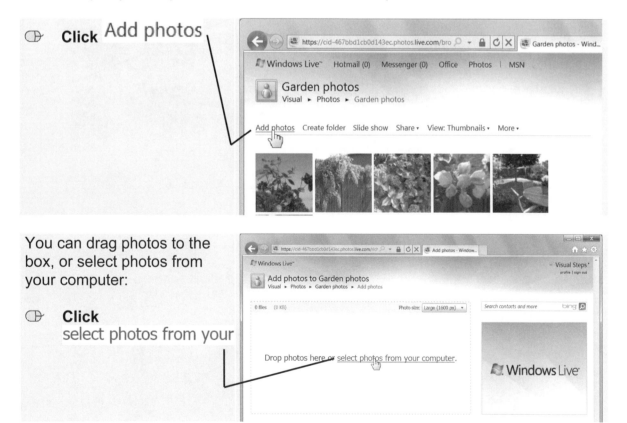

You can drag photos to the box, or select photos from your computer:

⊕ **Click**
select photos from your

You can add your own photos if you want. In this example, we will be using the practice photos that go with this book.

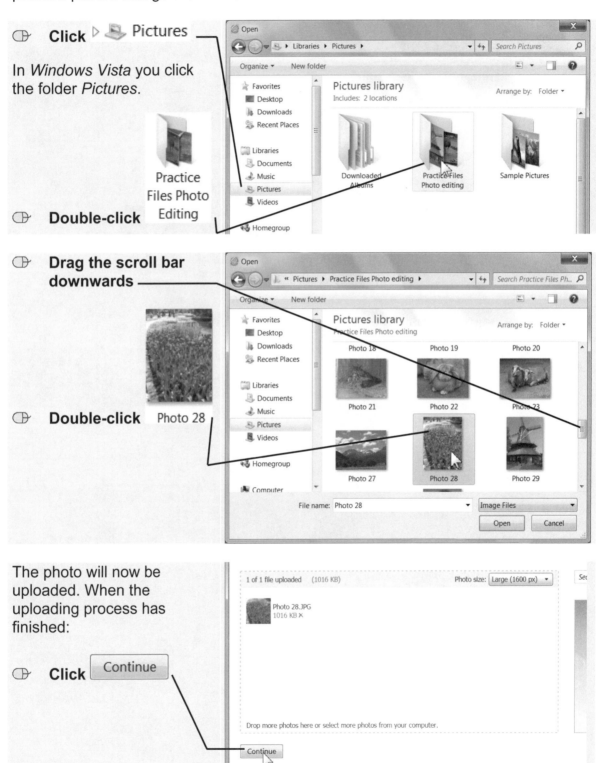

☞ **Click** ▷ 💻 **Pictures**

In *Windows Vista* you click the folder *Pictures*.

☞ **Double-click** Practice Files Photo Editing

☞ **Drag the scroll bar downwards**

☞ **Double-click** Photo 28

The photo will now be uploaded. When the uploading process has finished:

☞ **Click** Continue

You will see that the photo
has been added to the album:

Besides adding photos, you can also modify the photo album in other ways. For
instance, you can decide in what order your photos will be displayed:

☞ **Click** More ▼

☞ **Click**
Sort by: Date ▶

You can sort the photos in
various ways.

To sort the photos manually,
click Arrange photos....:

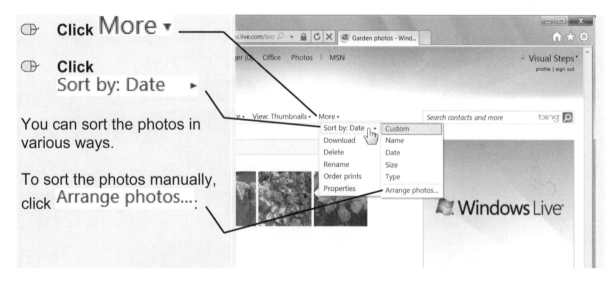

If you want to delete the entire album, click Delete:

To change the name of the photo album, click Rename:

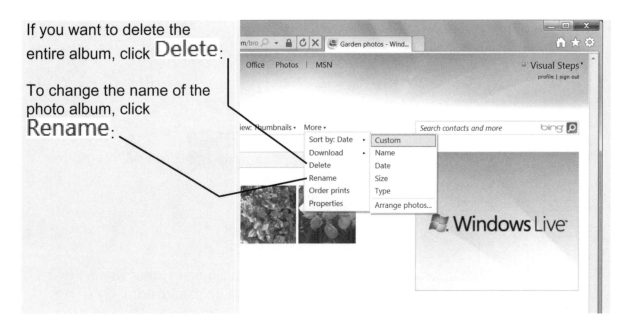

All the changes you make will be applied to the entire photo album. If you just want to edit one particular photo, you will need to select that photo first:

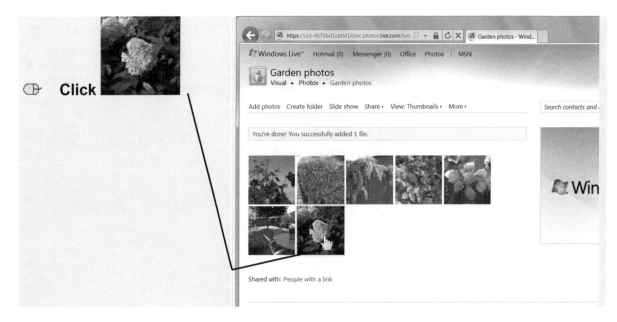

In this view you can delete the photo by clicking **Delete**:

There are even more options:

⊕ **Click More ▾**

For example, you can change the photo's name by clicking **Rename**:

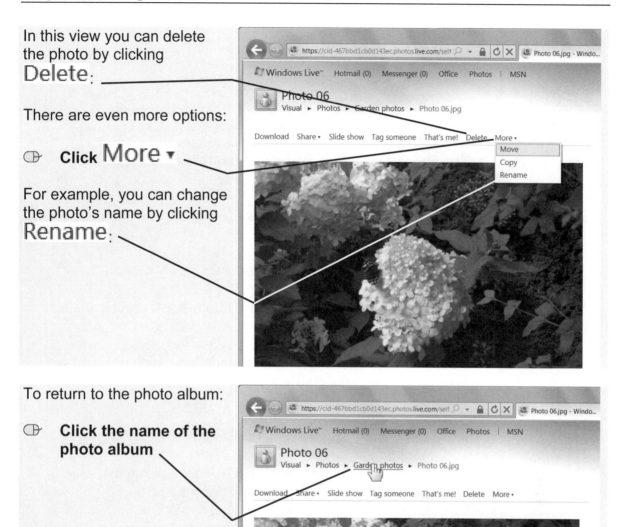

To return to the photo album:

⊕ **Click the name of the photo album**

☞ **Close** *Internet Explorer* 🦶🦶2

☞ **Close** *Photo Gallery* 🦶🦶2

In this chapter you have learned how to create an online photo album and how to upload it to *Windows Live SkyDrive*. You have also learned how to let other people know about your new album, by sending an e-mail link to them. And finally, you learned that it is always possible to modify your photo album later on, by adding or deleting photos, renaming them, or by changing the way in which they are ordered.

7.4 Background Information

Dictionary

Address bar	The *Internet Explorer* address bar contains the name of a website. You can also enter a website address here yourself.
Download	Copying a file from another computer or from the Internet to your own computer.
Hotmail	Free web-based e-mail service operated by Microsoft.
Internet Explorer	A program you can use to surf the Internet and view websites.
Link	Also called *hyperlink*. A link is a navigational tool that will take the user to another location after clicking a highlighted word or image.
Online	If you are online, you are connected to the Internet.
SkyDrive	*Windows Live SkyDrive* offers 25 GB online storage space for your own files, and for sharing files with others.
Upload	Copying a file from your own computer to another computer or to the Internet.

Source: Windows Help and Support, Wikipedia

8. Importing Photos to Your Computer

Copying photos from an external device, such as a digital photo camera, a video camera, a cell phone, an external hard drive or a USB stick, is called *importing*. You can use *Photo Gallery* to import photos to your computer.

There are two ways of importing photos made from your digital camera, video camera, or cell phone: by connecting the camera with the computer by means of a USB or firewire cable, or directly from the memory card (also called SD card) on which the photos have been stored. A memory card is a small card that can be removed from the camera.

If the photos you want to transfer are stored on a USB stick, external hard drive, or a CD, DVD or Blu-ray disk, then you can import them the same way, from within the *Photo Gallery* program. You can also use *Photo Gallery* to scan photos.

In this chapter we will first explain how to connect your digital camera, video camera, cell phone, external hard drive or USB stick to your computer. Next we will explain how you import photos from *Photo Gallery*.

In this chapter you will learn how to:

- connect the device to your computer;
- import photos to your computer;
- scan and import photos.

8.1 Importing Photos Using a USB or Firewire Cable

Most digital cameras, cell phones and external hard drives come with a USB cable that can be used to connect the device to your computer's USB port. Other types of digital cameras can be connected with a firewire cable to your computer's firewire port. Sometimes, older cameras use a serial cable. The opposite side of such a cable is connected to a smaller connection outlet on the camera itself.

The most common cable connection with a digital camera is the USB connection:

You can usually connect cell phones and external hard drives also with a USB cable.

Firewire is another alternative for connecting a digital camera with a computer. Firewire uses a smaller plug:

☞ **Make sure the device is turned off**

☞ **Connect the cable to the camera**

If you are using a cell phone or an external hard disk:

☞ **Connect the cable to the device**

☞ **Connect the USB or firewire cable to the matching port on the computer**

If your cable connector is not a USB or firewire connector, you need to connect the cable to the matching computer port on your computer (consult the device's manual).

☞ **If necessary, turn on the device**

Please note:

> Some digital cameras require that you turn on the connection mode or play mode first. In your camera's manual you will find the correct mode for your camera.

Windows will now try to connect to your camera or device.

If the device has never been connected to the computer before, *Windows* will try to install the device driver for it. The device driver ensures a stable connection between the camera, cell phone or external hard drive and the computer. A device driver is also just called a *driver*.

If the driver is available in the *Windows* program, the software will be installed automatically:

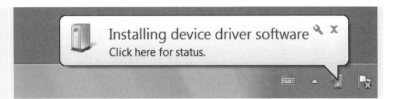

If *Windows* cannot find a suitable driver for your device, *Windows* will try to download the driver from the Internet. In that case you will see a message. If the driver is not available on the Internet, you will need to install the driver software in a different way.

Cameras that do not have a USB or firewire connection will not be automatically recognized by *Windows*. For that type of camera, you will always need to install the driver software yourself. Most camera packages include a CD or a DVD with the necessary software for using the camera with the *Windows* program.

If you still need to install the driver software yourself, then consult your device's manual first. It will explain what you will need to do to connect this device.
If the device does not come with a software CD or DVD, you can usually download the device driver from the manufacturer's website. In the manual you will often find the address for the manufacturer's website.

 Tip

> **Install a driver from the Internet**
> The CD or DVD that goes with the camera does not always contain the most recent version of the driver program. For instance, older devices will not yet have the drivers for *Windows Vista* or *Windows 7* available on CD. If you are experiencing problems with the connection between the device and the computer, it might be helpful to download and install the latest driver version from the manufacturer's website.

Look up the type of device you have on the website (as described in the manual, or on the device itself). Browse to the device's website and search for the words *download*, *driver*, or *device driver*. Normally, you will find the most recent device drivers on the website.

After you have downloaded the driver software, you can install it. First, check if the driver software includes a brief manual, usually in the form of a file called *readme*. Before installing the driver software, it is recommended that you close all other active programs in *Windows*. Open the installation program and follow the instructions on your screen.

If the device is properly connected and *Windows* has recognized the driver, you will be able to import the photos to your computer. In the following section you can read how to do that.

8.2 Importing Photos from a Memory Card

In the previous section you have learned how to connect your camera, cell phone or external hard drive to your computer by using a cable. But you can also transfer the photos directly from the memory card (also called SD card). However, for this you will need to use a card reader.

Many newer computers have a card reader already built-in. There are usually several slots available for various types of memory cards.

You can also buy portable card readers that can be connected to your computer's USB port. Before buying one, make sure the type of memory card you use is supported by the card reader.

If necessary, check your device's manual to find out where the card is located.

☞ **Connect the external device to your computer**

Apart from your camera or a memory card, you can also import photos from a USB stick, a CD, DVD or a Blu-ray disk.

☞ **Connect the USB stick to your computer**

Or:

☞ **Insert the disk into the disk drive**

8.3 Importing Photos with Photo Gallery

Now you are going to import photos from your camera, cell phone, external hard drive, USB stick, CD, DVD or Blu-ray disk with *Photo Gallery*. From this moment on, all operations will be exactly the same, no matter which device you use. When you connect an external device to your computer, the *AutoPlay* window will appear:

☞ **Click**

Import pictures and vid
using Windows Live Ph

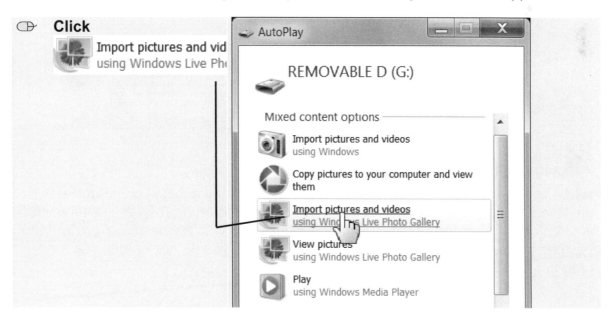

HELP! I do not see the AutoPlay window.

If the *AutoPlay* window does not appear when connecting your digital camera to the computer, it may mean that *AutoPlay* has been disabled. This is how to re-enable the *AutoPlay* setting:

Click , Control Panel

Click Hardware and Sound

Click Play CDs or other media automatically

Find your device and click ▼

Click ❓ Ask me every time

Click Save

 Turn the device off and then on again

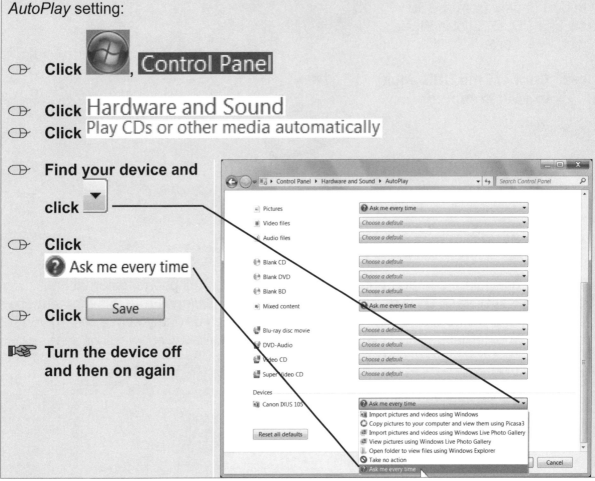

 ## HELP! I see a different window.

When you connect the device to your computer, this may result in one or more programs trying to start up automatically. Usually these programs were installed to your computer from the CD or DVD that was included with the device. If you want to, you can use such a program to import your photos. If you do not want to use the program, you can just close it.

☀ Tip

Import from *Photo Gallery*
You can also start the import operation from within the *Photo Gallery* program:

☞ **Click** *Import*

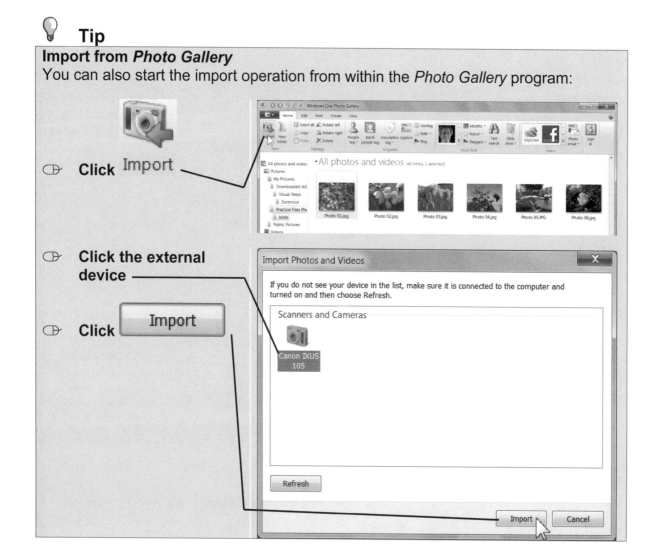

☞ **Click the external device**

☞ **Click** Import

Now you are going to select the photos you want to import:

☞ **Click** Next

You can also import all new photos at once, by clicking the radio button ◉ by Import all new items now.

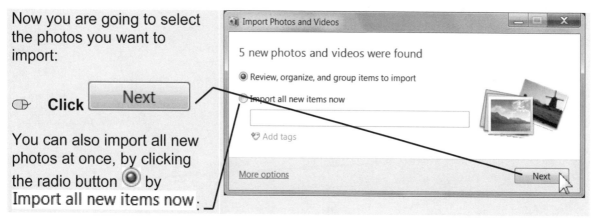

In the following window, the photos have been grouped according to their date and time. You can change this grouping by adjusting the days between the groups:

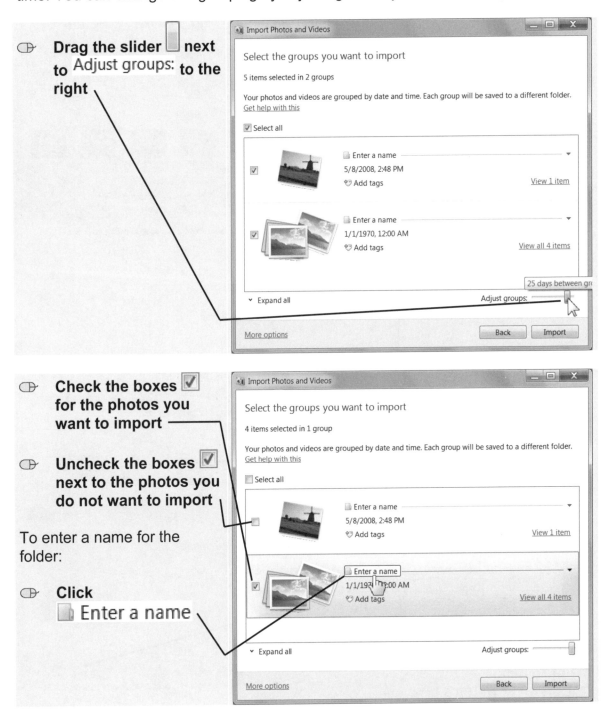

☞ **Drag the slider ☐ next to Adjust groups: to the right**

☞ **Check the boxes ☑ for the photos you want to import**

☞ **Uncheck the boxes ☑ next to the photos you do not want to import**

To enter a name for the folder:

☞ **Click ☐ Enter a name**

⌨ **Type a name** ⎯⎯⎯

☞ **Click** [Import]

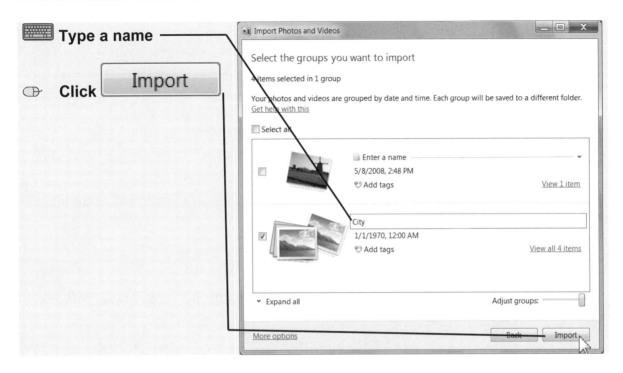

Now the photos will be imported and *Photo Gallery* will be opened:

You will see that the photos
have been imported to a
different folder in *Photo
Gallery*:

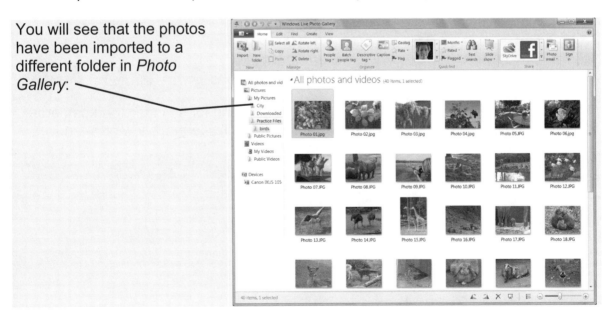

8.4 Importing Photos from a Scanner

In this section you can read about importing photos from your scanner. If you do not own a scanner, you can just read through this section.

☞ **Make sure the scanner has been installed correctly**

☞ **Make sure the scanner is turned on**

With some scanners, the corresponding scanning software program will automatically open. If that is the case:

☞ **Close the scanning program** ✌️²

☞ **Insert a photo into the scanner; the photo should be face down, with the printed side facing the glass plate**

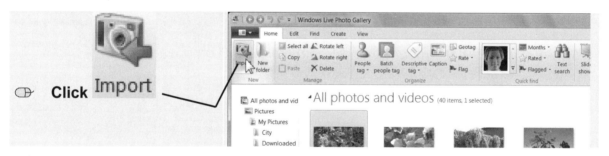

⊕ **Click** Import

The *Import Photos and Video* wizard will start searching for scanners and cameras connected to the computer. When this is done, you will see the following window:

If more than one device is found:

⊕ **Click your scanner**

⊕ **Click** Import

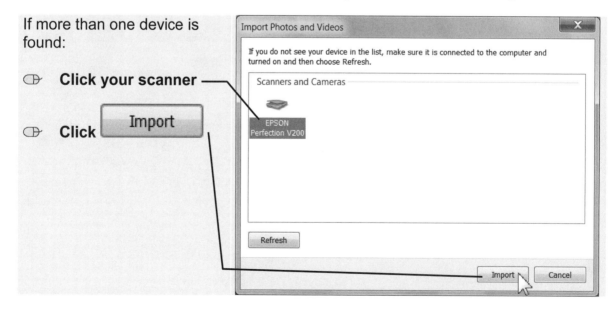

You will see the *New Scan* window.

The default setting is for scanning a photo:

Here you can set the scan color: in color, black and white, or greytones:

Here you can select the file type for the scan:

By Resolution (DPI): you can choose the number of dots (Dots Per Inch) that will be used for the scan:

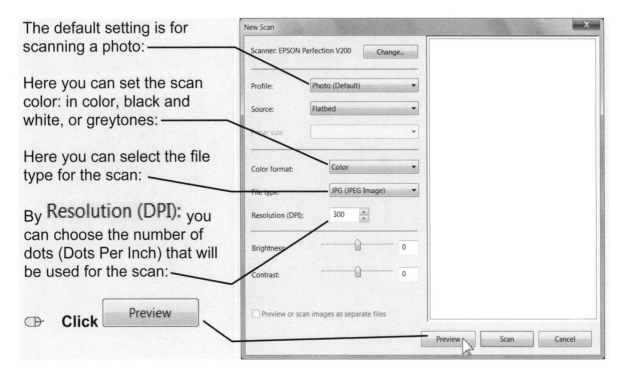

☞ **Click** Preview

💡 Tip

Scan quality and DPI
The scan quality is expressed in DPI: Dots Per Inch. This is also called the resolution. The setting that you choose will depend on the way you want to use the photo. The ranges are from 75 to a maximum of 2400 DPI.

For instance, if you want to display a photo on your website, you will not need a very high quality photo. 75 DPI will suffice. If you want to print a photo after scanning it, you can select a resolution that matches your printer's maximum resolution. If you intend to edit and enhance a photo after scanning it, you can scan it with the highest possible resolution. In the Background Information for this chapter you will find additional information.
But keep in mind that a 1200 DPI resolution, or higher, will produce an enormous file with a large number of megabytes.

First, a scan preview is made, and you will see an example of what the scanned photo will look like.

You will see the scan preview. A dotted frame will indicate the area that will be scanned. As you can see, a large part of the white area will also be included in the scan. But you can still adjust the scan area:

⊕ **Position the mouse pointer on a corner handle of the dotted frame**

⊕ **Drag the handle until you have reached the desired size**

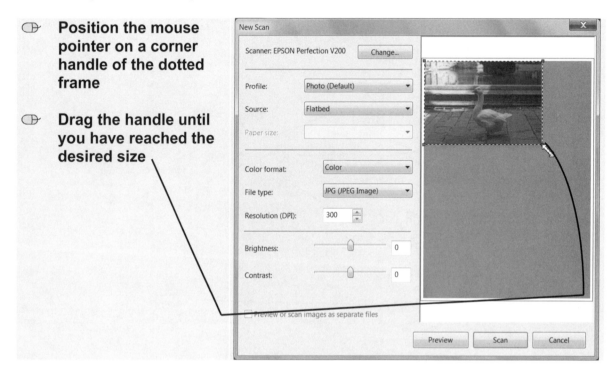

If you are satisfied with the changes, you can start the scan:

⊕ **Click** Scan

The photo will be scanned:

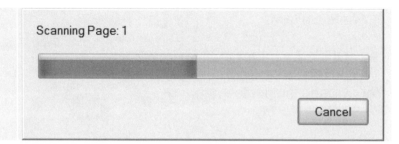

If you want, you can also add a tag for the scan. You can also just skip this step:

 **Click**

Windows Explorer will be opened and you will see the file for the scanned photo:

☞ **Close** *Windows Explorer* ∂∂2

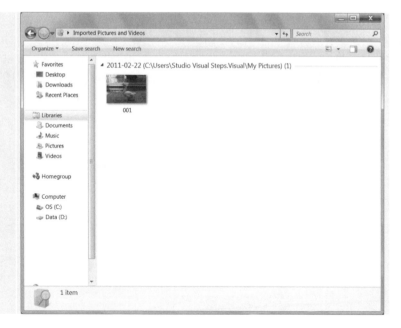

In *Photo Gallery*:

☞ **Click the folder**

You will see the photo in
Photo Gallery:

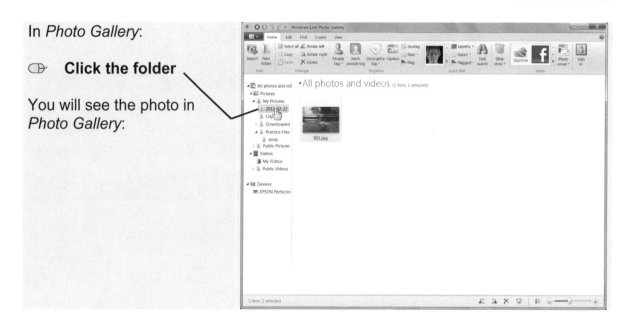

Now the photo has been imported in *Photo Gallery*. You can start editing the photo, by following the steps you learned in the previous chapters of this book.

☞ **Close** *Photo Gallery* 𝒪𝒪²

In this chapter you have learned how to connect your camera, cell phone, external hard drive or USB stick to your computer. Next, we have explained how to import photos in *Photo Gallery* from these external devices. And finally, you have learned how to scan a photo.

8.5 Background Information

Dictionary	
Driver	A special software program that is meant for operating a specific device, such as a digital photo camera.
External hard drive	An external storage device where you can store your programs and files. You can connect it to your computer with a USB cable.
Firewire	A fast cable connection between a computer and external devices, such as a photo camera or video camera.
Import	Copying files from a device, such as a digital camera, to your computer.
Install	Putting a program on your computer's hard drive.
Memory card	Storage device in the shape of a small card where you can permanently store data. There are various types of memory cards available. The storage capacity can vary from 128 MB up to 64 GB or more.
Memory card reader	A built-in device that enables you to read data on a memory card directly from your computer. You can also buy external card readers.
Scanner	A device that can convert a paper object into data that can be read by a computer.
Serial cable	A cable that can be connected to a serial port. Data is transferred at a much slower rate, which means this type of connection is slow.
USB	Rectangular communication port built-in to the computer, suitable for many purposes, such as connecting digital cameras.
USB stick	A storage device that is connected to the computer's USB port.

Source: Windows Help and Support, Wikipedia

Memory cards

Most digital cameras use memory cards to store photos. These cards have a storage capacity ranging from 128 MB up to 64 GB or more and can contain large numbers of photos.

The SD card is the most used memory card. Not only in digital cameras, but in cell phones, navigation devices, MP3 players and other portable media players as well. For the greater part, the CompactFlash card has become less popular due to the more inexpensive SD card. In spite of the ascent of the SD card, some manufacturers are still producing their own type of cards, for example, Fuji's xD card, and Sony's Memory Stick.

This is how you can retrieve the photos from such a memory card:

Remove the memory card from the camera:

Nowadays many computers have a built-in card reader. If your computer does not have one, you can also read the card from an external card reader, connected to your computer's USB port:

Windows identifies memory cards and the camera's memory as *removable media*. You can copy the files from these devices (the removable media) to your computer.

The camera's photo quality settings

On your digital camera, you can set the quality of the pictures you take.
A high resolution results in high quality photos, but also in larger files. If your memory card does not have a large storage capacity, it will quickly become full. Consider what you want to use the photos for in advance, and choose the relevant resolution.
For instance, if you just want to display your photos on screen, or send them to your friends by e-mail, then a lower resolution will suffice. But if you want to enlarge your photos and print them in a large size, you will need a much higher resolution. Consult your camera's manual for advice on setting the resolution.

Scanners

By far the easiest way of converting a printed photo to your computer is by scanning it. Apart from printed photos, it is also possible to scan your slides or negatives.
In scanning, the term *resolution* is used. The measurement for the resolution is the number of dots (points) per inch: also called *DPI*. The more DPI, the more definition the scanned photo will have. You can set this resolution in your scanning software program. Depending on the way you want to use the photo, you can select the relevant DPI setting. Always make sure you match the DPI setting to the purpose of the photo. A default setting for a very high resolution may result in enormous file sizes, which can barely be processed by your computer.
Beside the resolution, the so-called *color depth* is important as well. The color depth is the number of colors the scanner can distinguish. The quality of a scanner depends on the resolution, the color depth, and the scanning speed.

The so-called *flatbed scanners* are the most popular scanners. These scanners require you to place the photo on a glass plate, after which the photo is scanned by a device that moves along underneath the photo.

- Continue reading on the next page -

Some types of flatbed scanners can also scan slides and negatives, apart from photos and other documents. Often a special film adapter is included, in which you can insert transparent materials, such as slides or negatives. A useful feature is the possibility of scanning multiple photos at once. With the accompanying scanning software you can separate these images and store them as individual photos. This way, you can quickly digitize your old family photos and vacation snapshots.

There also exits special scanners for the sole purpose of scanning slides or negatives.

If you want to scan large numbers of slides, photos, or negatives, it will be definitely worth your while to buy a good scanner. You will also need to pay attention to the features of the software program that comes with the scanner. For example, if you buy a scanner which will let you scan multiple images at once; this will save you a lot of time. Ask the salespeople in the computer shop or other retail outlet for advice, before you buy such a scanner.

Scan slides and negatives
Scanners that are capable of scanning slides and photo negatives will always include a software program. In the program you can select the type of media you want to scan, such as 'negative film' or 'positive film'. The software program will automatically convert these files into regular photo files that you can edit and print.

Scan resolution

A photo's resolution is expressed in DPI. This stands for *dots per inch*. Depending on the purpose of the photo, you can determine the corresponding scan resolution. For example:

75 DPI	Monitor, Internet
200-300 DPI	Color print from an inkjet printer
720 DPI	High resolution inkjet printer
600-1200 DPI	Laser printer
2400 DPI	Professional prints

Let's say that you are going to select the resolution for a color photo, for instance 300 DPI.

The standard photo size is usually 4 inches high and 6 inches wide.

This will result in 4 x 300 = 1200 scanned pixels for the height, and 6 x 300 = 1800 pixels for the width of the photo.

The total amount is 1200 x 1800 = 2.160.000 pixels.

In actual practice these measurements will not exactly correspond to the scanned photo.

The video camera

Digital video cameras often come with a built-in option for taking pictures (stills), and store them to the video tape or memory card, in the same way that a digital photo camera does. There also exist digital video cameras that record the images on a DVD or a hard disk.

A digital video camera's memory card can be connected to the computer in the usual way. Many cameras have a USB connection. Nowadays, the photo quality of pictures taken with a digital video camera equals the quality of photos taken with a digital photo camera.

8.6 Tips

Tip

Adjust import options
You can change a number of import settings:

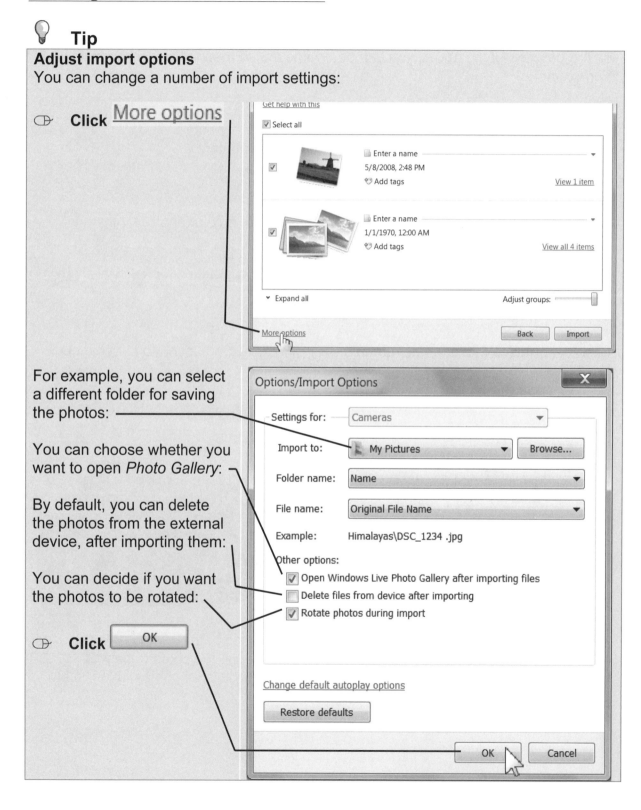

For example, you can select a different folder for saving the photos:

You can choose whether you want to open *Photo Gallery*:

By default, you can delete the photos from the external device, after importing them:

You can decide if you want the photos to be rotated:

9. Importing and Playing Video Recordings

In this chapter you will learn how to create an attractive movie from your video recordings. The *Windows Live Movie Maker* program offers many useful features and is easy to use.

You do not need to start by importing your own material. You can start editing right away, by using the practice files. In this way you can become familiar with all the options, step by step. You will be able to safely experiment with several different functions without the risk of damaging any of your own recordings.

After you have become familiar with the program, you will learn how to import your own video files. We will explain all about it in *Chapter 15 Importing Your Own Video Recordings*.

In this chapter you will learn how to:

- open *Windows Live Movie Maker*;
- use the various components of the program;
- add video files;
- select the standard or widescreen settings;
- adjust the size of the image;
- zoom in and zoom out;
- play a project;
- save a project.

9.1 Opening Windows Live Movie Maker

If the program is already installed on your computer, you can start it up like this:

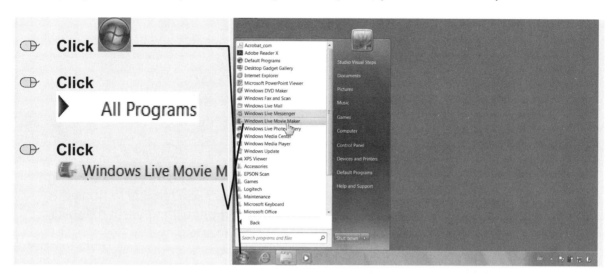

⊕ **Click** [Windows logo]

⊕ **Click**

▶   **All Programs**

⊕ **Click**

🎬 **Windows Live Movie M**

It is possible that you will see the Microsoft licensing agreement first; in that case, click **Accept**.

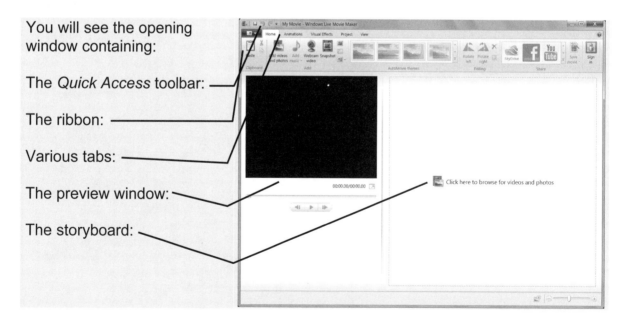

You will see the opening window containing:

The *Quick Access* toolbar: ──

The ribbon: ──

Various tabs: ──

The preview window: ──

The storyboard: ──

The ribbon has been designed to help you find all the necessary commands more quickly. The commands have been arranged in logical groups and tabs. Each tab is connected to a specific activity, such as changing the window settings, or adding effects.

For instance, take a look at the *Visual Effects* tab:

⊕ **Click the**

| Visual Effects | **tab**

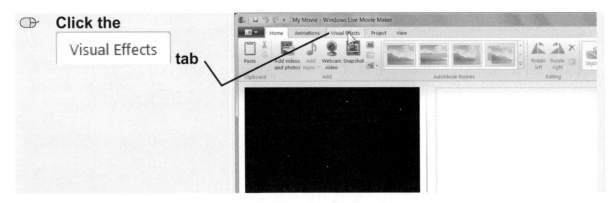

Now you will see the commands that are relevant to adding effects:

The commands are not yet active (light grey), because you have not yet selected any video files.

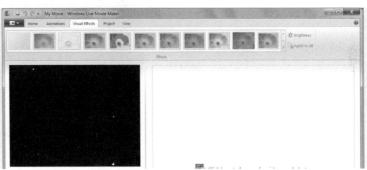

You can now go back to the *Home* tab:

⊕ **Click the** | Home | **tab**

Now you will see the *Home* tab once again.

If you want to execute a command on the ribbon, you usually need to click twice. First the tab, and then the command itself. If you find that you are using the same commands over and over again, this can be a nuisance. This is where the *Quick Access* toolbar comes in handy: ▭. This toolbar contains frequently used commands, which you can activate with a single click.

 Tip

Modify the Quick Access toolbar
You can decide which commands you want to add to the *Quick Access* toolbar. It is a good idea to add the commands you use most often to this toolbar, so you will not need to change tabs all the time or search for these commands. You can read how to modify the *Quick Access* toolbar in the *Tips* section at the back of this chapter.

9.2 Adding Video Files

A movie that is being edited in *Windows Live Movie Maker* is called a *project*.

If you want to make a movie, you start by adding one or more video or photo files to your project. This is called *importing*. You can start now by adding the practice files. Then you can follow the steps in this chapter and practice each action yourself:

Click Add videos and photos

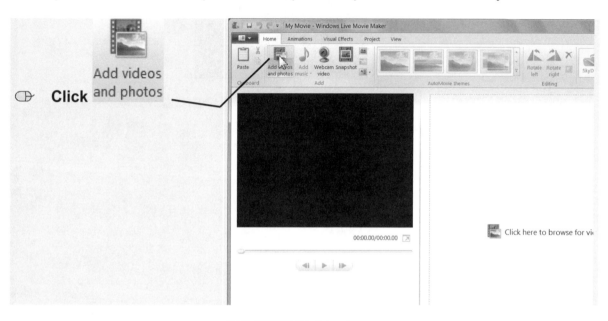

Click
▷ Documents

In *Windows Vista* you will need to click the folder *Documents*.

Click Practice Files Video ec

Click Open

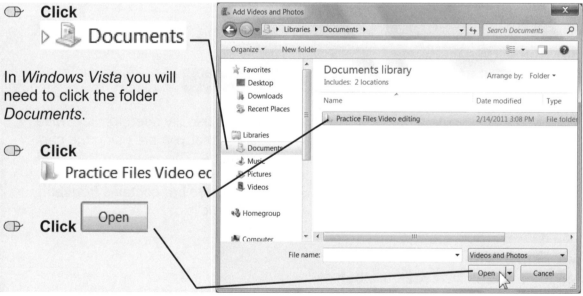

Now you will see the practice files. To display only the video files:

$\oplus$ **Click**

Videos and Photos

$\oplus$ **Click** Videos

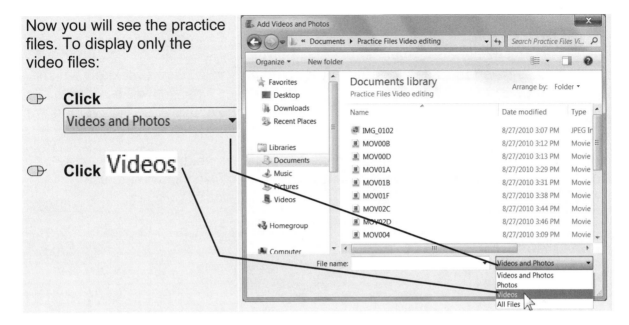

You are going to add all the video files:

$\oplus$ **Click** Organize ▼

$\oplus$ **Click** Select all

All videos have been selected:

$\oplus$ **Click** Open

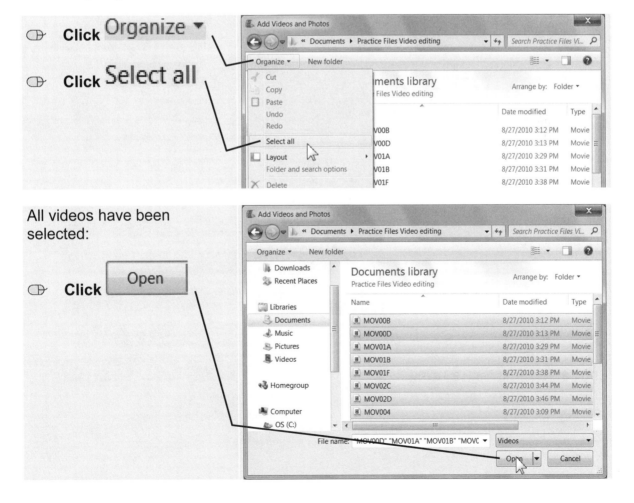

Tip

Select videos in Windows Live Movie Maker
You can just import the video files, but most of the time you will not yet know which scenes you will actually use. If you start by adding all the files, you will be able to view them in *Windows Live Movie Maker*, and then remove the video files you do not need.

If you are sure you do not want to use certain videos, for instance, because they refer to a different subject, you can select just the video files you want to use:

☞ **Click the first video file**

⌨ **Keep pressed down** `Ctrl`

☞ **Click the next video file(s)**

After the last video file:

⌨ **Release** `Ctrl`

☞ **Click** Open

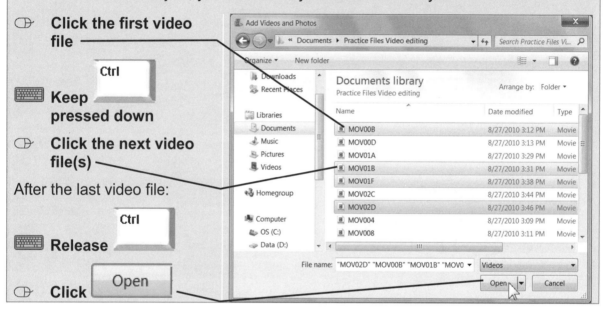

The video clips will now appear on the storyboard:

The storyboard is where you assemble your project.

The new Video Tools tab is now active:

Below the preview window you can see the total running time of the videos currently on the storyboard 03:44.06:

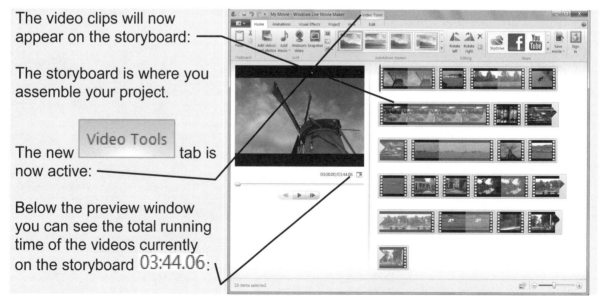

Please note:

The number of video clips shown on the storyboard will depend on your screen's resolution. If you are working on a laptop for instance, you may see fewer clips and will need to scroll down.

 Please note:

All the video clips you see here, are created with a digital camcorder. Each recording has been stored as a separate file. If you own a different kind of video camera, your recordings may be stored as a single movie, all together in one file. The movie will consist of different scenes. In *Chapter 15 Importing Your Own Video Recordings* you can read more about the various types of cameras, the way in which recordings are stored, and how to import them to your camera.

9.3 Playing a Video

In the preview window you will see the first frame of the first video clip. These clips have been recorded with a widescreen camera, which is why you see a black bar at the top and bottom of the frames. To correct this, you need to change the view to the widescreen view:

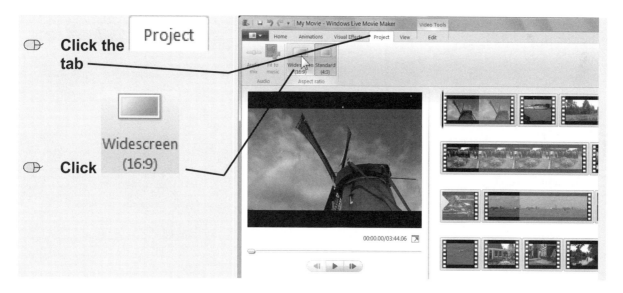

☞ **Click the** `Project` **tab**

☞ **Click** **Widescreen (16:9)**

If you do not own a widescreen camera yourself, you can change this setting

afterwards, and revert to the standard **Standard (4:3)** setting again. You will see an image from each video clip. To view the project, you can play it in the preview window:

The bars have disappeared:

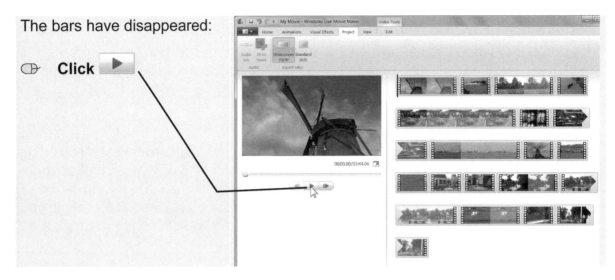

⊕ **Click** ▶

The playback indicator will show which part is being played:

You will see the time that has elapsed since the start of the video clip:

⊕ **Click** ❚❚

Play will stop.

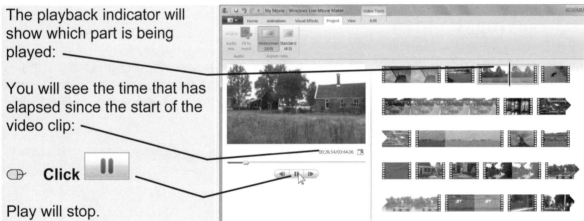

💡 **Tip**

Play and stop a video with the keyboard

Instead of clicking ▶ and ❚❚ you can also briefly tap the space bar on your keyboard.

You can also view the video one frame at a time:

Click [button] **a few times**

Depending on the video clip you might see the image changing a bit. But you will be able to see the playback indicator move along with the frames:

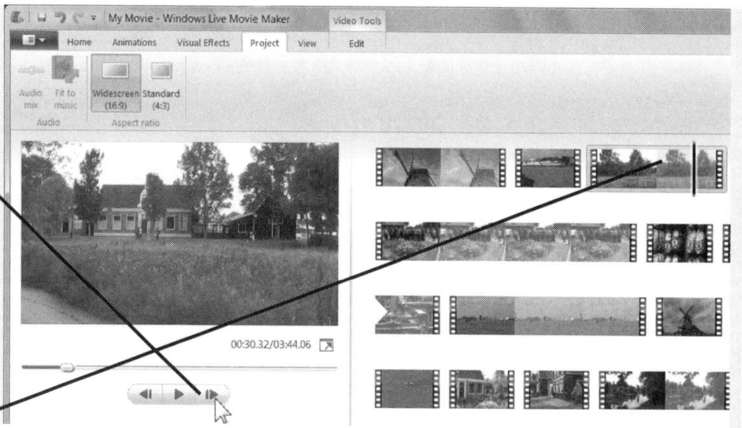

HELP! What is a frame?

A frame is the smallest unit of which a video clip is composed. A frame is also called an image.

Click [button] **a few times**

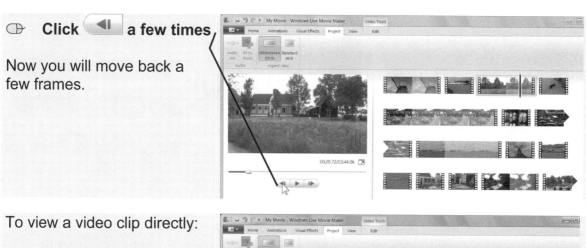

Now you will move back a few frames.

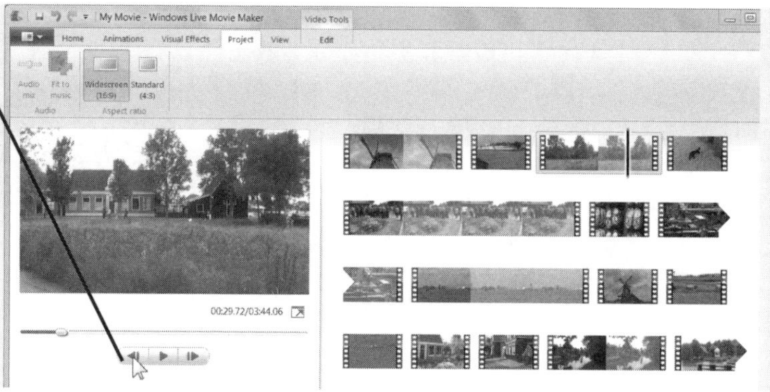

To view a video clip directly:

Click a clip

The playback indicator has moved to the beginning of the video clip:

If the clip is long, the playback indicator will be placed in the middle of the video clip.

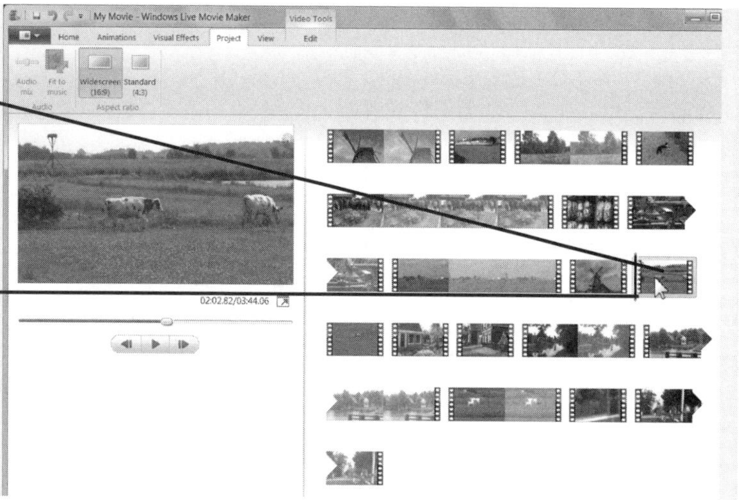

☞ **Click**

The project will start playing at the spot where the playback indicator is located.

☞ **In the next video clip, click**

A quick way to skip to a specific spot in the project is by dragging the playback indicator:

☞ **Drag the playback indicator to the desired location** ―――

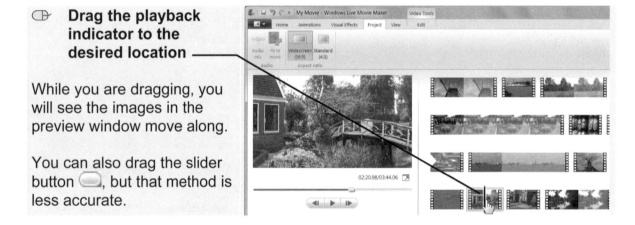

While you are dragging, you will see the images in the preview window move along.

You can also drag the slider button ⬭, but that method is less accurate.

9.4 Zooming In and Zooming Out

Depending on the size and settings of your screen, you will be able to see all the video clips, or just part of the project. To have a clear overview, you can display the video icons in a smaller size:

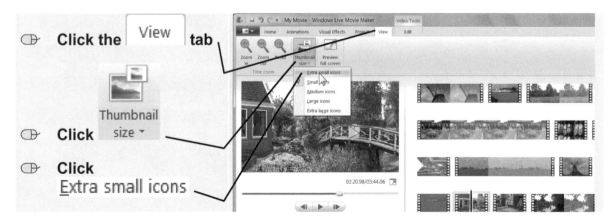

☞ **Click the** View **tab**

☞ **Click** Thumbnail size ▾

☞ **Click** Extra small icons

Now the videos have been made smaller but they are not as easy to recognize:

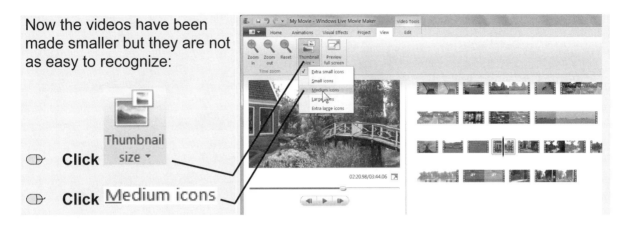

☞ **Click** Thumbnail size ▾

☞ **Click** Medium icons

Extra small icons will provide a good overview, but larger icons will let you see the video clips more clearly. A good overview can be useful when you are assembling the movie. Large icons are easier to work with when you are editing a video clip.

In order to edit your project more accurately, you can also zoom in. If you zoom in on the storyboard you will see more details for each video. You will be able to determine the exact spot where you want to make changes. This is how you zoom in:

The icons are displayed in the normal size:

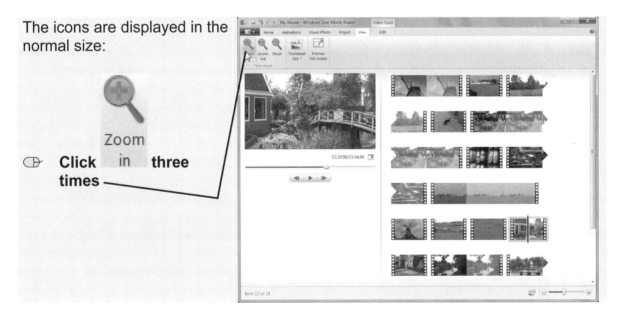

☞ **Click** Zoom in **three times**

☞ **If necessary, drag the scroll bar upwards**

Now the first video will consist of four parts, instead of two:

If you zoom out, the detail in the videos will diminish.

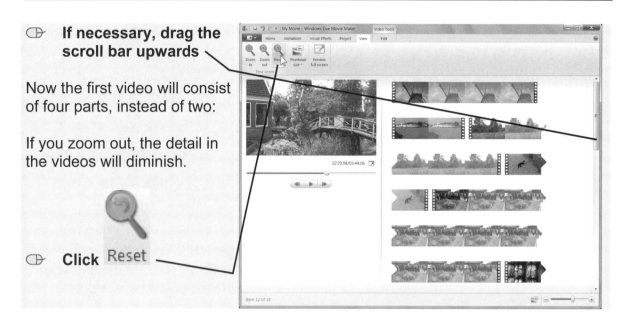

☞ **Click** Reset

Now you have disabled the zoom in function. Once again, the first video will be displayed with two frames.

💡 Tip

Enlarge the preview window or the storyboard
To enlarge the preview window or the storyboard, you can move the break line:

☞ **Position the mouse pointer on the vertical line**

The pointer will turn into ⬌:

☞ **Drag the line to the left or to the right**

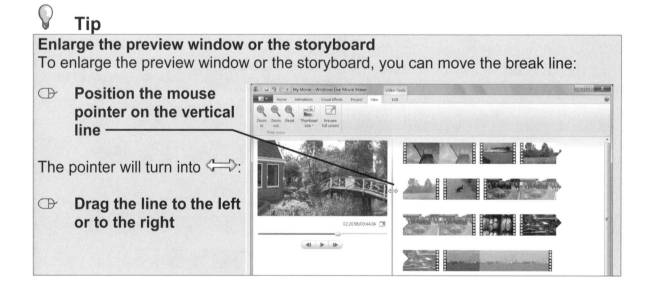

9.5 Saving a Project

Now you are going to edit the rough recordings. But first you are going to save the project:

In the top left of the window:

☞ **Click** 💾

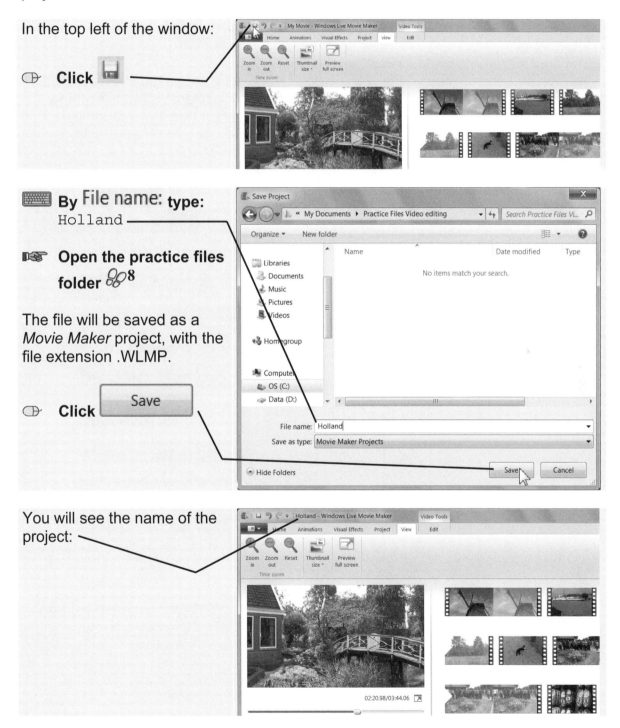

⌨ **By File name: type:**
Holland

☞ **Open the practice files folder** 👣8

The file will be saved as a *Movie Maker* project, with the file extension .WLMP.

☞ **Click** Save

You will see the name of the project:

Please note:

The project you have just saved contains only the references to the video files which are used in the project. The actual video clips are not stored in the project.

Never move, delete, or rename videos or other files that are used in a project which has not yet been closed. If you do this, *Windows Live Movie Maker* will no longer be able to retrieve the file and you may have to start all over again.

Pay close attention when you use any type of removable media, such as a USB stick or external hard drive. If you connect these devices to a different computer, they may be assigned a different drive letter, and this will mean that the project files cannot be found anymore.

Once you have saved or published a movie, the files will be included and stored within the movie and the original files are no longer required. But even then, it is recommended to save the files you have used for a while longer. Then you still have the chance to make additional changes to the movie later on, and save or publish the movie in a different way.

Close *Windows Live Movie Maker*:

☞ **Click** [X]

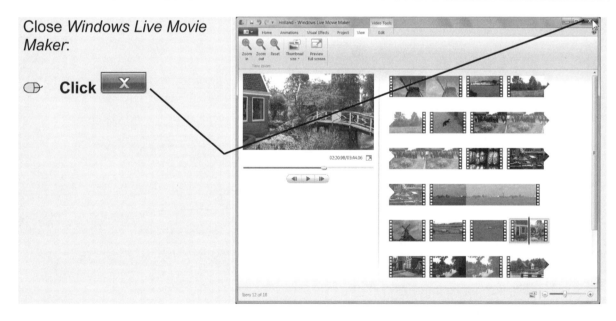

9.6 Background Information

Dictionary	
Frame	A frame is the smallest unit of which a video is composed.
Import	Transferring digital media files to *Windows Live Movie Maker*, so you will be able to use these files in various projects.
Movie	The final result of a project is a movie. A movie has the file type called .WMV.
Playback indicator	A black line on the storyboard that indicates the position in the project when the project is played or edited.
Preview window	The section in *Windows Live Movie Maker* that lets you display (part of) your project.
Project	A project is stored as a .WMLP file and contains links to all the videos, photos, and audio files that are used in the project. The project also contains the edits and the effects.
Storyboard	The section in *Windows Live Movie Maker* that displays the order of the photos, videos, audio files, and text in the current project. Here you can edit the photos, videos, music, and text.
Video	A file that contains a recording.
Zoom	Displaying more or fewer details of a video or a photo in a project. Per time unit, more or fewer frames will be displayed.

Source: Windows Live Movie Maker Help

Screenplay

Although you can enhance your video quite a lot by editing the clip, for the best results you will need to have a good recording. That is why it is recommended to write a screenplay before you start recording. Particularly if you want to make a movie of some special occasion. Such a screenplay or scenario constitutes the story of the movie, and is used as a guide while you are shooting the movie. Moviemakers who create documentaries and news reports always use a written screenplay, in which the story is written out in detail, and all the necessary props are listed.

In fact, for amateur moviemakers the same rules apply. Even if you want to record ordinary occasions, such as a wedding, a birthday party, or a holiday trip, it can be very useful to plan in advance, to determine which scenes you want to record. This will prevent your movie from becoming a mishmash of random shots.

It is not always necessary to use a written screenplay. If it is about a simple occasion, you can also think of nice images beforehand. For instance, you could start by filming the preparations for a daytrip, next you could shoot some scenes of the journey itself, and of the amusement park and finally the end when the family returns home again after a wonderful day. In itself this is already your story. Always try to film or take a picture of the entrance of a park, a nameplate and other relevant information. You can often use these shots as extra shots between the other shots. The current video cameras are very suitable for taking regular pictures of reasonable quality, so you will just need one device to shoot the movie and the stills.

If you want to make a movie of an important, unique occasion like a wedding, it is better to write the screenplay down and prepare everything in advance. Go through the screenplay with the master of ceremonies; this way, he will know what to say and do, and you will not be as surprised as the wedding couple, when they are being picked up by a beautiful old-timer. And do not forget to ask the wedding couple what they would like to have recorded.

Explore the place where the festivities are going to be and check out the possibilities and difficulties. Check if there is enough space and light, and try to find where all the people in the movie will be standing.

Think of the necessary resources (lighting, for example) and do not forget to bring enough memory cards and spare batteries, especially with these modern cameras.

- Continue reading on the next page -

But it is even better if such a hectic and important day is filmed by more than one person. One of the moviemakers can record the official part of the ceremony, while the other can roam around freely and record all the fun stuff. The guests, waiting for the wedding couple, the wedding cake being prepared, a sleeping child somewhere in a corner, etc. Afterwards you can assemble the recordings of both cameras and make a nice and entertaining movie.

File formats
In *Windows Live Movie Maker* you can import and use the following file formats:

Video: ASF, AVI, DVR-MS, M1V, M2TS, M2T, MOD, MOV, MP2, MP2V, MP4, M4V, MPE, MPEG, MPG, MPV2, QT, VOB, WM, WMV, WTV (You can find more information on these formats in the *Background Information* of *Chapter 10 Assembling the Movie*)

Audio: AIF, AIFF, ASF, M4A, MP3, WAV, WM, WMA

Images: BMP, GIF, JPEG, JPG, PNG, TIF, TIFF, WDP

Comments:

- You cannot use video and audio files which have been protected with DRM (Digital Rights Management) in *Windows Live Movie Maker*.

- You will only have support for the use of MPEG-2 and *Microsoft* TV-recordings in your movie if your computer is using one of the following editions of *Windows 7* or *Windows Vista*: *Windows 7 Home Premium, Windows 7 Professional, Windows 7 Enterprise, Windows 7 Ultimate, Windows Vista Home Premium* or *Windows Vista Ultimate*.

- You can use AVCHD video files with Dolby Digital audio in *Windows Live Movie Maker* if your computer is using one of the following editions of *Windows 7*: *Windows 7 Home Premium, Windows 7 Professional, Windows 7 Enterprise* or *Windows 7 Ultimate*.

- You can use MPEG-4 video files with AAC audio if you are working with *Windows Live Movie Maker* on a *Windows 7* computer.

- Some MPEG-4 video files can be used in *Windows Live Movie Maker* on a *Windows Vista* computer, but only if the necessary audio and video codecs have been installed.

Camera movements

You can make quite an interesting movie by shooting a series of images from a fixed camera position. But the movie will be much more entertaining if you use some camera movements. There are various kinds of movements.

The most frequently used movement is the *pan*. Panning means moving the camera from the left to the right, or from the right to the left. You are creating a kind of panoramic overview. By panning you will be able to show your viewers a complete image of relatively large subjects. For instance, some scenery, or a wall with a lot of different paintings in a row. You can also use the panning technique to follow a moving object, such as a car.

Yet another camera movement is called the *tilt*. With the tilt you move the camera upwards or downwards. You can use the tilt to film a high subject, such as an apartment building. And you can also use this movement to follow an airplane taking off.

A special camera movement is the *dolly*. With this technique the camera itself is moving; it is used to follow a subject, like you were filming from a car. But you can also hold the camera and walk by the subject. A dolly will add extra motion to a scene.

No matter which camera movement you are using, it is important not to move the camera too fast, otherwise the image will become blurred. You also need to move the camera steadily and avoid shaking it. You can use a tripod to keep the camera steady.

Camera positions

Many amateur movies are shot from a single camera position. That is to say, the position of the eyes of the camera man. Actually this is not really odd, because the camera man is nearly always standing up while he is filming, and most of the time he is looking through the viewfinder or the LCD screen in front of him. The advantage of this camera position is that the audience can easily identify with it. After all, this is the same view they would have had themselves, had they been present.

However, it might be interesting to choose a different camera position once in a while. It will make the movie much livelier, but can also add an extra dimension to the movie. For example, while you are filming a children's party, you could record everything from a lower position. This way, you will show everything from a child's viewpoint. It can be very surprising, to an adult audience, but to the kids as well.

There exist two camera positions that are often used without people being aware of it; that is when the subject is filmed from below, or from above. Usually these positions do not have the effect the moviemaker intended, but quite a different one. Filming a person from above might relay the message that this person is in an inferior position (you are looking down on him). On the other hand, filming somebody from below can create the image of somebody who is authoritarian and dominant (you are looking up to him). It is a good idea to realize the effect of such a camera position. For example, if you want to give an impression of the height of a tower, you can start filming the tower from a low position, close to the ground.

A position that can create a strange, alien effect, is the position in which the camera is skewed. The result is that everything that is recorded seems to be lopsided. In this way you can make a recording of narrow, ancient city alleys look very oppressive.

Normal　　　　*Low*　　　　*High*　　　　*Skewed*

Outside exposure

Film and light are firmly tied to one another. No light, no movie. No good exposure, no good movie. If you are filming outdoors in daytime, you will always have a great light source: the sun. The sun always provides sufficient light for shooting your film without too many problems, even on a cloudy day.

If you intend to film outdoors, make sure you adjust the camera setting to this type of filming. Your camera will have a special knob for this, which you can switch to the 'sun' setting.

However, you may experience problems while filming outside, even if there is plenty of sunshine. And even if you use a modern camera with built-in options for automatically selecting the best exposure in various circumstances.

One of those problems is backlight. Backlight means that you are filming while the light source shining into the lens is very intense; this will make the other subjects in the picture look very dark and shadowy. For example, if you are filming a person with his back to radiant sunshine, this person's face will become a dark blur.

An easy way of preventing backlighting is not to shoot straight into the fierce lamp light or sunlight. If you are filming a certain subject, try to keep the sun or the light source at your back. If this is not possible, you can use the backlight correction option on your camera. This feature will filter the backlight and render the rest of the image lighter and more distinct.

Another problem can occur when you are shooting your movie in a place where there are sharp contrasts between bright and shadowy areas. For instance, while you are filming someone who comes walking out of a tunnel, or when you film somebody who is walking from the shadows into bright sunshine while you are in the shadow yourself. The automatic exposure settings of the camera will not be adjusted correctly, because these settings take into account the entire picture's exposure and not just the person you want to film. In the case of the tunnel this will result in an unclear image of the person. While the recordings of the person who comes into view from the shadows will often display rather unpleasing light effects. These problems can be partly solved by disabling the camera's automatic exposure settings, and adjusting the exposure manually.

Inside exposure

If you want to record your movie indoors, you will often experience exposure problems. It is not very hard to shoot some good scenes in a room where the sun shines through the windows. But the results can be very depressing if the room is dark, or when you are shooting at night.

A lot of video cameras are equipped with a knob for selecting indoor or outdoor recording modes. That is, for selecting the exposure in bad lighting conditions. The video camera will adjust the settings according to the amount of light available. This will improve the result, but the image can still be a bit grainy and have a reddish color.

There is a simple solution. Make sure there is enough light. It is best to use special video lights. These lights will provide a clear white light.
Often just a single light is used. If you have a large camera, the light can be fixed on a socket, on the camera. In this way the subject will always be exposed from above, and a bit slanted. This type of exposure method is used for television recordings that are shot at night, on location. The result is a good, clear image. But on the down side, the subject is often displayed in a very intense and harsh way.

You can also hold such a video light in your hands. This way, you can expose the subject from a different angle, from in front and slanted, for example. And you can use such a portable light to create special effects. For instance, shining the light on somebody from below, which will give this person quite a creepy look.

Using multiple lights is much more elaborate, but will yield much better results. By positioning two or three lamps all around the subject in the right places, you can create exactly the right atmosphere. An advantage of using multiple lamps is that you will be able to get rid of shadows. This will render the image of the person or subject less harsh.

Exposure from the top right   *Exposure from below*   *Exposure from the left and right*

Framing and composition

It seems so simple. You point your camera towards the object you want to record and you press the record button. Nevertheless, you will create much more interesting movies by taking into account how the image is composed.

Image composition means that you pay attention to the image that is captured within the frame, while you are filming. The frame consists of the borders around the image. You can stick to capturing a person in the center of the frame all the time, but sometimes it can be better to position a person to the left or right of the center.

For instance, if somebody is crossing the street from the left to the right side, it is recommended to film this person on the left side of the frame and leave some open 'leading' space on the right-hand side. This will make it easier to keep track of the person, but you will also leave some space open for the person to walk into.

Are you filming a conversation between two people who are standing opposite each other? And do you want to edit (or 'cut') it in such a way that alternating close-ups of one person's face and then the other will be shown? Then keep framing one person at the left-hand side of the frame, and the other at the right-hand side. When you are editing the images later on, they will fit together nicely. You will still see two people talking to each other, one on each side of the frame. If you would have filmed both persons on the same side of the frame, it would seem as if these people were not talking to each other at all, after the cutting operation.

Left side of the frame   *Right side of the frame*

By positioning subjects or people a little off-center instead of exactly in the middle of the frame, you can often get nicer results. You will have left some extra space, in which you can include another object. For example, if you are filming a blacksmith, you can include the anvil in the foreground. You will not only give extra information on your subject, but you will also add extra depth to the image.

There are endless possibilities. For example, you can film somebody though the bushes, film two people with one of them sitting in the foreground, and the other standing in the background, etc. By watching closely how professional moviemakers do it, you can pick up lots of ideas.

Cut-outs

If you want your movie to tell the story properly, and in an interesting way, it is important to use various types of cut-outs. A cut-out is the part of the subject that you want to focus on. In the movie business they use standard names for these cut-outs: extreme long shot, long shot, medium shot, and close-up.

Extreme long shot: this will display an overview of the surroundings of the subject.

Long shot: the subject will be entirely visible. This is a good way of introducing the main character in a movie.

Medium shot: the subject is only partially visible, so the focus is on that part of the body. For example, the main character's upper body.

Close-up: a very detailed image of the subject. In this way you can show a lot of information on the subject. For example, the main character's face.

By arranging the various cut-outs in the right way, you can provide your audience with clear information and tell a proper story. For instance, you could start with a close-up of a place name sign, and then use an extreme long shot to film an overview of the place itself.

If you want to be able to edit the images properly and create a good movie, it is important to use different cut-outs while filming your subjects.

Focus the camera

If you want to shoot attractive scenes, make sure the image is focused. It is not always easy to tell whether the image is focused enough, when using a viewfinder or an LCD screen. This can be especially difficult in extreme wide shots where you need to zoom out a great deal, like in a total body shot. Often the images do not prove to be as focused as you expected, when you view the images on a larger screen later on.

All cameras come with an autofocus function. In many cases this is not the ideal solution, because by default, the camera will focus on the most obvious element in the picture. Sometimes the camera focuses on a specific element, while you would have liked to focus on a different object. This can occur when you want to film somebody through the branches of a tree, for instance. The camera will automatically focus on the branches, while you would prefer to focus on the person who is a bit further away. If you do not want this to happen, you will need to use the manual focus. Most cameras offer this possibility.

But there is a trick to make sure the image is always focused as much as possible. First, you need to disable the camera's automatic focus function. Next, you zoom in very closely to the object you want to focus on. This object will often be quite blurry. Now you can use the manual focus to adjust the picture. Usually by turning the focus ring until the picture is sharp. Then you can zoom out again, to the required framing.

Zoomed in and blurred   *Zoomed in and sharp*   *Zoomed out*

Zooming

Most video cameras have a zoom lens which allows you to draw the object closer. There is a distinction between the *optical* zoom and the *digital* zoom. The optical zoom uses the lens; the digital zoom is an electronic zoom function.

In actual practice, the optical zoom produces better results than the digital zoom. A digital zoom only enlarges part of the image digitally, and the picture will lose quality. If you want to zoom in very closely, it is recommended to use a tripod. You will see that when you zoom in, each (unexpected) movement you make will be intensified.

Every camera has some kind of zoom button. You can use this button to zoom in to an object, make the image larger, for example, from a long shot to a close-up shot. Or you can zoom out and distance yourself away from the image, for instance, from a close-up shot to a long shot.

Because of this special zoom button, many people think they can make their movie look prettier by zooming in and out a lot. On the contrary, frequent zooming in and out will often get on people's nerves. This is because people use the zoom function indiscriminately, without adding substantial meaning to the movie.

Often it is a better idea to pass from a long shot to a close-up shot without zoom action. A long shot of a specific subject, immediately followed by a close-up of the same subject, will have a much greater impact. If you want to use this technique, you can stop filming for a short moment, after you have filmed the long shot. Next, you can use the zoom button to quickly zoom in on the subject. And then you start filming again. But you can also keep filming during the zoom action and cut out this action later on, when you are editing the movie.

Be very economical with the zoom function; only use it if you have something meaningful to say in the movie. For example, an interesting effect might be created by filming a face in close-up first and then very quickly zooming out; this way, the audience will suddenly get to see the person's environment. This can give quite a surprise.

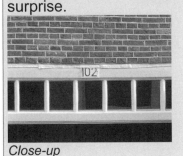
Close-up

Zooming out medium shot   *Zooming out long shot*

9.7 Tips

 Tip

Modifying the Quick Access toolbar
The commands in *Movie Maker* are arranged in various tabs. This means you sometimes need to click several times before a command is executed. If it is a command you use very often, this can be a little annoying. If you add this command to the *Quick Access* toolbar, you will be able to execute it with just one click. This is how you add a command to the toolbar:

You will see the commands on the toolbar:

☞ **Click**

☞ **Click the command you want to add**

Now the command has been added:

If you click the command in the menu once again, the button will be removed from the toolbar.

Here is another way of adding a command:

☞ **Right-click the button**

☞ **Click**
Add to Quick Access Toolb

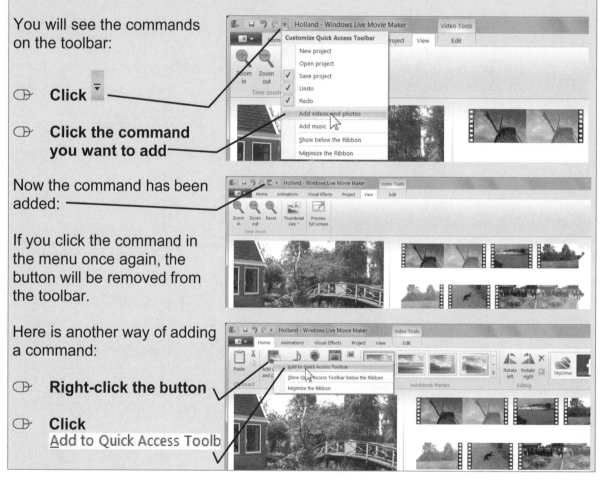

 Tip

Do not delete video files from your camera
Usually you will not need to use all the video footage you record. It is still a good idea to transfer the files to your computer, and it is much easier to view a video on a computer screen. You may find that you can still use a certain bit of footage after all. You can decide to delete the videos later on. If your camera runs out of storage space, however, it might be necessary to delete any unsatisfactory recordings.

10. Assembling the Movie

Now that your video material has been imported, it is time to arrange the images and turn them into a logical story. The order in which the scenes were recorded does not matter. You can arrange your recordings any way you like. You probably will not need every scene that you shot. You can trim some of the scenes at the beginning, middle or at the end of your movie.

In this chapter you will learn how to work with a number of features built into *Windows Live Movie Maker*. To trim your video clips, you will learn how to use the trimming tool and you will see how easy it is to adjust the display order by dragging the clips or photos into position until they are arranged in just the order you want.

In this chapter you will learn how to:

- make a movie plan;
- delete videos;
- move videos;
- cut and paste;
- insert a photo into a project;
- trim videos;
- use the *Trim tool*;
- set a start and an end point;
- split a video;
- set the duration for displaying a photo.

 Please note:

To work through all the exercises in this chapter, you will need to download the relevant practice files from the website to the (My) *Documents* folder on your computer. In *section 1.3 Download the Practice Files for Movie Maker* you can read how to do this. If you have completed *Chapter 9 Importing and Playing Recordings,* you will already have these files imported.

10.1 Making a Movie Plan

The scenes you have recorded will form the basis of your movie. This is your project's rough material. Take a look at what you have so far.

☞ **Start** *Windows Live Movie Maker* ⌇⌇7

Open the *Holland* project:

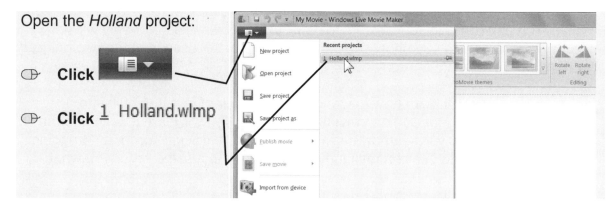

☞ **Click** [≡ ▾]

☞ **Click** 1 Holland.wlmp

🩹 HELP! I do not see the project.

If you have been editing other projects in the mean time, or have re-installed the program, you will see different projects or possibly no projects at all. If that is the case, you can open 1 Holland.wlmp like this:

☞ **Click** [≡ ▾]

☞ **Click** 📁 Open project

- Continue reading on the next page -

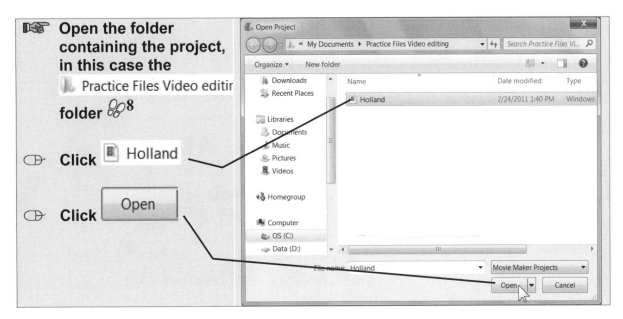

☞ **Open the folder containing the project, in this case the**

📁 Practice Files Video editir

folder 👣8

☞ **Click** 🖼 Holland

☞ **Click** Open

You will see the project:

Before you start assembling the movie, you can take a look at the various scenes that are available:

☞ **Play the entire project** 👣10

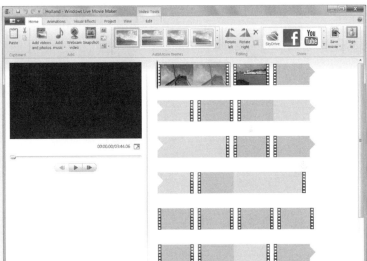

 Please note:

Make sure the speakers from your computer are turned on, so you can hear any sounds that have been recorded.

Now that you have gathered together the material you will need for your movie, you can begin by making a *movie plan*. A movie plan is a general plan that states the content of the movie, and the scenes you plan to use. If you have written a screenplay you will also be able to use that, but this movie plan is based on the actual material you have shot. This may be different from the screenplay; for example, if you have not filmed a certain event, or if you want to add different (unexpected) events.

Tip

Use the file names

A project may contain video clips that seem very similar to one another. To avoid using the wrong clip, or accidentally deleting the clip, it is recommended to use the file names in your movie plan. You can add a brief description and a few comments.

When you position the mouse pointer on the video, you will see the file name:

☞ **Point the mouse to a video**

You will see the file name:

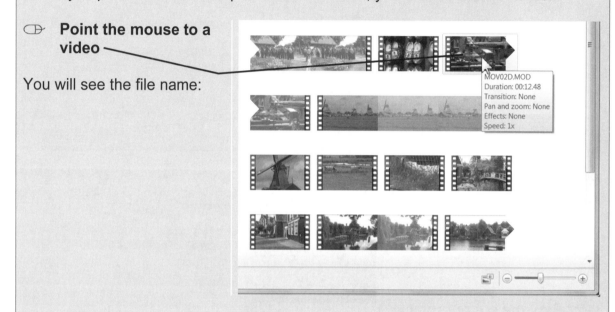

In your movie plan you can refer to this video in the following way:
MOV023.MOD   *goats and windmill*   *background music by choir*

You can make it even shorter, because the name starts with *MOV* and ends with *.MOD*:
023   *goats and windmill*   *background music by choir*

It is not necessary to write out a detailed plan for the entire movie. You could start by looking at the scenes you want to use in the beginning of the movie, and then assemble the movie bit by bit. But it is a good idea to make a general plan, in order to create a logical story.

In the *Background Information* for this chapter you will find an example of a movie plan for the movie that is discussed in this chapter. You can use this plan in the subsequent parts of this chapter.

10.2 Deleting Videos

Before you begin putting your scenes in order, it is a good idea to delete the video clips from the storyboard that you know you will not be using. Return to the beginning of the movie:

 Press `Home`

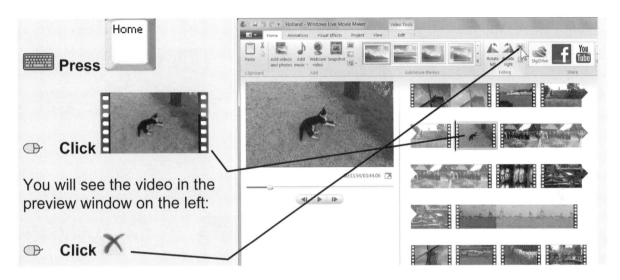

☞ **Click**

You will see the video in the preview window on the left:

☞ **Click** ✗

➥ Please note:

When you delete a video from a project, it is not deleted from your computer. It still remains in the folder where it was originally imported.

The video has been removed:

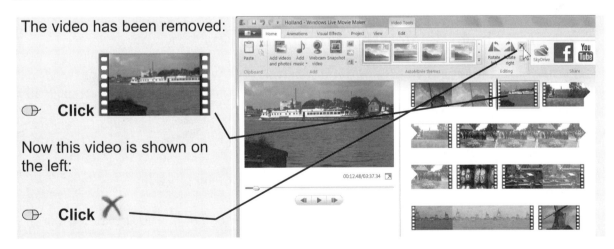

☞ **Click**

Now this video is shown on the left:

☞ **Click** ✗

✖ HELP! I have deleted the wrong video (1).

Did you accidentally delete the wrong video but haven't changed anything else yet?

Then just use the *Undo* button to restore the deleted video.

Now the next fragment has been selected. You can delete that clip also:

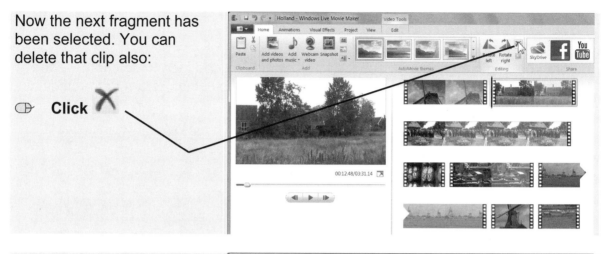

☞   **Click** ✗

The video has been deleted.

The overall length of the movie is now shorter:

🩹 HELP! I have deleted the wrong video (2).

Did you delete the wrong video are unable to restore it with the Undo button ?
The videos that you remove from a project are not deleted from your computer. You

can retrieve the video once more by clicking the button **Add videos and photos**.

Now you have removed the videos that you do not need. While you are assembling the movie, you can still delete other unwanted scenes, if you need to.

10.3 Moving Videos

The scenes that you see now on the storyboard (or timeline) are probably not arranged in the sequence that you want. You can put them in the correct order by moving them. Start by arranging the videos for the first part of your movie:

👆 **Click**

You will see the preview:

👆 **Drag the clip to the right of the first video**

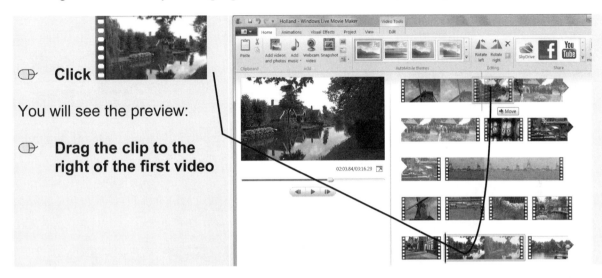

The video has been moved:

Dragging is the most useful way of moving videos over short distances.

👆 **Click**

You will see water, with a fish swimming in it:

👆 **Click** ✂

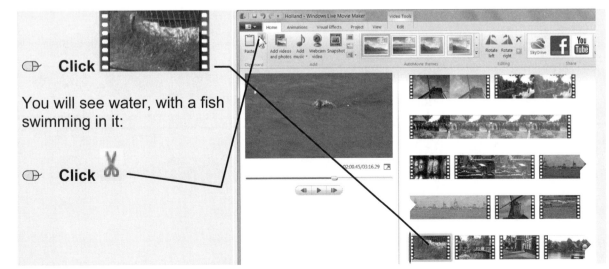

The video you have just cut is light-colored: ─────

⊕ **Click the second video**

You will see the second video. The playback indicator (long black vertical line) is shown on top of the second video.

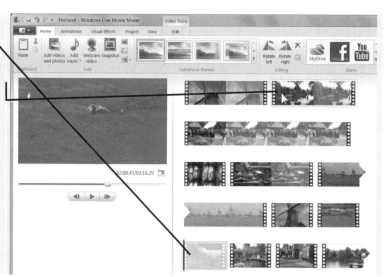

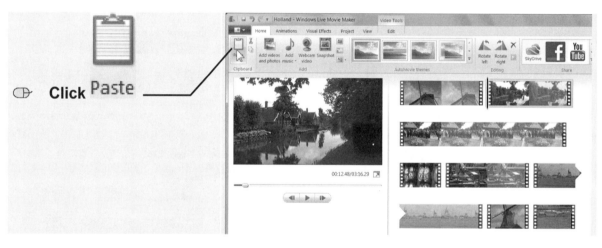

⊕ Click Paste ─────

The video will be inserted after the second clip: ─────

In this method, the clip is automatically inserted into the timeline *after* the clip you have selected. Surrounding clips will automatically shift on the timeline accordingly.

Click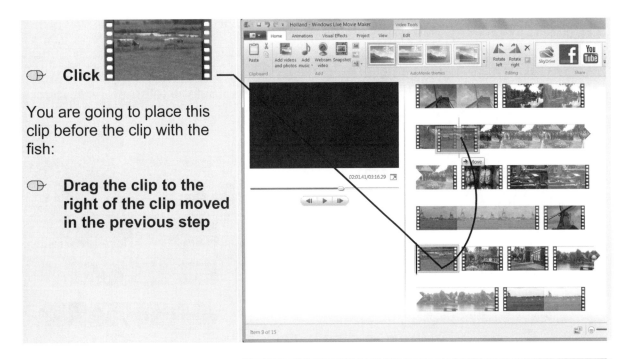

You are going to place this clip before the clip with the fish:

⊕ **Drag the clip to the right of the clip moved in the previous step**

The video has been moved. Now the sequence at the beginning of the project looks like this:

Save the project for now:

⊕ **Click**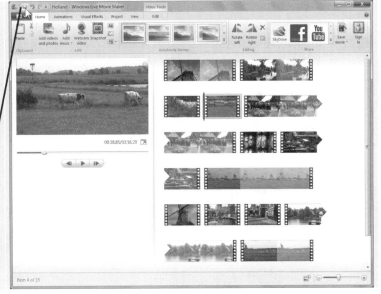

10.4 Inserting a Photo

You can also insert photos into a project. These can be photos that were made with a video camera, a regular photo camera, or even photos from the Internet. First you position the playback indicator on the spot where you want to insert the photo. Then you can add the photo:

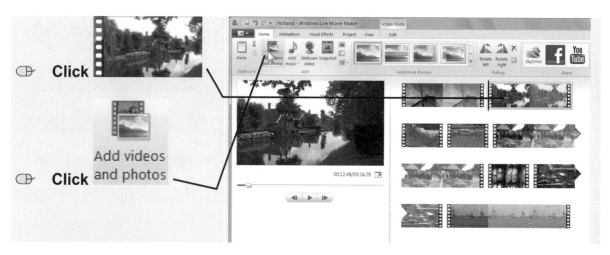

 Click

Click Add videos and photos

Please note:
The photo will be inserted after the second clip on the timeline.

You will see the practice files:

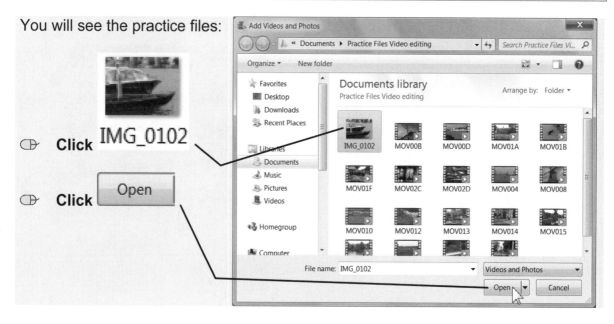

Click IMG_0102

Click Open

Now the photo has been placed between the video's:

Tip

Photo or video

You will be able to tell whether a picture is a photo or a video by looking at the borders:

Photo:

Video:

A video that continues on the next line appears like this:

10.5 Trimming Videos

Now you can view the first part of the movie, the part that includes the photo:

👉 **Go to the beginning of the movie** 𝒞𝒞14

👉 **Play the movie** 𝒞𝒞10

The photo will be displayed for a while.

When you see the choir:

👉 **Stop the movie** 𝒞𝒞11

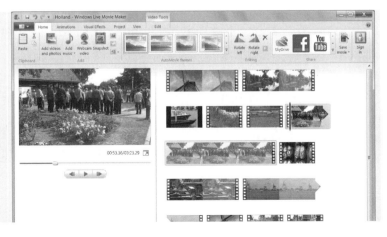

Often, a video will contain some inconvenient scenes at the beginning or the end. For instance, perhaps some unrelated person walks through the scene or your introduction is a bit too lengthy. The second video ends with such a scene, with people sitting on a bench:

You want to end this scene before the people enter the picture. To do this, you can set an end point:

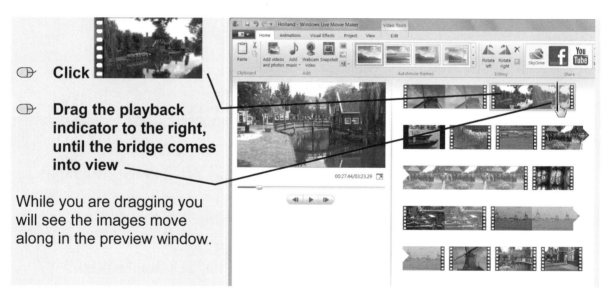

☞ **Click**

☞ **Drag the playback indicator to the right, until the bridge comes into view**

While you are dragging you will see the images move along in the preview window.

If you have dragged the playback indicator too far, then drag it back a little.

 Tip

Accurate positioning

If you want to position the indicator more accurately, use the previous ◀ and next ▶ buttons. They allow you to advance forward or back one frame at a time.

⊕ **Click the**

Edit **tab**

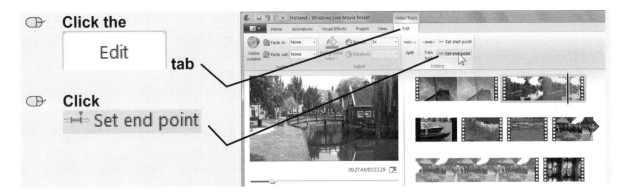

⊕ **Click** ⊢ Set end point

Now the video has been trimmed at the end point you have selected.

🩹 HELP! This was not the correct spot.

The video will only be trimmed within this project. The original file will not be edited.

If you have trimmed the video in the wrong spot, then click [image] to undo the trimming. If this button is disabled, or if you have already performed other operations which you do not want to undo, then read the section below. Here you can read how to change the end point afterwards.

Play this video once again:

⊕ **Click** [image]

☞ **Play the video** 🦶10

Now you will no longer see the section you have trimmed:

When you see the photo:

☞ **Stop the video** 🦶11

At the beginning of the scene you will also see a small glitch. The camera may have shaken a bit. You can improve this by trimming off a small portion of the beginning of the clip:

⊕ **Click**

⊕ **Drag the playback indicator to the right a little, until you see** 00:16.00

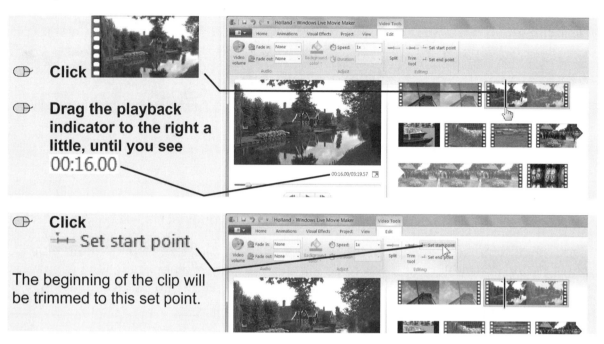

⊕ **Click**
 ⊢ **Set start point**

The beginning of the clip will be trimmed to this set point.

🩹 HELP! The video looks different from the storyboard.

When you trim a video, its duration becomes shorter. The number of frames you see on the storyboard depends on the length of the video. You may see fewer frames after you have trimmed the video.

Before trimming, you see two frames:

After you have trimmed the video, just a single frame remains:

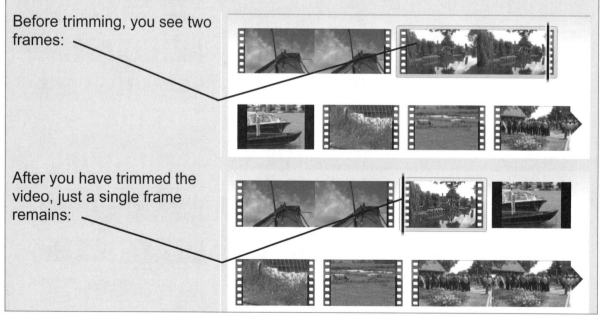

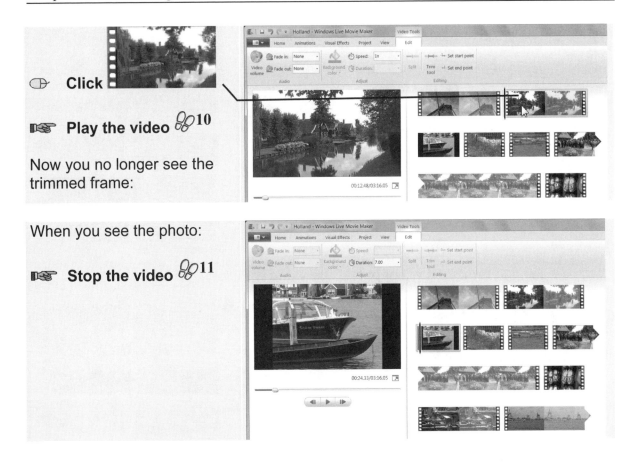

⊕ **Click**

☞ **Play the video** 🦶🦶**10**

Now you no longer see the trimmed frame:

When you see the photo:

☞ **Stop the video** 🦶🦶**11**

10.6 Using the Trim Tool

If you want to be more accurate while trimming a video, you can use the *Trim tool*. This tool lets you set the exact time for the frames you want to trim, and select them one by one:

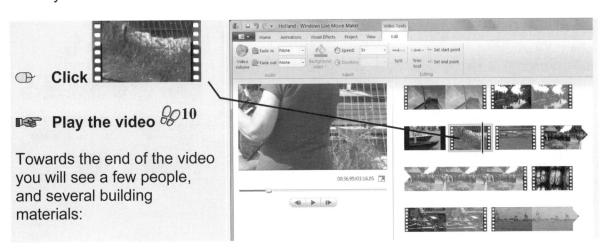

⊕ **Click**

☞ **Play the video** 🦶🦶**10**

Towards the end of the video you will see a few people, and several building materials:

When the next clip starts to play:

☞ **Stop the video** ⚘11

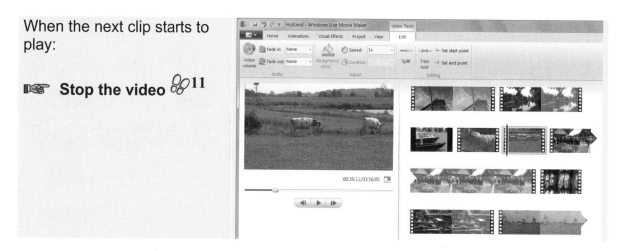

You are going to remove the last part of the video with the *Trim tool*:

⊕ **Click** [filmstrip]

⊕ **Click** [Trim tool]

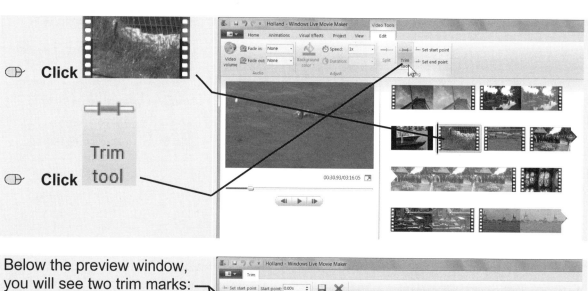

Below the preview window, you will see two trim marks:

By dragging the trim mark on the right you can move the end point.

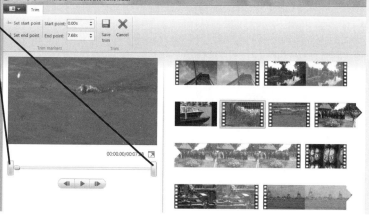

Drag the trim mark on

the right ⬜ **to the left, until you see the corner of the fence**

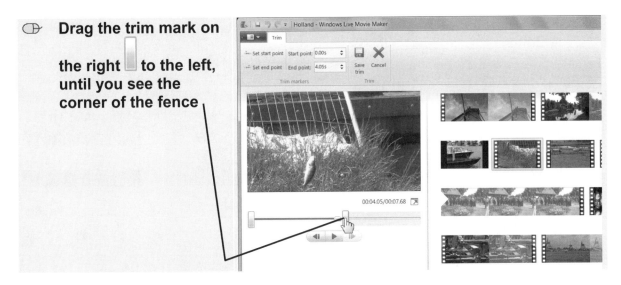

🢂 **Please note!**

The images may move a bit jerky. In order to find the right frame, you may need to drag the trim mark a little to the right and then back again to the left. You can also try using the previous ◀▌ button to find the right frame.

If you want to set a fixed duration for a specific scene, you can set a time for the start and end points, in seconds:

You will see the end time by End point:.

By End point: click
▼ until you see 2.85s

Now the time set for the end point is 2.85s:

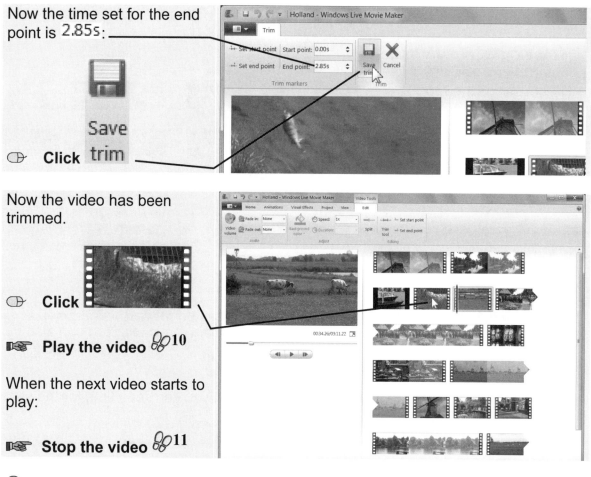

⊙ **Click** Save trim

Now the video has been trimmed.

⊙ **Click**

☞ **Play the video** 👣10

When the next video starts to play:

☞ **Stop the video** 👣11

💡 **Tip**

Set the start point
You can set the start point in the same way as the end point.

You can still change the start and end points by using the trim marks, or by setting a fixed time:

⊙ **Click**

⊙ **Click** Trim tool

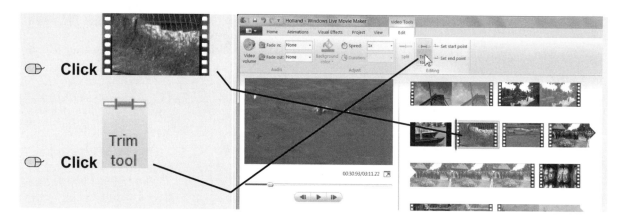

Click 2.85s

Type: 3.5

Press Enter ↵

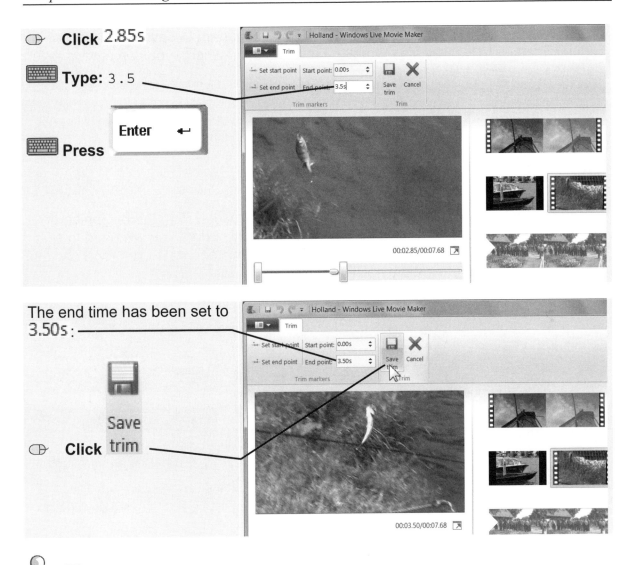

The end time has been set to 3.50s:

Click Save trim

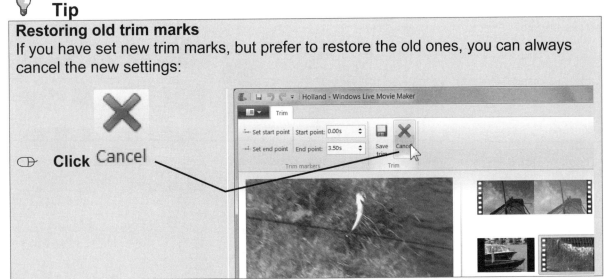

💡 **Tip**

Restoring old trim marks
If you have set new trim marks, but prefer to restore the old ones, you can always cancel the new settings:

Click Cancel

If you have been editing the video for a while, it is important to save the project at regular intervals. This way, if you make a mistake somewhere, you can always revert back to the version that has been saved.

☞ **Save the project now** ✇¹³

10.7 Splitting a Video

In the last section you learned how to trim parts of the video from the beginning or end. If you want to remove a part from the middle of the video, you will need to split the video first. This means the video will be split into two separate clips. You can use the playback indicator to set the splitting point for the video:

Click

Please note: in your window, this video clip may wrap to the next line. If that is the case, take into account the frames occurring on that line as well.

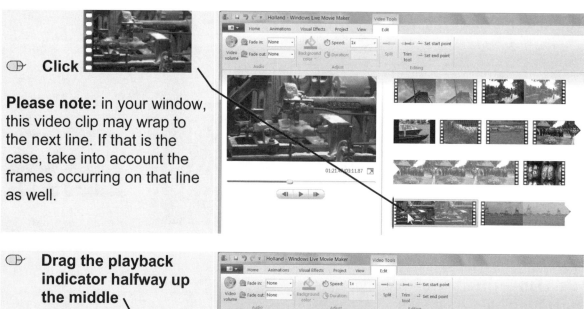

Drag the playback indicator halfway up the middle

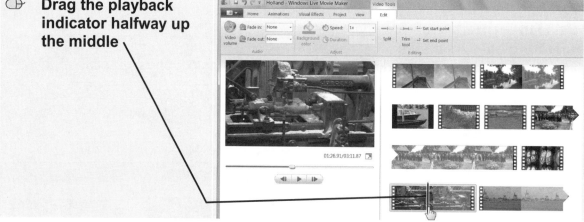

⊕ **Click** Split

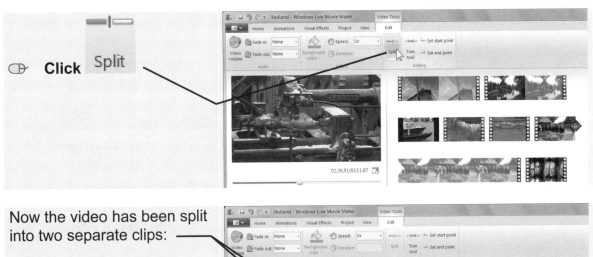

Now the video has been split into two separate clips:

By adjusting the starting or ending points of the new clips, you can trim the middle part.

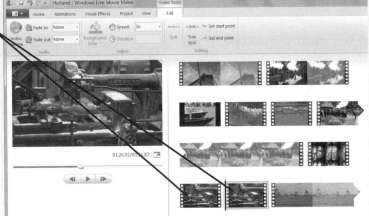

Please note:

Splitting a video in *Windows Live Movie* will not affect the master copy of the video. The video file is still stored in its original folder on your computer.

After you have split the video, you can move both of the clips individually or insert other video clips in between:

⊕ **Click**

⊕ **Drag the video between both parts of the split video**

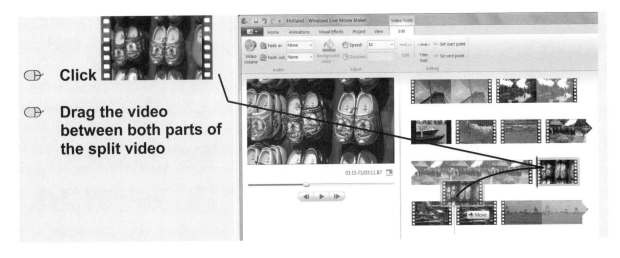

The video has been inserted:

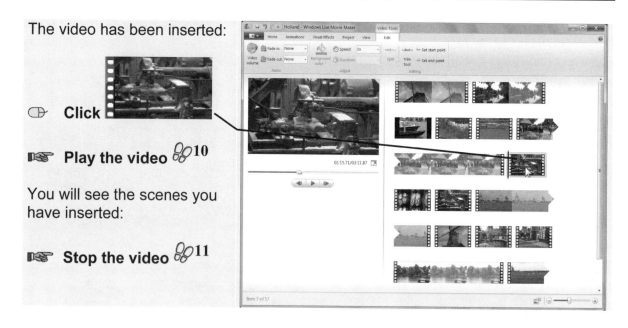

☞ **Click**

☞ **Play the video** 🐾10

You will see the scenes you have inserted:

☞ **Stop the video** 🐾11

10.8 Set the Duration for a Photo

When you insert a photo into your project, it will be displayed in the video for seven seconds. This is the default duration. Since the photo is motionless, you may feel that this is a little too long. To adjust the duration:

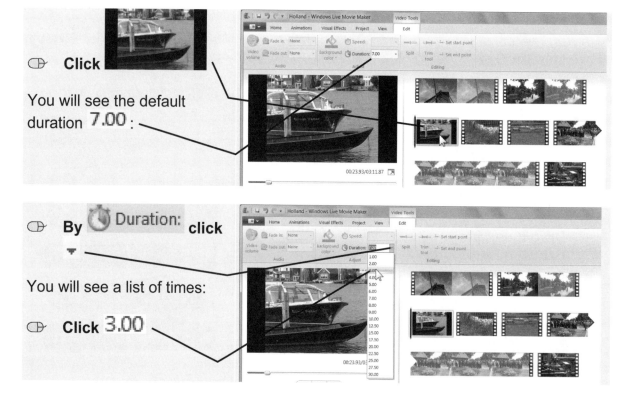

☞ **Click**

You will see the default duration **7.00** :

☞ **By** ⏱ **Duration:** **click** ▼

You will see a list of times:

☞ **Click 3.00**

Tip

Longer display time for photos with a lot of information
If you want to insert a photo that contains a lot of text, for example an information sign by a National Park or other point of interest, then it may be necessary to display the photo for a while longer. This way, the audience will have a chance to read the text.

☞ **Play the video from** ℘℘**10**

Now you will see that the photo is only displayed for a brief moment.

☞ **Stop the video after you have viewed the photo** ℘℘**11**

☞ **Save the project** ℘℘**13**

10.9 The Final Assembly Operations

In the previous sections of this chapter, you have learned how to arrange the scenes in the movie, by deleting, moving, trimming, and splitting the videos. Now you are going to finalize the assembly process, by referring to the movie plan at the end of this chapter. For each video listed you will see a description, comment and if it's used in the movie, what section it belongs to.

 Please note:

In the following operations you will be using the file number that is associated with the video file. Since the name of these files begins with *MOV* and ends with *.MOD*, we will omit those letters here. So, just like in the movie plan, we will simply refer to the *MOV004.MOD* video file as *004*.

If you prefer using file names, you will need to rename the video files before adding them to your project. If you change the file name afterwards, *Windows Live Movie Maker* will no longer be able to find the file.

 Please note:

Always check if the preview window displays the correct video, before moving or deleting such a file. If you accidentally delete or move the wrong video, then use to revert back to the previous action.

Delete clips that are not needed:

☞ **Delete video 004**

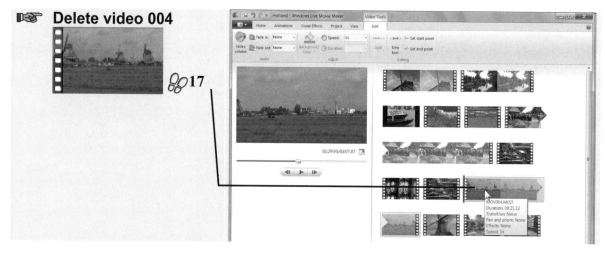

☞ **Delete video 008**

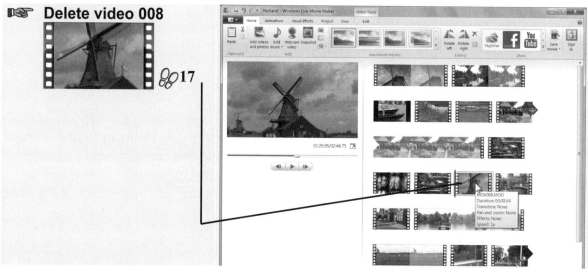

☞ **Delete video 013**

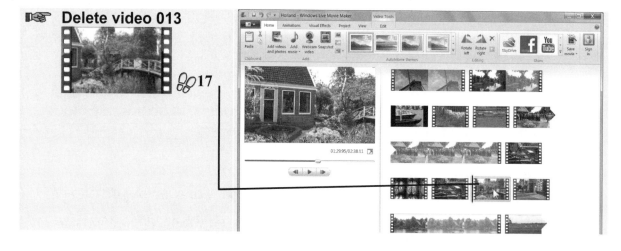

👉 **Delete video 014**

👣17

👉 **Move video 018**

to the end 👣16

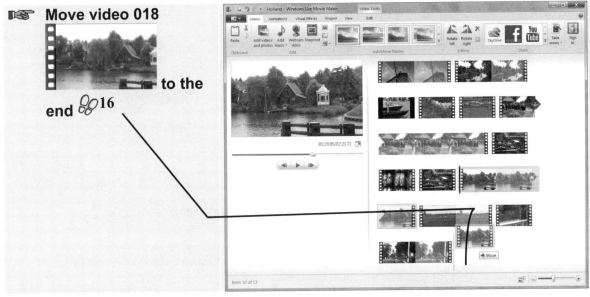

👉 **Move video 023**

so that it displays after the choir 👣16

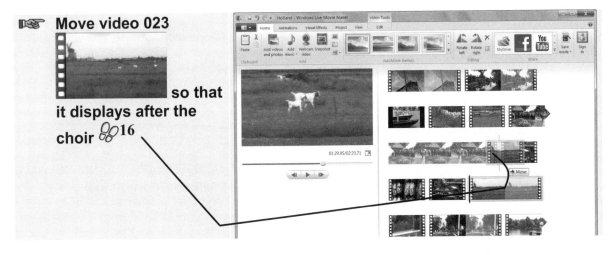

☞ **Delete video 026** 👣17

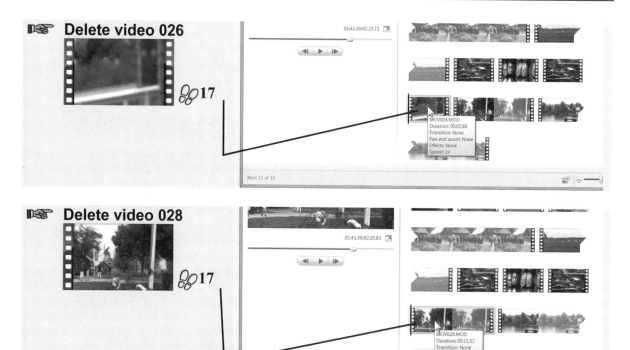

☞ **Delete video 028** 👣17

Now the project looks like this:

☞ **Save the project** 👣13

Please note: the exact order on your screen may differ somewhat, but that does not matter.

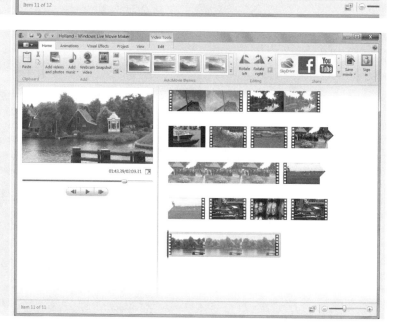

Now you have finished assembling the movie. In the next couple of chapters we will explain how to add sounds and effects, to make your movie more attractive.

☞ **Close** *Windows Live Movie Maker* 👣6

10.10 Background Information

Dictionary

Assembling	Arranging and trimming the videos and photos within a project.
Movie plan	An overview of all the available videos and photos.
Screenplay	The movie story or outline, used as a guide for shooting the movie. The screenplay often includes an overview of the required locations and props. Is also called a script.
Split	Dividing a video into two parts; the split will be made at the frame that is displayed in the preview window.
Trim mark	A slider on the timeline, used to set the start or end point of a video.

Source: Windows Live Movie Maker Help, Wikipedia

Taking pictures
Many video cameras will let you take snapshots, as well as record videos. The camera has a special button for this option.

The photo will be stored in a separate storage location, or in a separate folder on your camera's hard drive or memory card. Compared to video recordings, photos take up much less space.

With most video cameras, the photo quality is not as good as that of modern digital cameras. If you use such a photo in a movie, the quality should be good enough, but if you want to enlarge the photo, the image may become blurry.

Movie plan

Here is an overview of all the available videos for the movie. The column *Order* indicates where the clip will occur in the movie if it is used. The name of these files begins with *MOV* and ends with *.MOD*. For simplification, we have omitted those letters in the column *File* and have listed only the variable part of the file name.

File	Description	Comment	Order
00B	top of windmill	sound of windmill	start
00D	ship		x
01A	houses		x
01B	cat		x
01F	choir	singing	6
02C	clogs	engine sounds	9
02D	clog maker	engine sounds	part 8 and 10
004	scenery with windmills		x
008	windmill		x
010	cows		5
012	fish		4
013	bridge		x
014	street		x
015	houses on the waterfront		2
018	view from the bridge		end
023	goats in front of windmill	background choir music	7
026	??	blurry image	x
028	vista of windmill		x
	photo		3

When you point the mouse to a video, you will see the file name:

MOV010.MOD
Duration: 00:06.72
Transition: None
Pan and zoom: None
Effects: None
Speed: 1x

- Continue reading on the next page -

If the total duration is important to you, you can add a separate column to your plan and list that as well. All the files in this list have been arranged by their number, except the first and the last file. You can decide how to arrange the videos in your own plan. You may prefer to list them by the section of the movie they belong to, for example, *beginning*, *middle* or *end*. Or you can list them by event or location, such as *departure*, *town hall*, *church*, *party*. Once you start assembling a particular section, you can always make further adjustments as needed.

Video files

The film footage that you transfer from your video camera to your computer is saved as a video file. There are several types of video files available. Each type has its own advantages and disadvantages. These are the most commonly used types:

AVI - Audio Video Interleaved. This is a file format for sound videos, developed by *Microsoft*. You will frequently see this type of file in *Windows*. You can play an AVI video with the *Windows Media Player*. The image quality may vary, from reasonable to good. Higher quality files need more storage space. AVI files can often be played on older computers.

MPG - (also called MPEG, or Motion Pictures Expert Group). This is a file format for sound videos that uses a very high compression factor for the images without a substantial loss of quality. It is the standard format for video images and is used the most. The quality is good, especially with the development of the second edition, MPEG-2. With this edition you can store sound and vision in CD quality. MPEG-4 provides even higher quality.

MOV – a special video format, developed by *Apple,* for *Quicktime players*. It is available for both *Windows* and *Macintosh* computers.

WMV - *Windows Media Video*. This is a video file format that is developed by *Microsoft* and is especially suitable for *Windows Media Player*.

Deleting video files from your computer

Never move or delete the files (the master copy) from their original folder on your computer while you are still editing them in *Windows Live Movie Maker*. Remember that in a *Windows Live Movie Maker* project, only the links to the original files will be stored, along with the edits you make. When you start coding and publishing, this material is gathered together along with the edits and stored as a single unit in a new format. If you were to move, delete or rename the original files, the program would not be able to find them anymore. In that case, you would have to start all over again.

When you have finalized the movie and you are satisfied with it, you *can* delete the original file(s). But before deleting them, consider creating a backup, in case you want to use the files again later on. If you want to make a backup, you can use a burn program to burn the original files to one or more DVDs, or copy them to another storage device such as an external hard drive, before permanently removing them from your computer.

Jump cuts

You can assemble an entire movie from unrelated scenes. But be aware of a noticeable jump or sudden shift in the action, when assembling your movie. This occurs when people or objects in the movie appear to be jumping from one shot to the other. This is called a *jump cut* in the world of professional video editors. For example: in the first shot, somebody is standing in front of a door, and in the next shot he is standing on the doorstep, all of a sudden. This can be quite disconcerting for your viewers.

- Continue reading on the next page -

Fortunately, a movie allows you to skip certain periods of time and move from one action to another. Lengthy, boring sections can be left out. A shorter movie will hold your viewer's attention longer. In a holiday movie, you can film a shot of a car driving away from home, followed by a shot of the same car, arriving at the holiday destination. The viewer will automatically presume that a whole journey has taken place in between these shots. This sequence of shots will have a smoother transition because the shots are taken at different locations. If your camera angle stays the same and you cut out some footage, the resulting cut may look like a time cut where the action jumps from one point to another.

You can avoid these sudden shifts in the action by using so-called *inserts*. An insert will fill up the time that has elapsed between a specific shot and the next one. If we take the example of the person and the doorstep, this would be the time it took for him to stand in front of the door, walk towards the door and step up onto the doorstep. If you do not have a shot of him stepping onto the doorstep, you can use a different shot. In this case that could be a shot of the door, for example. While we see a shot of the door, the person could have stepped up onto the doorstep; there is a more logical progression of the action and it is less jerky.

Try to change camera angles when you shoot your films. It's not that hard when you are shooting your video, to stop the shot and move five or six feet to either side and re-size the shot before you resume shooting. Also make sure you have enough material. It is better to film more shots than you need, then to find you have not shot enough material.

10.11 Tips

 Tip

Rotate photos and videos
If you have shot a few frames, or a photo, in vertical position, you can always rotate the frame a quarter turn when you are assembling the movie:

☞ **Click the file**

On the Home tab:

☞ **Click** Rotate left

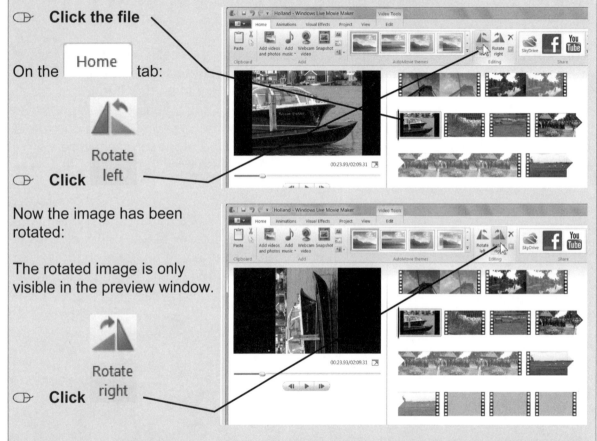

Now the image has been rotated:

The rotated image is only visible in the preview window.

☞ **Click** Rotate right

Now the image is positioned horizontally once again:

If you click once more, the image will be rotated to the other side.

💡　Tip

Change the size of the thumbnails and zoom in on the storyboard

You can also change the size of the thumbnails in the following way:

In the bottom right of the window:

☞　**Click**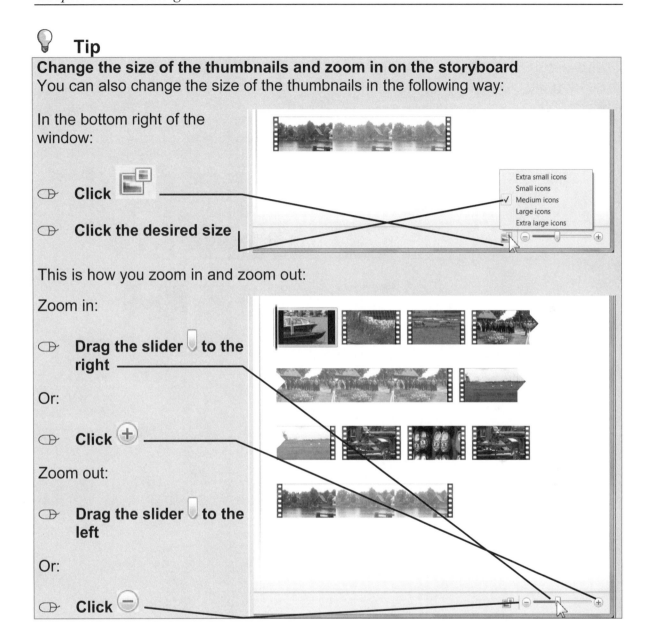

☞　**Click the desired size**

This is how you zoom in and zoom out:

Zoom in:

☞　**Drag the slider to the right**

Or:

☞　**Click ⊕**

Zoom out:

☞　**Drag the slider to the left**

Or:

☞　**Click ⊖**

Tip

Windows Live Movie Maker Help pages
The program includes a help option, which you can open if you have an Internet connection:

In the top right of the window:

☞ **Click**

Help and Support for Windows Live Movie Maker will be opened in your internet browser.

Click the relevant topic for more information.

11. Adding Effects and Transitions

One of the most striking differences between the tools that were used to assemble movies in the past and the digital types that are used today is the vast array of special effects and transitions that have become available. These options will enhance your movie; make it look more professional and more entertaining for your viewers.

With the effect tools you can change the colors of the movie, or turn it into one that looks like an old classic black-and-white film. You can apply these effects to the entire movie, or just to a single scene. Furthermore, you can add motion to your images, for example, allowing them to fade in and out.

Transitions are image effects that can be inserted between the scenes in your movie. They are actually a special kind of animation which makes the flow between the scenes very smooth. Transitions are not just pretty; they can also be very functional. They are very effective when applied to areas where the movie changes subject or location, or where the scenes differ widely in brightness or contrast.

In this chapter you will learn how to:

- correct the brightness;
- apply artistic effects;
- make images look older;
- mirror the image;
- add extra motion;
- use the fade effect;
- fade in and fade out a video;
- join together various effects;
- set transitions between videos;
- set a transition for the entire project;
- change the duration of a transition;
- use panning and zooming.

 Please note:

In this chapter we will be applying many different effects to the practice movie, so that you can understand how they work. However, you should try to limit the number of effects you apply to your own movies. Too many effects can make you movie harder to watch.

11.1 Correcting Brightness

A video clip can sometimes appear too dark, or obscure, the same way photos do. You can adjust the brightness with *Windows Live Movie Maker*:

☞ **Start *Windows Live Movie Maker* 𝒫7**

☞ **Open the *Holland* project 𝒫18**

You will see the project:

☞ **Play the last video 𝒫10**

The last section is very dark.

The video will automatically stop playing when it reaches the end.

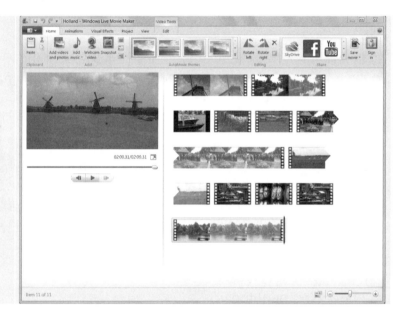

👆 **Click the**

| Visual Effects | **tab**

👆 **Click ☼ Brightness**

👆 **Drag the slider ▢ to the right, until the image becomes brighter**

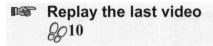 **Replay the last video**
$\mathcal{QQ}$10

Now the end has more light but the first section has become a little too bright. The typical green color is hardly recognizable. Also details, such as clouds and waves, are barely visible:

👆 **Click** ☼ Brightness

👆 **Drag the slider ▯ a little to the left**

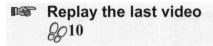 **Replay the last video**
$\mathcal{QQ}$10

If you are not satisfied:

👆 **Adjust the brightness once again**

In the upper left corner of the
video you will see :

⬤ **Position the mouse
   pointer on the video**

In the information frame you
can see that the brightness
has been adjusted:

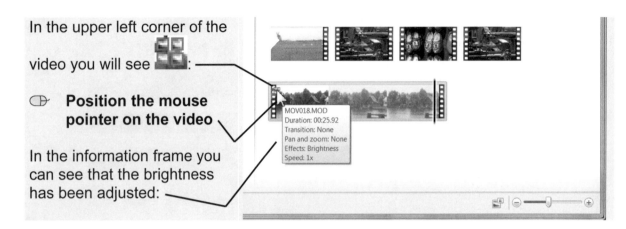

MOV018.MOD
Duration: 00:25.92
Transition: None
Pan and zoom: None
Effects: Brightness
Speed: 1x

💡 **Tip**

Different brightness settings within a single video
You can only adjust the brightness for the entire video at once, not for a specific
section of the video. If you want to correct extremely large contrasts, you can split
the video. Then you will be able to edit the two clips and set the brightness for each
one separately:

⬤ **Position the playback
   indicator on the spot
   where you want to spit
   the video**

Pay attention to the preview
window.

⬤ **Click the** Edit **tab**

⬤ **Click** Split

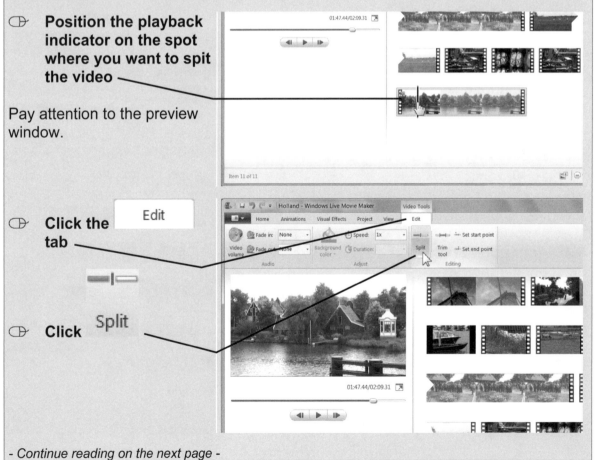

- Continue reading on the next page -

The video has been split:

Now you can set the brightness for both clips separately.

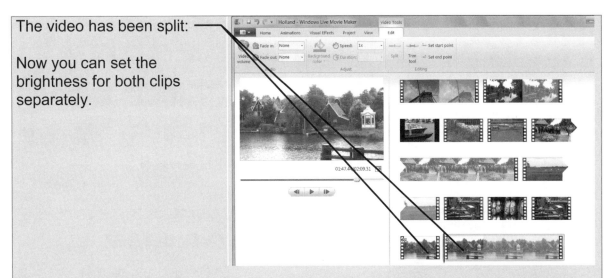

Since these videos follow one another, be careful not make too big of a difference in brightness. If you need to correct the brightness further, it is better to split the video into three or more sections, and adjust the brightness step by step.

And you can add transitions between the parts you have split. We will learn how to do this later on in this chapter

☞ **Save the project** ✂️13

11.2 Artistic Effects

To make your movie more entertaining you can use a large number of different effects. The effects have been arranged in several categories. First, you are going to take a look at an artistic effect:

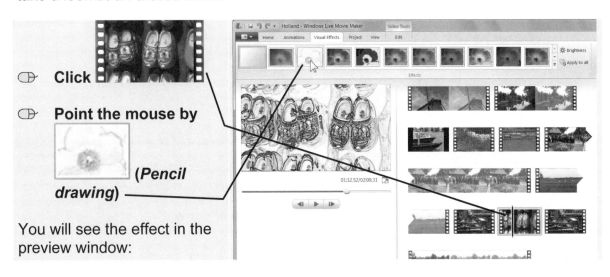

👆 **Click**

👆 **Point the mouse by**

(Pencil drawing)

You will see the effect in the preview window:

To set the effect:

⊕ **Click**
(Pencil-drawing)

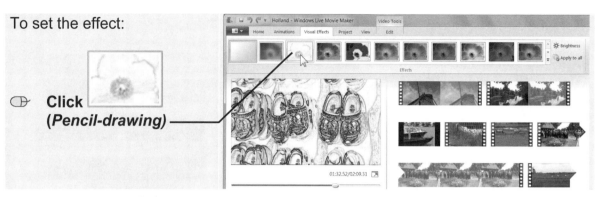

⊕ **Click**

☞ **Play the project** 🐾¹⁰

Watch the effect. Afterwards:

☞ **Stop playback** 🐾¹¹

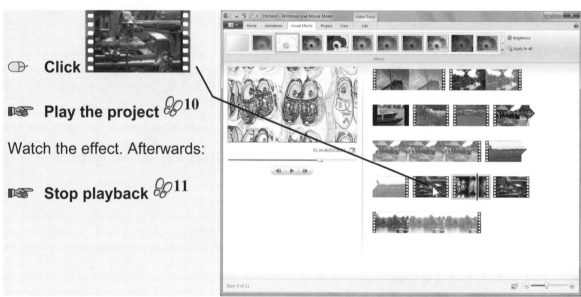

⊕ **Position the mouse**
pointer on

In the information frame you
will see the effect you have
inserted:

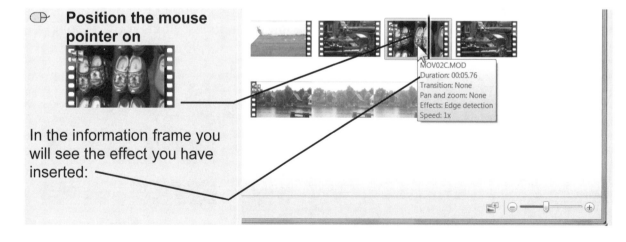

It is easy to disable the effect, if you do not like it:

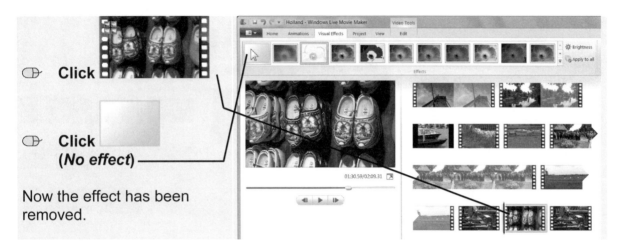

☞ **Click**

☞ **Click**
   (*No effect*)

Now the effect has been
removed.

11.3 Aging Effects

To view various categories of effects, you can use the ⏷ button:

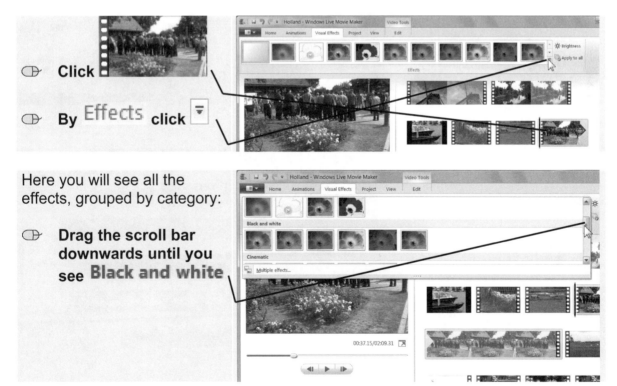

☞ **Click**

☞ **By** Effects **click** ⏷

Here you will see all the
effects, grouped by category:

☞ **Drag the scroll bar
   downwards until you
   see** Black and white

⊕ **Point the mouse to the first effect in** **Black and white**

The effect will be applied to the bottom part of the preview window:

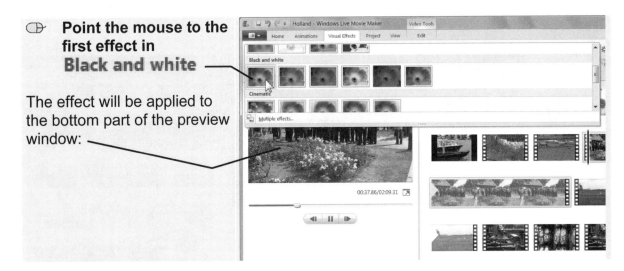

☞ **Take a look at the other effects in the** **Black and white** **category**

Select *Sepia tone*:

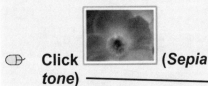

⊕ **Click** **(Sepia tone)**

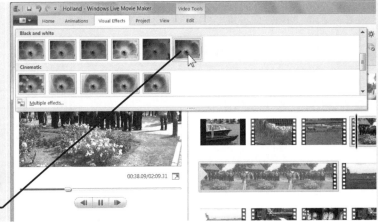

☞ **Play the video** 𝄞10

The video looks like an old fashioned movie:

☞ **Stop playback at the end of the clip** 𝄞11

11.4 Mirroring the Image

Sometimes a video will look better when the direction of motion is changed. For instance, from right to left, instead of from left to right. To do this, you will need to rotate or mirror the video. This will make the video look less awkward and can result in a smoother transition from the previous video, or to the next video. You can practice applying this effect with the photo of the boat:

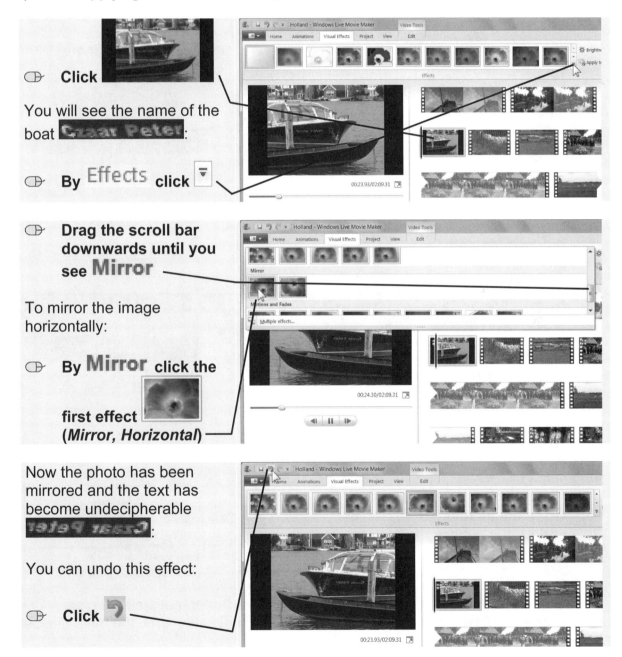

☞ **Click**

You will see the name of the boat **Groor Peter**:

☞ **By** Effects **click** ⬇

☞ **Drag the scroll bar downwards until you see Mirror**

To mirror the image horizontally:

☞ **By Mirror click the first effect (*Mirror, Horizontal*)**

Now the photo has been mirrored and the text has become undecipherable **Groor Peter**:

You can undo this effect:

☞ **Click** ↺

This type of effect us also used on television, to render advertisements less clear.

The second effect ![small image] (*Mirror, Vertical*) will let you mirror the image vertically.

Sometimes you can even mirror moving images, without it resulting in a strange effect:

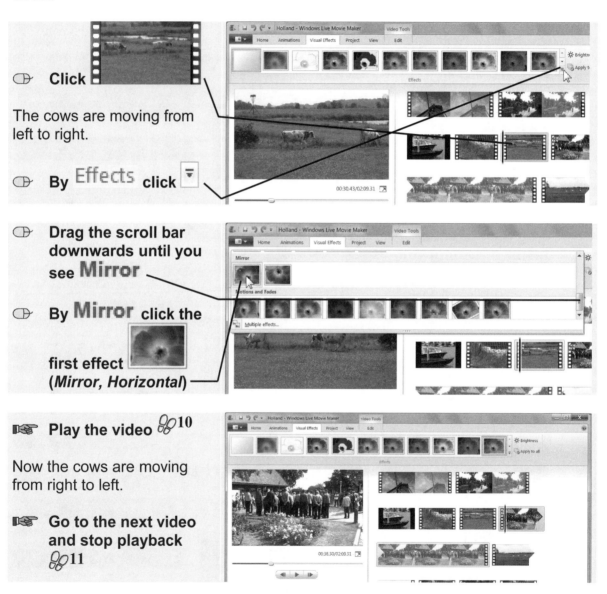

👆 **Click**

The cows are moving from left to right.

👆 **By** Effects **click** ⬇

👆 **Drag the scroll bar downwards until you see** Mirror

👆 **By** Mirror **click the first effect** (*Mirror, Horizontal*)

☞ **Play the video** 🦶10

Now the cows are moving from right to left.

☞ **Go to the next video and stop playback** 🦶11

You can use this mirror effect if the direction of motion better matches the other videos, or if the video has been filmed from a different direction than the other videos.

☞ **Save the project** 🦶13

11.5 Motions

By using motions you can sometimes add extraordinary effects to a movie.

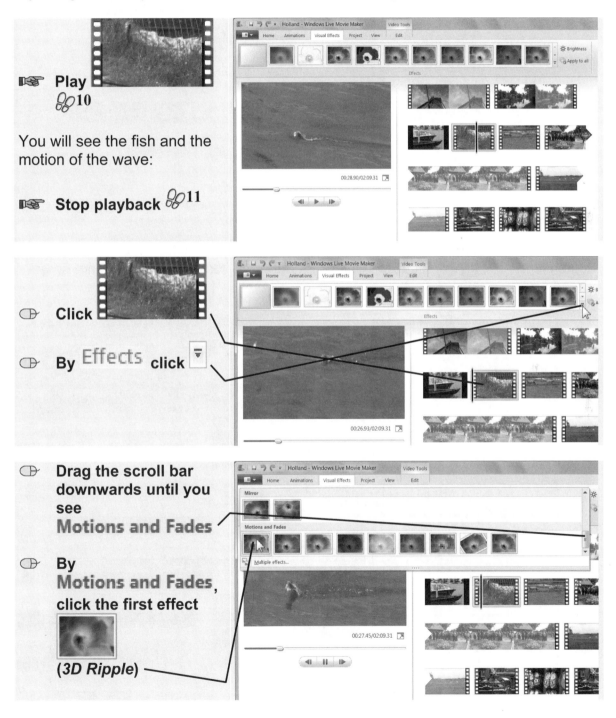

☞ **Play** ᗡᗡ10

You will see the fish and the motion of the wave:

☞ **Stop playback** ᗡᗡ11

👉 **Click**

👉 **By** Effects **click** ⧩

👉 **Drag the scroll bar downwards until you see**
Motions and Fades

👉 **By**
Motions and Fades,
click the first effect

(3D Ripple)

☞ **Play the video** 👣**10**

Now the rippling motion has become much stronger:

☞ **Go to the next video and stop playback** 👣**11**

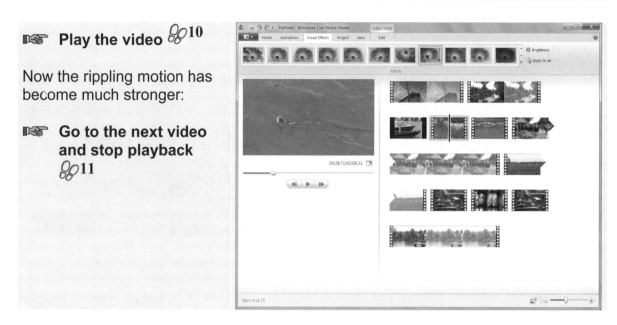

As a rule, it is better to be economical with these motion effects. Otherwise, your audience may get a little seasick. But for the moment you are just practicing, so go ahead and try another effect:

👆 **Click** [thumbnail]

👆 **By** Effects **click** [icon]

👆 **Drag the scroll bar downwards until you see** Motions and Fades

👆 **By** Motions and Fades [icon] **click** (*360° Rotation*)

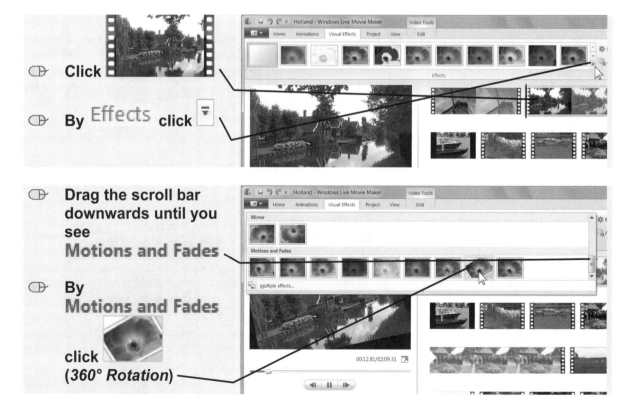

☞ **Play the video** 👣10

You will see the rotation:

☞ **Go to the next video and stop playback** 👣11

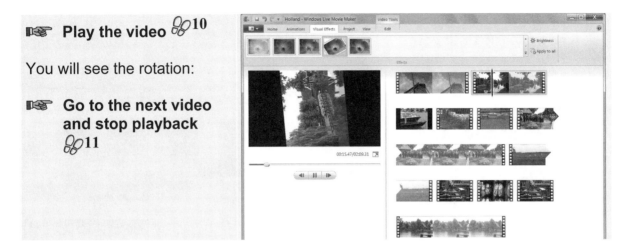

Sometimes such an effect can be useful in a slide show, but a movie already displays enough motion by itself. Adding this type of effect to a movie clip may be too much. For the time being you are going to leave this effect in place, but you can remove it later on.

☞ **Save the project** 👣13

11.6 Fading In and Out

If you want to achieve a smooth transition between videos, you can use *fades*. The colors in a clip will slowly change to other colors, or to a neutral color such as black or white. You can insert a fade at the end or at the beginning of a clip. You could start for example, with a particular color and allow the real colors to slowly emerge.

Fades are an excellent way of making the beginning or ending of a video less abrupt. You can practice using this transition, by applying a *fade in* to the first video in the project:

👆 **Click**

👆 **By** Effects **click** ▼

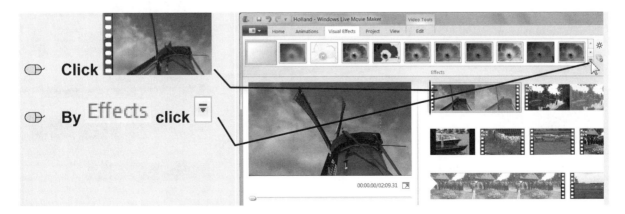

Drag the scroll bar downwards until you see **Motions and Fades**

By **Motions and Fades** click the second effect

(Fade in from black)

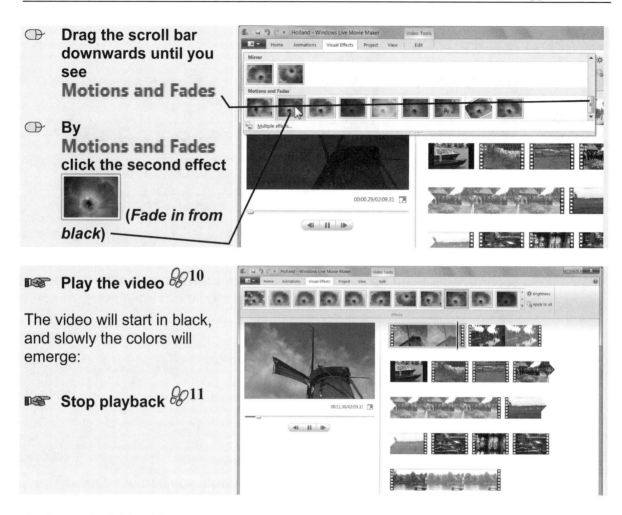

☞ Play the video 👣10

The video will start in black, and slowly the colors will emerge:

☞ Stop playback 👣11

At the end of this video, you can insert a *fade out* effect:

Click

By Effects click ▼

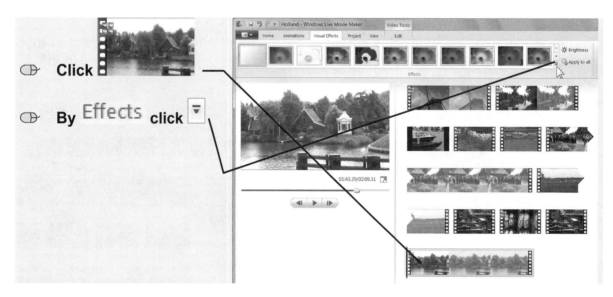

⬚ **Drag the scroll bar downwards until you see Motions and Fades**

⬚ **By Motions and Fades click the fourth effect**

(*Fade out to black*)

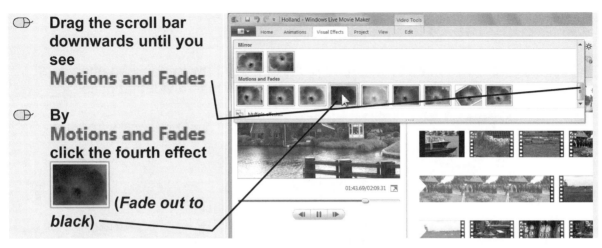

☞ **Play the video** 👣10

At the end of the movie, the video will turn black:

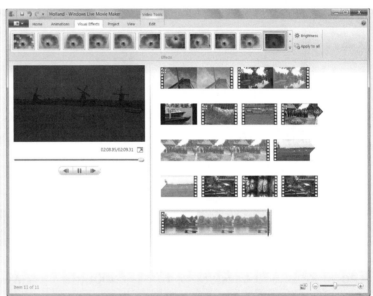

☞ **Save the project** 👣13

11.7 Applying Multiple Effects

All the methods previously demonstrated showed you how to apply an effect to a *single* photo or video. But you can apply multiple effects to a video at once:

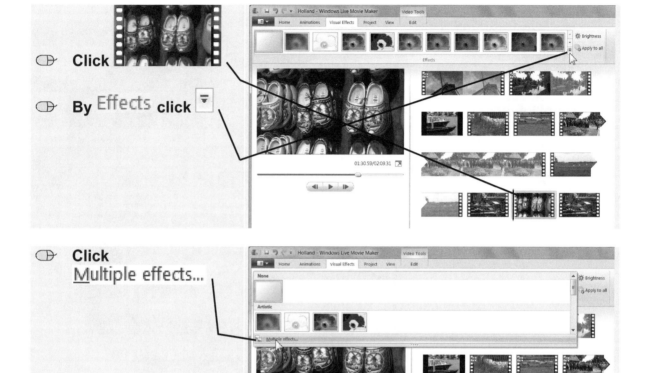

☞ **Click** 🖐️

☞ **By** Effects **click** ▼

☞ **Click**
  Multiple effects...

The window *Add or Remove Effects* appears. You will see the effects that are available. You can try using two of them now:

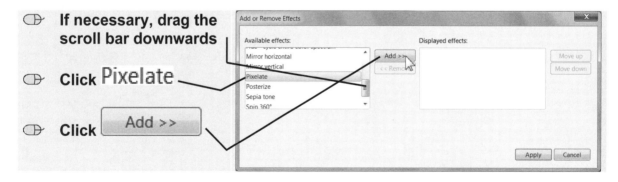

☞ **If necessary, drag the scroll bar downwards**

☞ **Click** Pixelate

☞ **Click** Add >>

The effect has been added:

⌖ **Drag the scroll bar upwards**

⌖ **Click**
Black and white

⌖ **Click** [Add >>]

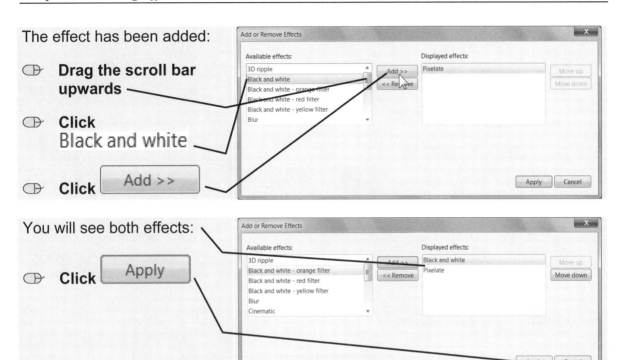

You will see both effects:

⌖ **Click** [Apply]

In the preview window, the clogs are now displayed in black and white:

☞ **Play the video** 🥿🥿10

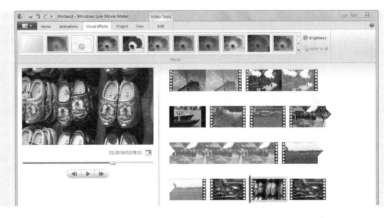

The image will turn into pixels:

☞ **Stop playback** 🥿🥿11

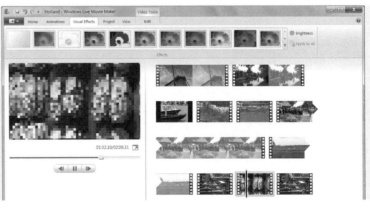

If you do not like a specific effect, you can delete or change it:

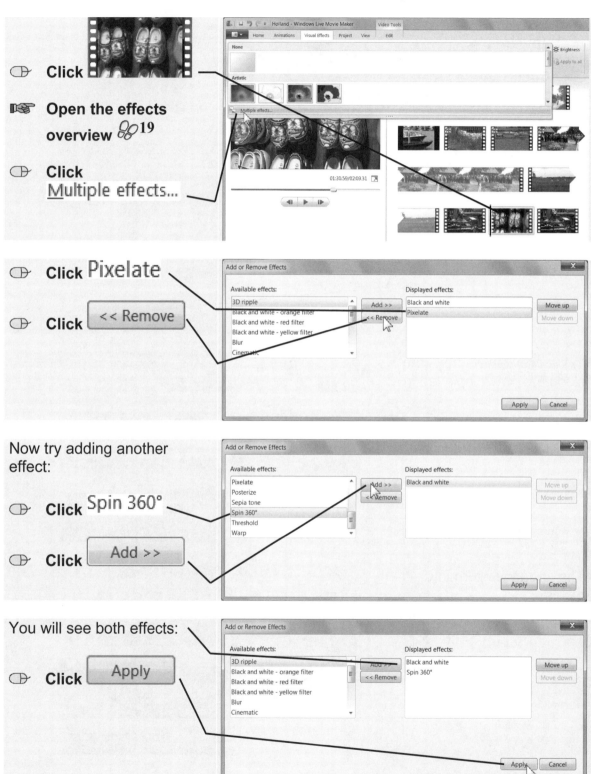

👆 **Click**

☞ **Open the effects overview** 👣19

👆 **Click** <u>M</u>ultiple effects...

👆 **Click** Pixelate

👆 **Click** << Remove

Now try adding another effect:

👆 **Click** Spin 360°

👆 **Click** Add >>

You will see both effects:

👆 **Click** Apply

Tip

Change the order of the effects
If you are using multiple effects, the order in which they are applied can make a difference. This is how you change the order:

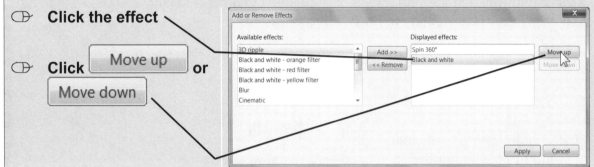

⟳ **Click the effect**

⟳ **Click** [Move up] **or**
   [Move down]

👉 **Play the video** 👣10

The image will revolve:

👉 **Stop playback** 👣11

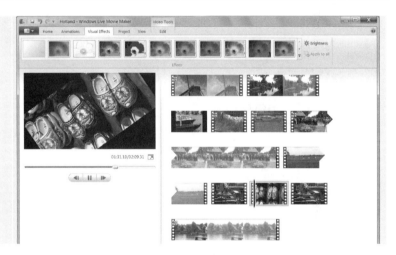

⟳ **Position the mouse pointer on the video**

You will see both effects:

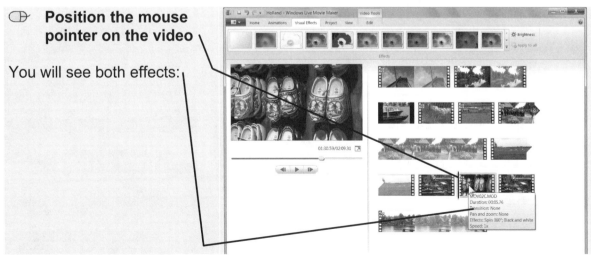

👉 **Save the project** 👣13

11.8 Setting Transitions

A transition allows you to switch smoothly between one video clip or photo and the next. Without using transitions you may see very abrupt breaks, especially if there is a lot of difference in the brightness of the videos. You can select various transitions and apply them individually to each video or photo:

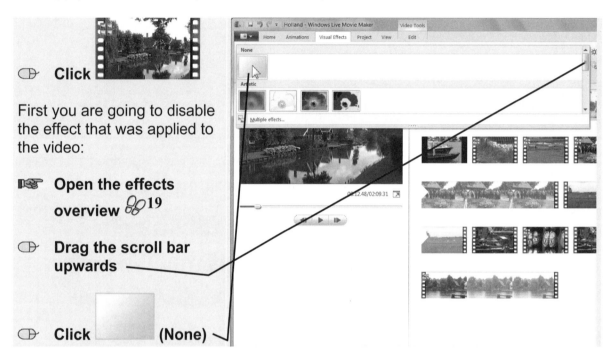

☞ **Click** [📷]

First you are going to disable the effect that was applied to the video:

☞ **Open the effects overview** 👣[19]

☞ **Drag the scroll bar upwards**

☞ **Click** [ ] **(None)**

Combinations of effects and transitions can sometimes result in a very crowded and turbulent image. A rotating effect had been applied to this particular video. This makes it difficult to properly view the transition.

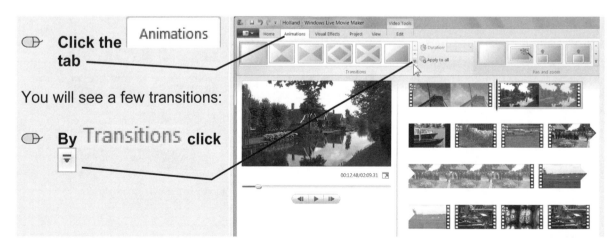

☞ **Click the** [Animations] **tab**

You will see a few transitions:

☞ **By** Transitions **click** [▼]

The transitions are arranged in categories, just like the effects. If you point the mouse to a specific transition, you will see an example of the transition in the preview window:

Point the mouse to *(Diagonal cross)*

You will see the transition:

Take a look at some of the examples in the other categories:

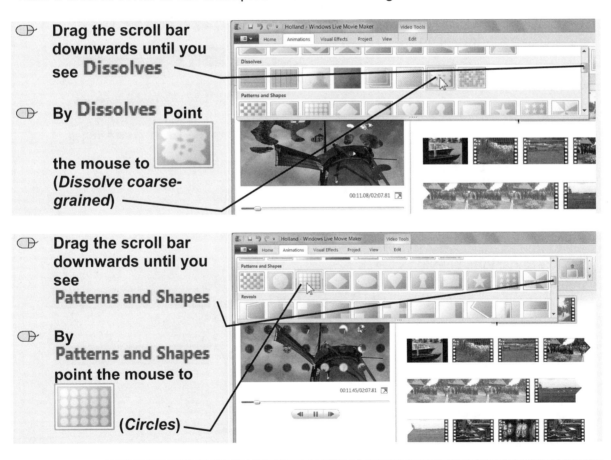

Drag the scroll bar downwards until you see Dissolves

By Dissolves Point the mouse to *(Dissolve coarse-grained)*

Drag the scroll bar downwards until you see Patterns and Shapes

By Patterns and Shapes point the mouse to *(Circles)*

☞ **Browse through other examples in this category, and then take a look at some of the other categories**

If you have found a suitable transition, then you can insert it in the following way:

By **Dissolves** click

(Cross fading)

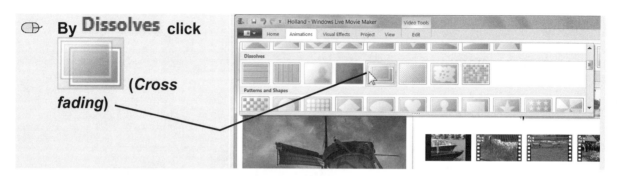

Play the project, starting with the first video ✂10

You will see the transition:

Stop playback ✂11

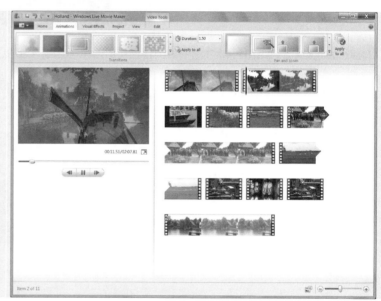

When a transition is set for a specific video, a gray triangle will appear in the bottom left of the frame:

Save the project ✂13

Skip to the beginning of the project ✂14

11.9 Set Transitions for the Entire Project

If you want your movie to look calm and steady, try to refrain from using too many different transitions. It is recommended to set a default transition for the entire project, and only change this transition for a few specific videos. Now you are going to set the transition you have previously set for the second video, and apply it to the entire project, as a default transition:

☞ **Click the** Home **tab**

☞ **Click** ⬜

Now all the videos and photos have been selected:

🡆 Please note:

If you have set a transition for a certain video, you will not see the first frame of that video in the preview window anymore; when you select such a video, you will see the image of the previous video.

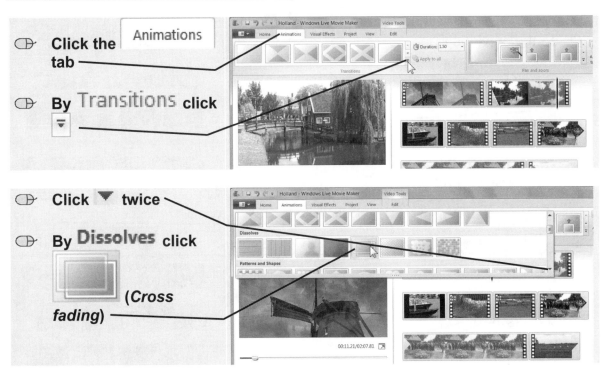

☞ **Click the** Animations **tab**

☞ **By** Transitions **click** ⬇

☞ **Click** ▼ **twice**

☞ **By** Dissolves **click**

⬜ **(Cross fading)**

☞ **Go to the beginning of the project** 🐾14

☞ **Play the entire project** 🐾10

You will see all the transitions:

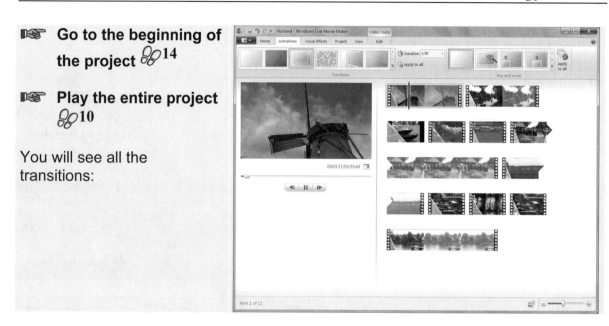

You can still insert a different transition for each individual video or photo:

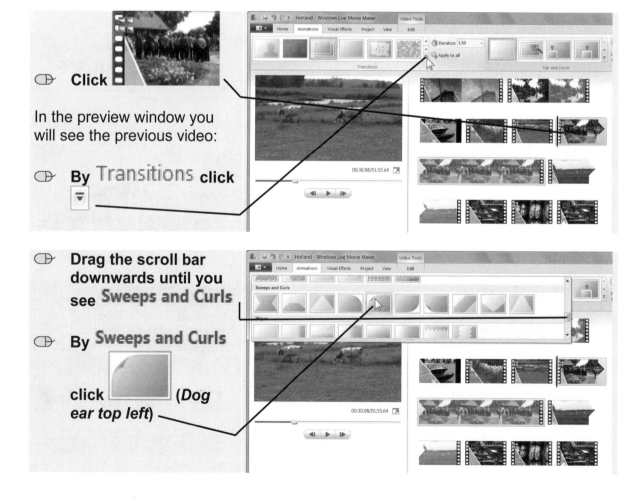

⊕ **Click**

In the preview window you will see the previous video:

⊕ **By** Transitions **click**

⊕ **Drag the scroll bar downwards until you see** Sweeps and Curls

⊕ **By** Sweeps and Curls **click** *(Dog ear top left)*

☞ **Play the project starting at the previous video** 👣10

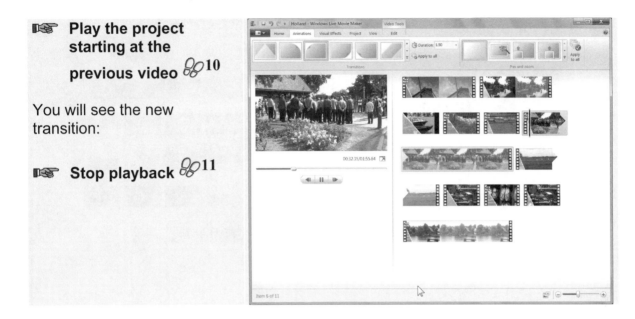

You will see the new transition:

☞ **Stop playback** 👣11

11.10 Setting the Transition's Duration

Usually, a transition takes 1.5 seconds. If that is too long or too short, you can change its duration:

☞ **Click** [thumbnail]

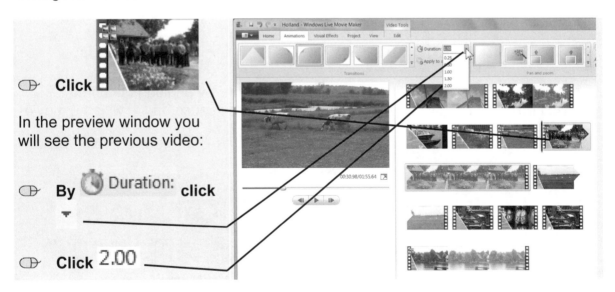

In the preview window you will see the previous video:

☞ **By** ⏱ **Duration:** **click** ▼

☞ **Click** 2.00

☞ **Play the project starting with**

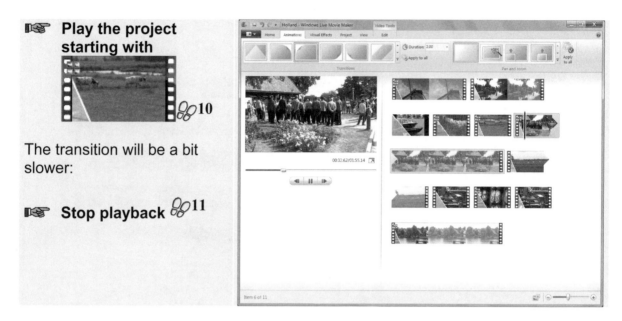

₁₀

The transition will be a bit slower:

☞ **Stop playback** ₁₁

The length of the video fragment can also influence the length of the transition. If you use a lengthy transition with a short video clip, you will not see a whole lot of the actual video; if that is the case, then it might be wiser to select a shorter transition.

☞ **Save the project** ₁₃

11.11 Panning and zooming

A still image does not really fit in a movie full of motion. By panning the photo (moving it), or zooming in on the photo, it will be more in accordance with the movie:

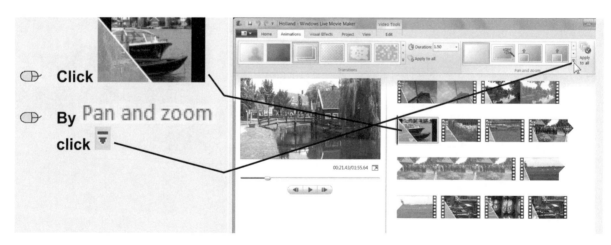

⊕ **Click**

⊕ **By** Pan and zoom

click ▼

By **Pan only** position the mouse pointer on

(*Pan to the right*) —————

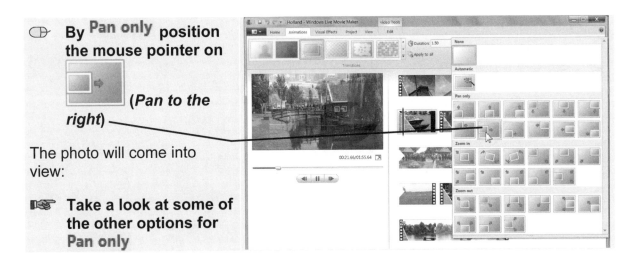

The photo will come into view:

☞ **Take a look at some of the other options for Pan only**

With the movements will be alternated. Each time you play the video, you will see a different movement.

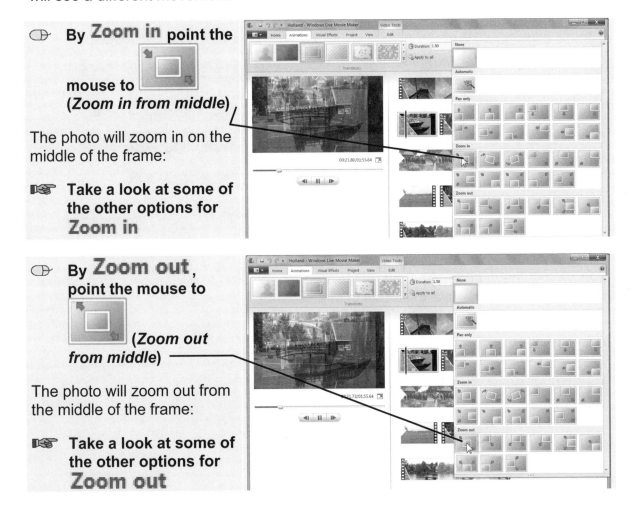

By **Zoom in** point the mouse to (*Zoom in from middle*)

The photo will zoom in on the middle of the frame:

☞ **Take a look at some of the other options for Zoom in**

By **Zoom out**, point the mouse to (*Zoom out from middle*) —————

The photo will zoom out from the middle of the frame:

☞ **Take a look at some of the other options for Zoom out**

Apply the *zoom in from the middle* option to the photo:

By **Zoom in** click

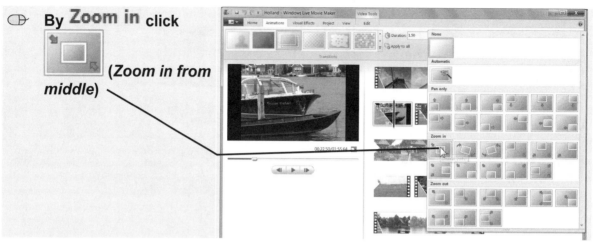

(Zoom in from middle)

Play the project, starting with

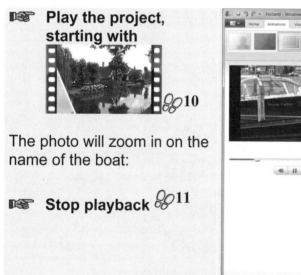

The photo will zoom in on the name of the boat:

Stop playback 𝒐𝒐11

By now, you have added enough effects and movements to your movie. In the next chapter you will learn how to add titles and captions.

Save the project 𝒐𝒐13

Close *Windows Live Movie Maker* 𝒐𝒐2

11.12 Background Information

Dictionary	
Aging effect	To render color recordings in black and white, or in sepia (brown) tones, which give them a classic old fashioned look.
Effects	Changes in the colors or motion of the original recording, in order to create a particular atmosphere, or correct recording errors.
Fade	Type of transition where the scene *fades out* at the end, or slowly *fades in* at the beginning.
Mirroring	Turning over the image (you can mirror horizontally or vertically). With moving images, the direction of the motion will be reversed.
Panning	Horizontal movement of a scene; this effect is similar to shaking the camera. For example, the image will be moved from one corner to another.
Transitions	Special image effect that can be inserted between consecutive scenes. You can use it to take a time leap, to display a different angle, or to soften large differences in brightness.
Zooming	Displaying a photo in a larger or smaller size.

Source: Windows Live Movie Maker Help, Wikipedia

11.13 Tips

 Tip

Available animations
The number of transitions you see on the *Animations* tab depends on the file type and its position in the project.

If the video is in the *middle* of your project, you will see:

- all of the transitions

- panning and zooming will be disabled

Panning and zooming is only possible with still images, such as a photo.

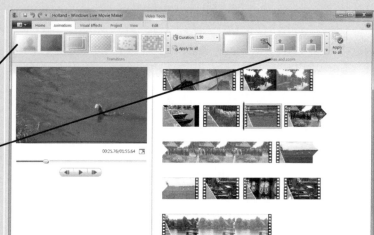

If the video is the *first* video in your project, you will see:

- only the transitions suited to the beginning of a video

- here, panning and zooming will be disabled as well

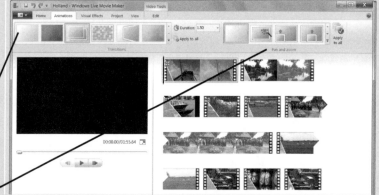

In case it is a photo, you will see:

- the transitions

- the options for panning and zooming

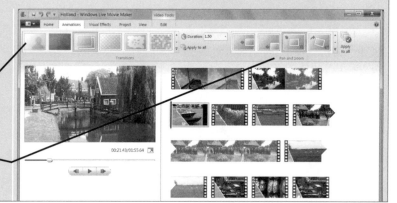

Tip

Creating a slide show
The effects and animations you have learned to use in this chapter are also very suitable for creating an entertaining slide show with your photos.

☞ **Add the photos to a project** ⌘²⁰

☞ **Arrange the photos in the right order**

☞ **Add effects and animations**

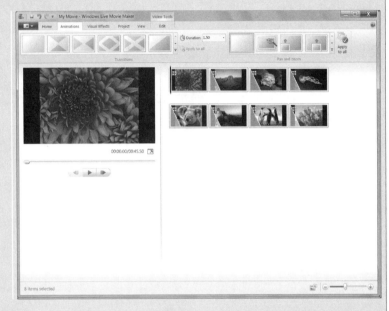

You can also edit, save, and publish a slide show project. In the following chapters you will learn how to do this.

 Tip

Right mouse button
You can display frequently used functions by right-clicking a video or a photo:

☞ **Right-click a video or photo**

You will see a context menu:

Tip

Shortcut keys

Many of the operations in *Windows Live Movie Maker* can also be executed by using the shortcut keys. Many of the keyboard shortcuts in *Windows Live Movie Maker* are the same as those used in *Microsoft Office*. You can also find them by clicking *Help* and searching on the word 'keyboard'. Here is a list of the keyboard shortcuts:

General shortcut keys

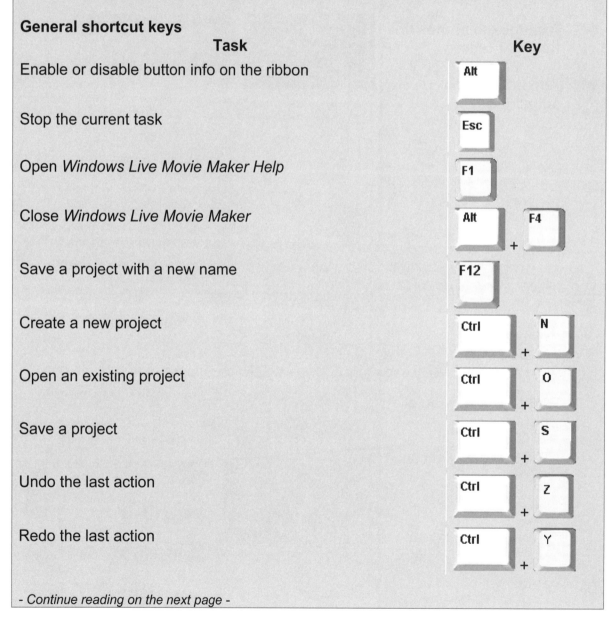

Task	Key
Enable or disable button info on the ribbon	Alt
Stop the current task	Esc
Open *Windows Live Movie Maker Help*	F1
Close *Windows Live Movie Maker*	Alt + F4
Save a project with a new name	F12
Create a new project	Ctrl + N
Open an existing project	Ctrl + O
Save a project	Ctrl + S
Undo the last action	Ctrl + Z
Redo the last action	Ctrl + Y

- Continue reading on the next page -

Shortcut keys for examples and editing

Task	Key

Play or pause

Space bar or K

Go to previous frame — J

Go to next frame — L

Cut the video to start it at the current position in the video — I

Cut the video to end it at the current position in the video — O

Split the video at the current position in the video — M

Shortcut keys for the storyboard

Task	Key

Cut the selected item — Ctrl + X

Copy the selected item — Ctrl + C

Paste — Ctrl + V

Delete selected items — Delete

Select next item in the direction of the arrow — ← , → , ↑ or ↓

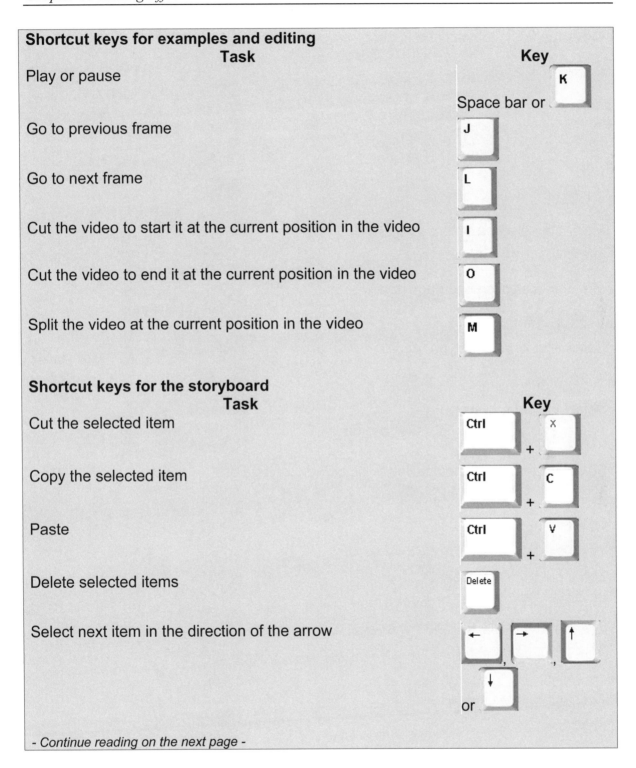

- *Continue reading on the next page -*

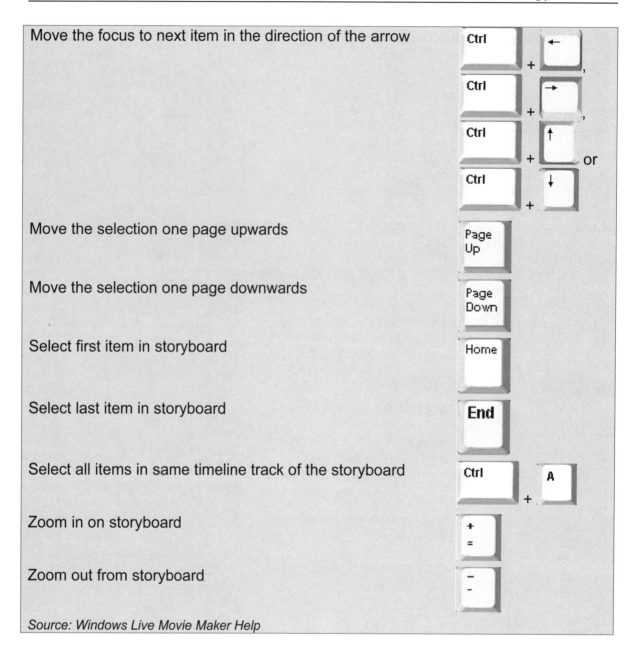

Move the focus to next item in the direction of the arrow	
Move the selection one page upwards	
Move the selection one page downwards	
Select first item in storyboard	
Select last item in storyboard	
Select all items in same timeline track of the storyboard	
Zoom in on storyboard	
Zoom out from storyboard	

Source: Windows Live Movie Maker Help

12. Titles and Captions

If you have created a movie yourself, you will know what the movie is about. But your audience will not know that. It is a good idea to start your movie by showing the title of it. Try to find a title that explains the content of the movie. It can also be very useful to add short text fragments every now and then, that will explain certain events or show the name of a person or a location. Otherwise it may take a while before your audience understands what is happening.

In *Windows Live Movie Maker* you will find various options for adding titles and captions. You can add a title at the beginning of the movie, in between the scenes, or in the movie itself. And you can end the movie with closing credits.

You can also choose different text colors and set special effects for the text.

In this chapter you will learn how to:

- add a title to a project;
- move titles;
- choose title colors;
- set title effects and animations;
- add intermediate titles;
- edit titles;
- add a caption to a video;
- change the time settings for a caption;
- add credits.

12.1 Adding Titles

Unless you want to surprise your audience, you will usually want to start your movie by displaying a title. The title could be the name of the movie (*Holidays 2010*), or even a short description of the occasion (*Wedding Day of…*). Here is how to add a title to your movie:

☞ Start *Windows Live Movie Maker* ⑥⑥⁷

☞ Open the *Holland* project ⑥⑥¹⁸

On the │ Home │ tab:

⊕ Click

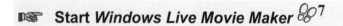

HELP! The preview window is dark.

You are about to insert an animation. The screen will be black at the beginning (to show your title), then slowly the video will emerge. The first shot will be black.

A title slide has been inserted before the first slide:

You will also see a new tab

Text Tools

Format

☞ Select **Holland**
⑥⑥27

⌨ **Type:** Holiday Holland 2010

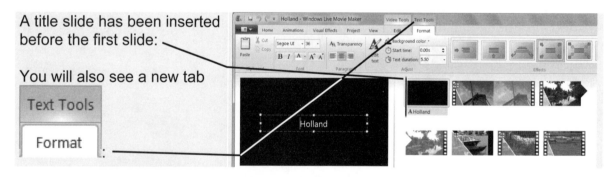

⊕ **Click somewhere next to the text box**

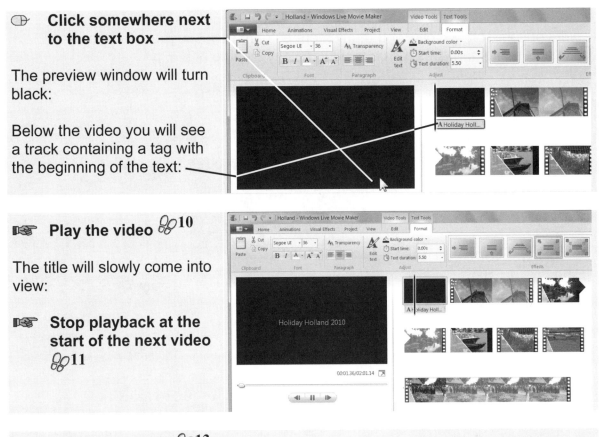

The preview window will turn black:

Below the video you will see a track containing a tag with the beginning of the text:

☞ **Play the video** 🐾**10**

The title will slowly come into view:

☞ **Stop playback at the start of the next video** 🐾**11**

☞ **Save the project** 🐾**13**

12.2 Changing Colors

You can easily change the background color of the title slide. If you change the background color to a darker blue, it will more closely match the clip that follows:

⊕ **Click the title video**

⊕ **If necessary, click the** Format **tab**

⊕ **Click** 🎨 Background color ▾

⊕ **Click ■ (Blue, darker 50%)**

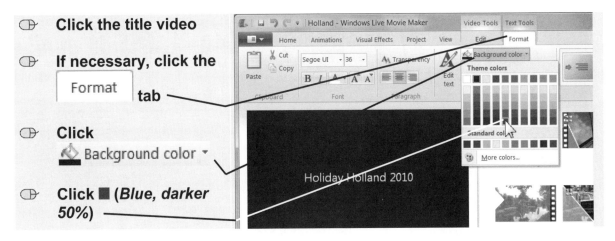

Instead of selecting one of the default colors shown, you can also click the *More colors* option. This will give you many more colors to choose from. First, select a text color that sort of matches the color you actually want to use:

Now the background color is blue:

You want the text color to be light blue:

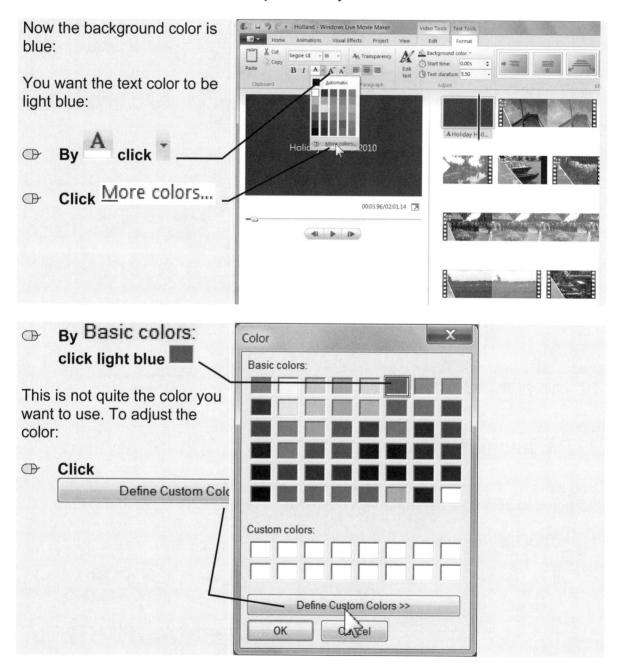

⊕   **By** A **click** ▾ ————

⊕   **Click** More colors...

⊕   **By** Basic colors:
     click light blue ▢ ——

This is not quite the color you want to use. To adjust the color:

⊕   **Click**
     Define Custom Col

⊕ **Drag ◀ upwards until you see the right color**

⊕ **Click**

Add to Custom Colors

Now the color has been added: ————

⊕ **Click** OK

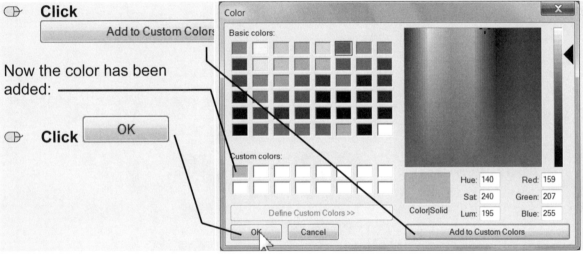

The text color has been modified:

You can also add effects to the text:

⊕ **By** Effects **click** ▼

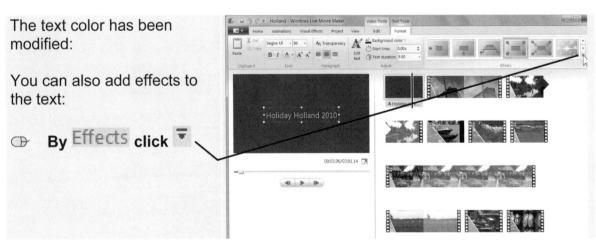

For titles you cannot select the regular visual effects. Instead, you can use special title effects:

⊕ **Move the mouse over a few of these effects**

You will see the effects in the preview window:

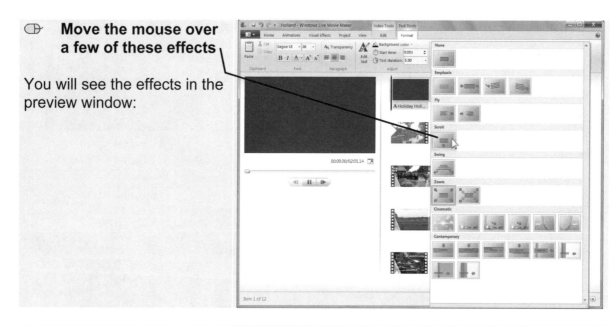

⊕ **By Swing click**

(Turn downwards)

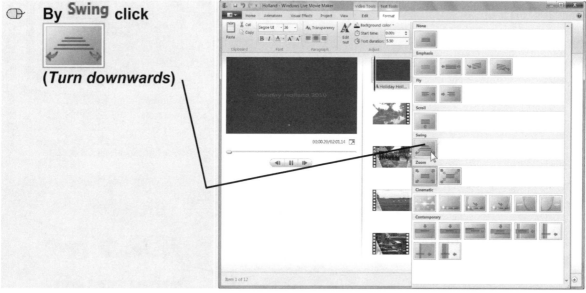

☞ **Play the video** ✂10

You will see the colors and the effect.

☞ **Stop playback at the start of the next video** ✂11

12.3 Setting the Title Duration and Adding Animations

You can set the duration for the title clip, as well as the text. By default, the title clip is displayed for seven seconds, and the text for 5.5 seconds. This is quite a long time for a short title, but you can shorten this period:

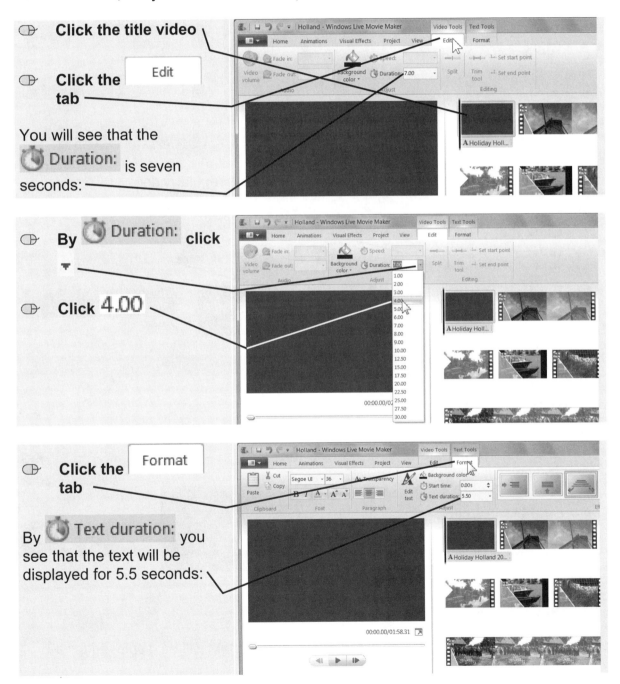

Click the title video

Click the Edit **tab**

You will see that the Duration: is seven seconds:

By Duration: **click** ▼

Click 4.00

Click the Format **tab**

By Text duration: you see that the text will be displayed for 5.5 seconds:

It will look nicer if the text appears a little while later, and disappears from view just before the end.

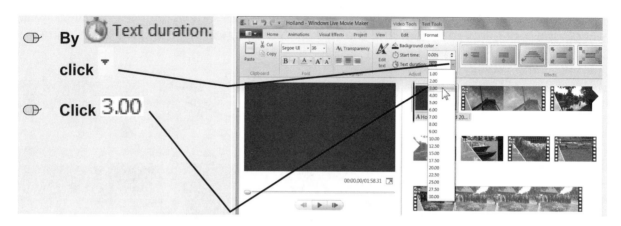

☞ By ⏱ **Text duration:** click ▾

☞ **Click** 3.00

You can also add animations to the title clip, just like a regular video:

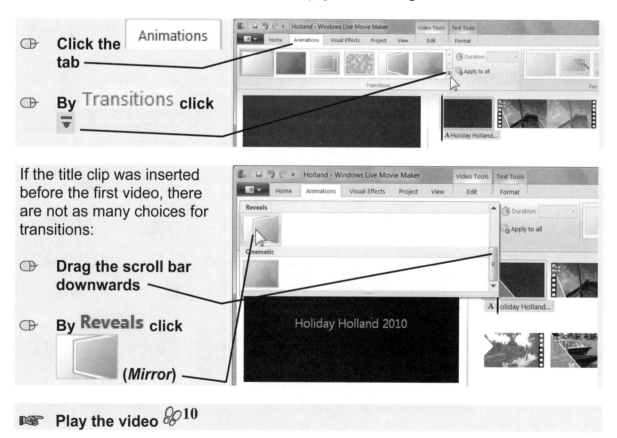

☞ **Click the** Animations **tab**

☞ **By** Transitions **click** ▾

If the title clip was inserted before the first video, there are not as many choices for transitions:

☞ **Drag the scroll bar downwards**

☞ **By** Reveals **click**

(*Mirror*)

☞ **Play the video** 🐾¹⁰

The title clip will start with the selected effect, and the text will be displayed for a shorter period of time.

☞ **Stop playback at the start of the next video** 🐾¹¹

☞ **Save the project** ⬷¹³

12.4 Add an Intermediate Title

A title does not always have to be placed at the start of a movie. You may often see a movie with a few introductory shots at the beginning, followed later by a title. You can insert the title for example after the first video:

👆 **Click the title clip**

👆 **Drag the title clip to the right of the first video**

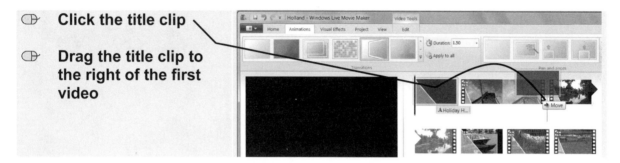

The transition to the title clip is now very sudden. But you can adjust that. Since the title clip is no longer at the beginning of your movie, you also have a wider choice of transitions:

👆 **If necessary, click the** Animations **tab**

👆 **By** Transitions **click** ▼

👆 **Drag the scroll bar upwards a little**

👆 **By** Dissolves **click**

⬚ **(Dissolve)**

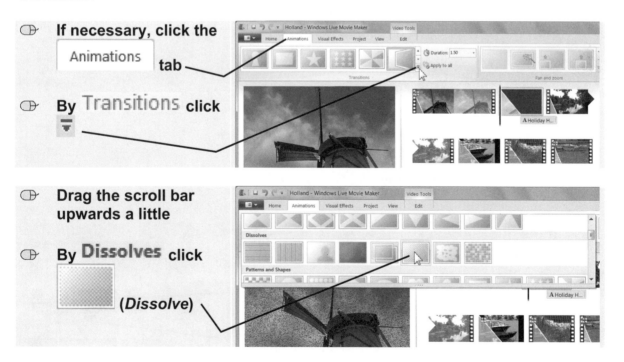

You can add the same effect for the transition from the title to the next video:

⊕ **Click**

☞ **Set the same** (*Dissolve*) **transition for this video** &021

☞ **Go to the beginning of the project** &014

☞ **Play the video** &010

The movie will start with an introduction, after which the title will be displayed.

☞ **Stop playback in the video** &011

☞ **Save the project** &013

12.5 Edit Titles

If you want to change the text or formatting of a title later on, you will need to select it first:

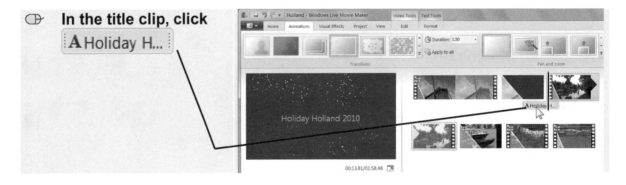

⊕ **In the title clip, click**
A Holiday H...

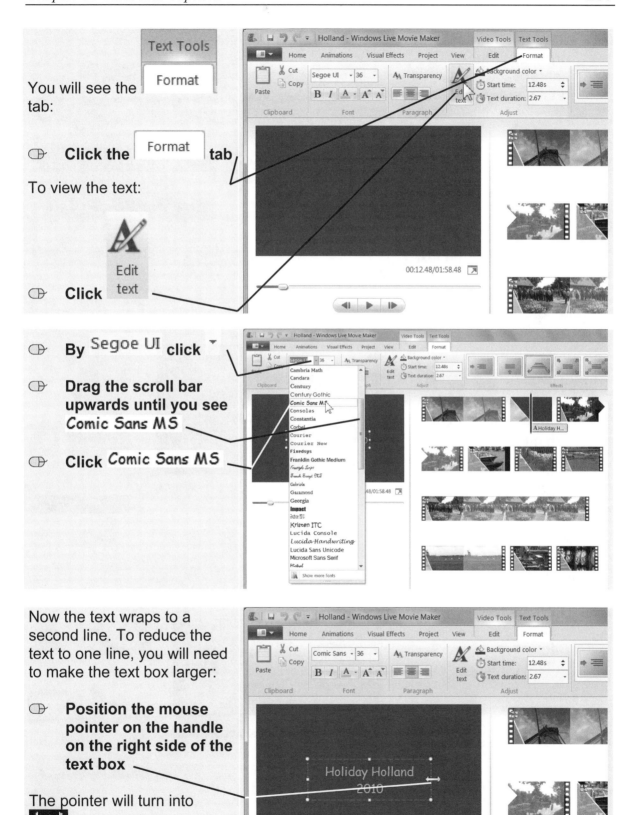

You will see the Format tab:

⊕ **Click the** Format **tab**

To view the text:

⊕ **Click** Edit text

⊕ **By** Segoe UI **click**

⊕ **Drag the scroll bar upwards until you see** Comic Sans MS

⊕ **Click** Comic Sans MS

Now the text wraps to a second line. To reduce the text to one line, you will need to make the text box larger:

⊕ **Position the mouse pointer on the handle on the right side of the text box**

The pointer will turn into
⟷ :

⬭ **Drag the pointer to the right, until the sentence is displayed on a single line**

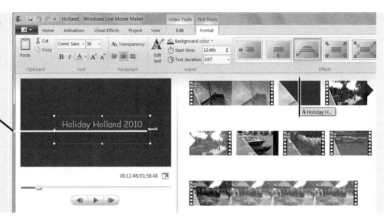

Now you can center the text:

⬭ **Position the mouse pointer on the border of the text box**

The pointer will turn into ✛:

⬭ **Drag the text box to the middle of the frame**

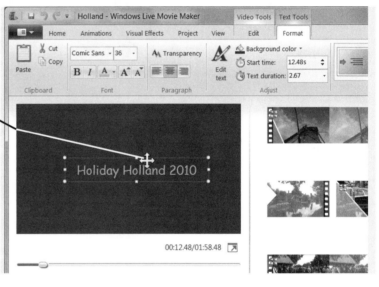

You will see the font:

The formatting you have chosen will be applied to the entire title.

⬭ **Click somewhere outside the text box**

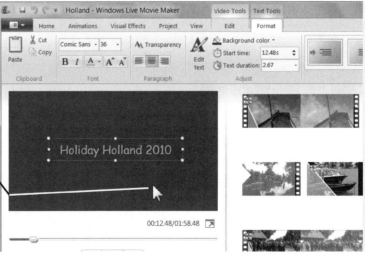

☀ Tip

Transparency

Use the $\mathbf{A_A}$ Transparency button to make the title less conspicuous:

☞ **Click**
   $\mathbf{A_A}$ Transparency

To make the text even more transparent:

☞ **Drag the slider ▯ to the right**

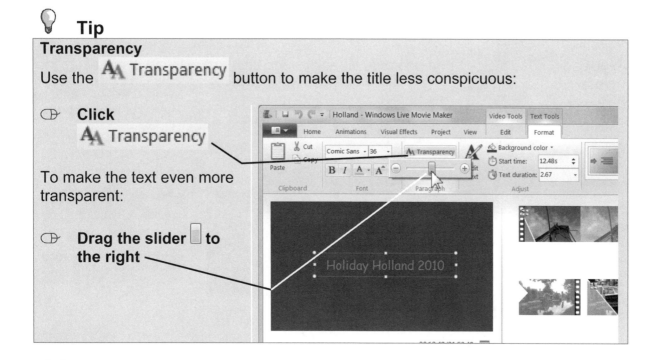

✂ HELP! Now the title has become too big or too small.

Each font has its own size. You can adjust the size of the text:

To make the text bigger:

☞ **Click** $\boxed{\mathbf{A^{\blacktriangle}}}$

To make the text smaller:

☞ **Click** $\boxed{\mathbf{A^{\blacktriangledown}}}$

☞ **Save the project** ✀¹³

12.6 Captions

You cannot use a video or a photo as a background title. But you can insert a caption into a video or a photo:

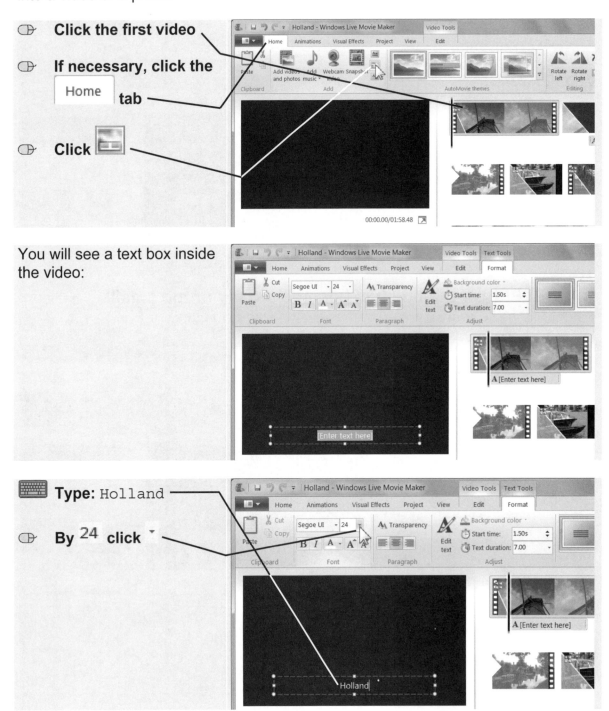

⊕ **Click the first video**

⊕ **If necessary, click the** Home **tab**

⊕ **Click** ▣

You will see a text box inside the video:

⌨ **Type:** Holland

⊕ **By** 24 **click** ˅

> **Click** 72

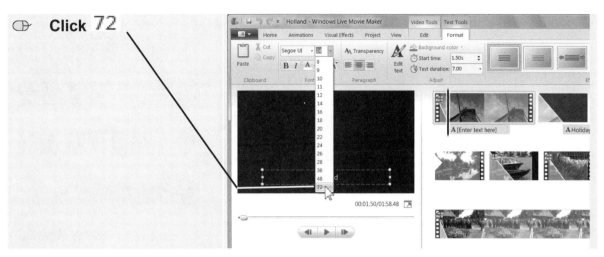

You can make the text bold:

> **Click** B

Move the text to the top, and center it:

> **Point the mouse to the border of the text box**

The pointer will turn into :

> **Drag the text box upwards, and to the middle**

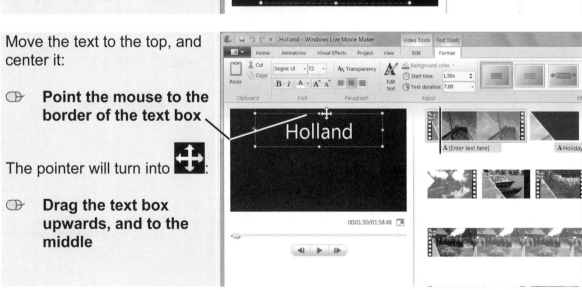

☞ **Click next to the text box** ——

☞ **Go to the beginning of the project** 𝒫14

☞ **Play the video** 𝒫10

☞ **Stop playback right after the title video has been displayed** 𝒫11

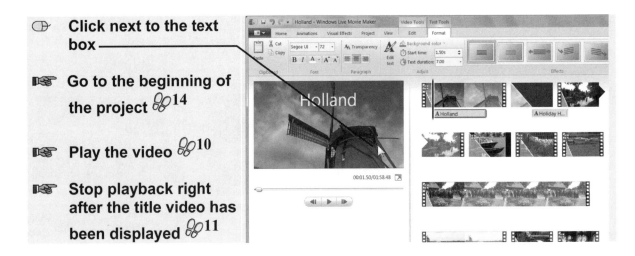

12.7 Change the Caption's Timing

The caption is shown at the beginning of the video, but disappears before the video has finished. Because of that, it does not really match the title clip. You can set the caption to display a little bit later, and for a longer period of time:

☞ **Click** **A Holland**

☞ **If necessary, click the**

Format **tab** ——

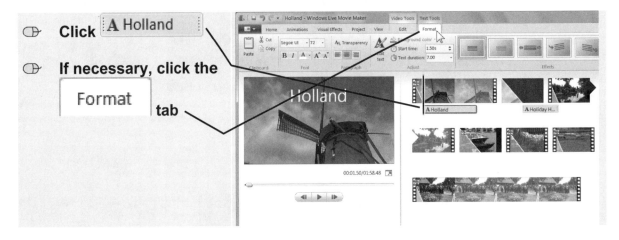

 Tip

Watch the text tag
The text tag in the track below the video will indicate approximately when the text will emerge, and for how long. By watching the tag you can quickly tell when a title or caption will appear in the video.

The start time is 1.5 seconds from the beginning of the movie. You can set the text to display a little bit later:

⊕ **By** 🕐 **Start time: click 1.50s**

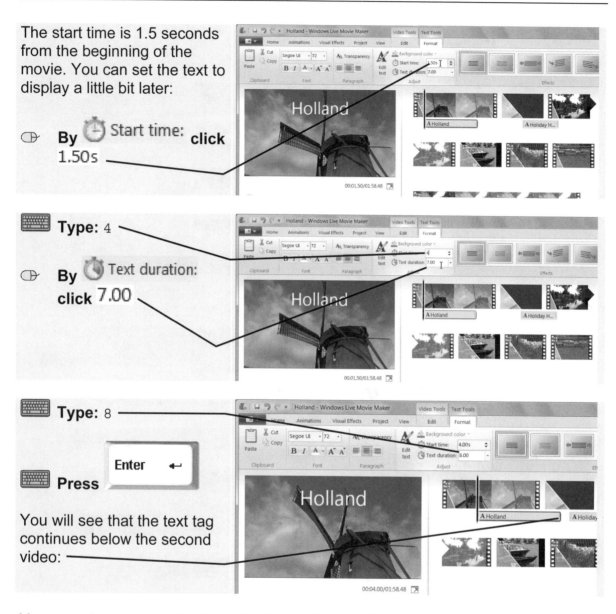

⌨ **Type:** 4

⊕ **By** 🕐 **Text duration: click 7.00**

⌨ **Type:** 8

⌨ **Press** Enter ↵

You will see that the text tag continues below the second video:

You can also use an effect to make the text gradually appear and disappear again:

⊕ **By** Effects **click** ▼

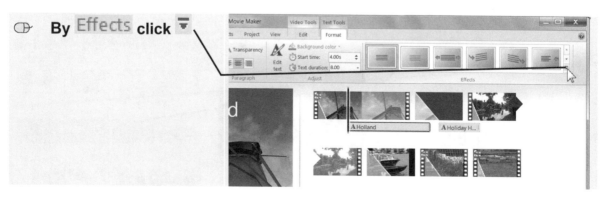

By **Zoom** click

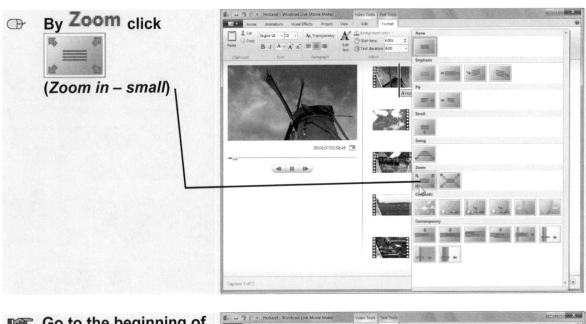

(Zoom in – small)

☞ **Go to the beginning of the project** 👣14

☞ **Play the video** 👣10

☞ **Stop playback after the title clip has been displayed** 👣11

You can also use captions to add a comment or description.

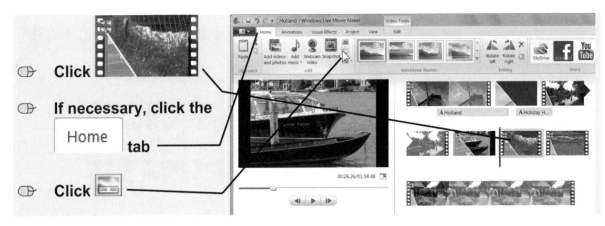

Click

If necessary, click the
Home tab

Click

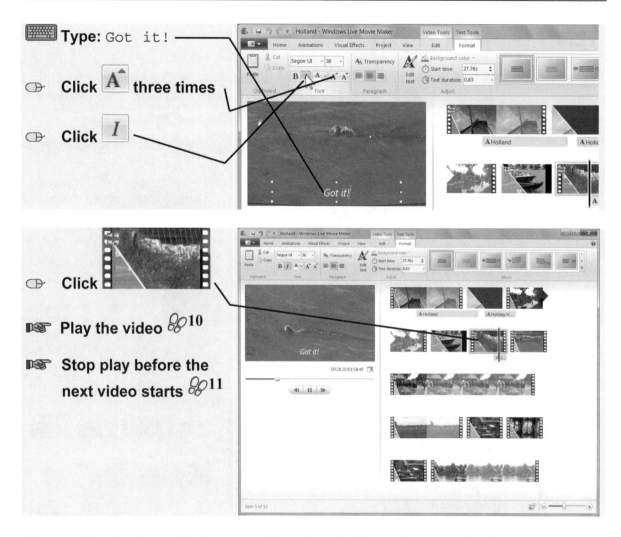

Type: Got it!

☞ Click **A⁺** three times

☞ Click *I*

☞ Click

☞ Play the video 👣10

☞ Stop play before the next video starts 👣11

Use captions to insert brief comments or descriptions. For example, the name of a town or a person. Captions are not very suitable for writing long texts especially if your video has a lot of motion in it. It is better to use a title clip for such a purpose.

☞ Save the project 👣13

💡 **Tip**

Telling a story
You can also use captions to tell a serial story. Enter a number of short texts and display them one after the other, in consecutive videos. You can cut up a longer video in several pieces, so you can display multiple captions after each other. If necessary, you can adjust the timing of the captions, the same as you did in the previous steps.

12.8 The Credits

Towards the end of a movie you will usually see the credits, with a closing text and maybe some information about the creator(s) of the movie. This is how you make the credits:

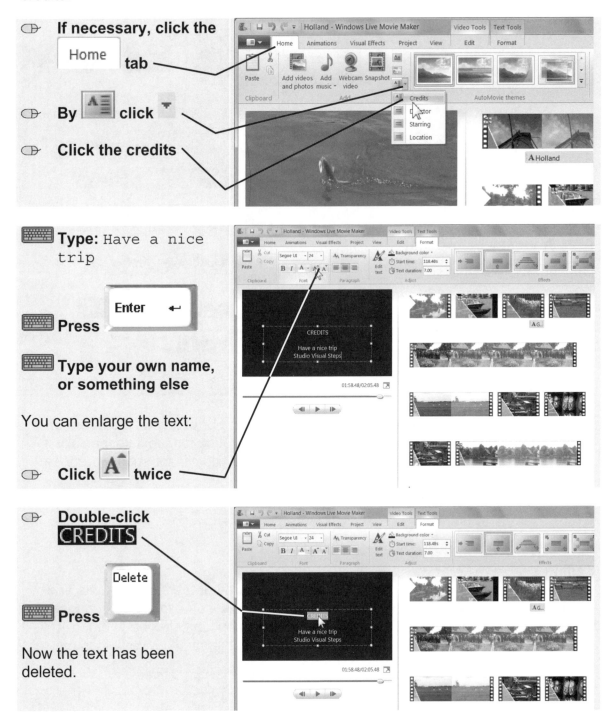

☞ **If necessary, click the** | Home | **tab**

☞ **By** 🔲 **click** ▼

☞ **Click the credits**

⌨ **Type:** Have a nice trip

⌨ **Press** | Enter ↵ |

⌨ **Type your own name, or something else**

You can enlarge the text:

☞ **Click** A▲ **twice**

☞ **Double-click** **CREDITS**

⌨ **Press** | Delete |

Now the text has been deleted.

☞ **Play the video** ☍☍**10**

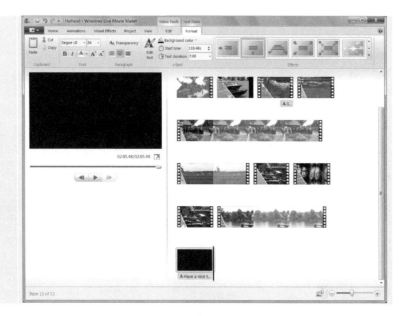

Playback will stop
automatically.

If you want to, you can
change the effect, the same
as you did in the previous
steps.

Titles and captions can be very useful, but use them wisely. The focus should be on
the movie, and too much text will draw the attention away from the content of the
movie.

☞ **Save the project** ☍☍**13**

☞ **Close** *Windows Live Movie Maker* ☍☍**6**

12.9 Background Information

Dictionary

Caption	Text that is added to a video, and which can provide additional information. Also called an overlay title.
Credits	Text at the end of the movie, displayed in a separate video fragment, intended to provide additional information. Usually, the credits are use to convey a message, or list all the contributors.
Title	Text, added to the movie in a separate video fragment; you can use this text to provide additional information. At the beginning of a movie, the title usually states the name of the movie.
Track	An overview that displays all the titles that have been added to the movie, in chronological order (title track). It can also provide an overview of all the sound clips that are added to the movie (sound track). A track may be displayed above or below the video images, in the preview window.

Source: Windows Live Movie Maker Help, Wikipedia

12.10 Tips

 Tip

Make a copy with Save As
Making a movie can take up a lot of time. That is why it is important to save a copy of your project at regular intervals. For instance, after you have finished assembling the movie, or after you have added the effects and titles.
If any problems occur in the following stage, you can always revert to the previous stage. A simple way of making a copy is the *Save project as* option:

☞ **Save the project** $\mathcal{QQ}^{13}$

Afterwards:

☞ **Click**

☞ **Click** Save project as

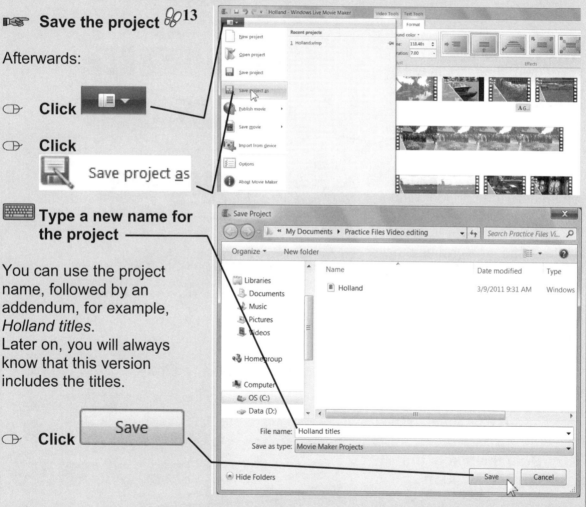

⌨ **Type a new name for the project**

You can use the project name, followed by an addendum, for example, *Holland titles*.
Later on, you will always know that this version includes the titles.

☞ **Click** Save

Afterwards, you can close this project $\mathcal{QQ}^{2}$ and open the original project again. $\mathcal{QQ}^{18}$

Please note: this is an extra precaution, apart from the regular saving of the original project, which is something you should always do at regular intervals. $\mathcal{QQ}^{13}$

Tip

How long can a caption be displayed?
If you want to determine a caption's duration, it is useful to know the total length of the video:

⊂ฺ **Point the mouse to a video**

You will see the duration of the video:

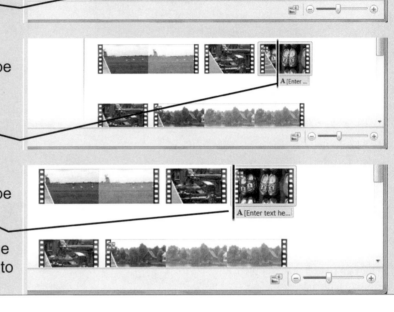

If the video contains an animation, the caption will be displayed after that animation:

If you have not added an animation, the caption will be displayed right away:

In this case, you can use the entire duration of the video to display the caption.

 Tip

Move a title or a caption
You can move a title or caption by dragging it along the title track:

⊂ฺ **Position the mouse pointer on the text**

⊂ฺ **Drag the text to the desired location**

You can also move (part of) the text to another video.

If you move a title to a different video, it will turn into a caption.

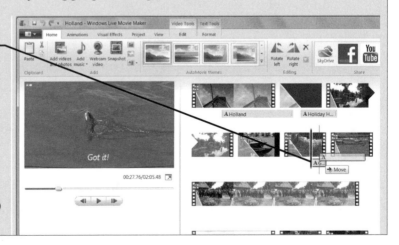

13. Sound and Music

Usually, the emphasis in a movie is on the moving images or stills, but the sound can also play an important part. It can create a certain atmosphere and add an extra dimension to your movie. It can also provide additional information. Furthermore, you can use sound to connect the scenes in your movie. In this way you can make an attractive movie, in which sound and vision merge fluently.

Windows Live Movie Maker distinguishes two types of sound:
* the sound that you have recorded with your video camera while filming;
* the sound that you add to your movie later on; for example, background music, or spoken commentary (*voice-over*).

You can mix both types of sound, and add transition effects as well.

You can add sound to the movie from an audio file on your computer. An audio file can be downloaded from the Internet, copied from an audio CD, or it may consist of your own commentary, recorded by microphone.

In this chapter you will learn how to:

* analyze the sound you have recorded;
* set the sound level;
* let the sound fade in and fade out;
* add background music;
* move sound files;
* mute the video sound, or the background noise;
* set a start time for the music;
* trim the background noise;
* record commentary.

 Please note:

Start editing your movie's sound after you have assembled the movie and added the titles. If you want to add background music, in particular, the length of the video is important; if you still need to edit the video, the length of the movie could change.

 Please note:

You cannot use *Windows Live Movie Maker* to edit the sound that you have recorded with your video camera. You will only be able to adjust the sound volume.

13.1 Analyzing the Sound

Before changing the setting for the sound, it is a good idea to review your project and play it again once more. Pay special attention to the sounds you hear:

☞ **Start** *Windows Live Movie Maker* ✂️[7]

☞ **Open the** *Holland* **project** ✂️[18]

☞ **If necessary, make sure your computer's speakers have been turned on**

You will see the project:

☞ **Play the project**
    ✂️[10]

☞ **Listen to the sound that was recorded while filming the videos**

Playback will automatically stop at the end of the project.

If the movie is made up of a number of different videos, you will often experience these problems:
- the sounds are too loud or too soft;
- some sections do not contain any sounds (titles, for example);
- during the transition from one video to another the sound level may vary a great deal;
- you hear annoying (background) noises.

First, you are going to determine which video sounds are best suited to your movie. In this project, these are:
- the opening video with the windmill;
- the choir;
- the clog maker.

Next, you are going to determine what to do with the other sections. To prevent silence during playback, you can add background music to the silent sections.

Tip

Add commentary
You can also add spoken commentary (your own or somebody else's). You can read more about this a little further on in this chapter.

13.2 Setting the Sound Level

It is important to synchronize the sound level of the various videos. If the differences are too great, this will disturb playback and you will have to keep adjusting the sound level while viewing the movie.

The sound of the clog maker-scenes is much louder than the sound of the other videos. You can adjust the sound level like this:

⊕ **Click**

☞ **Play this video, and the next two videos** ✂10

The sound is very loud.

☞ **Stop playback** ✂11

You can reduce the sound level for these three videos. First, you will need to select all three videos:

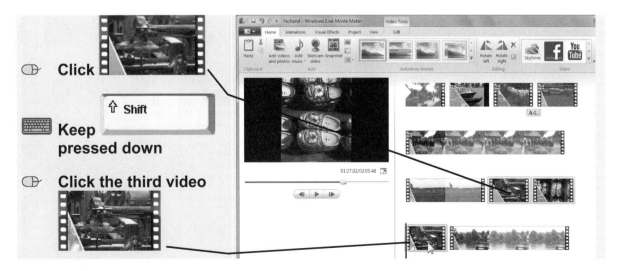

⊕ **Click**

⌨ **Keep pressed down** [⇧ Shift]

⊕ **Click the third video**

Now you have selected all three videos.

 Tip

Select multiple videos
You can select consecutive video files by clicking the first video, keeping the

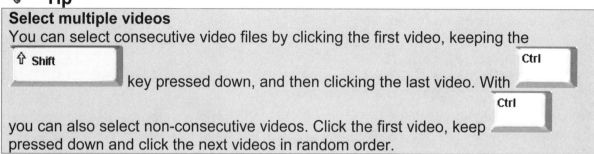

⇧ **Shift** key pressed down, and then clicking the last video. With **Ctrl**

Ctrl you can also select non-consecutive videos. Click the first video, keep pressed down and click the next videos in random order.

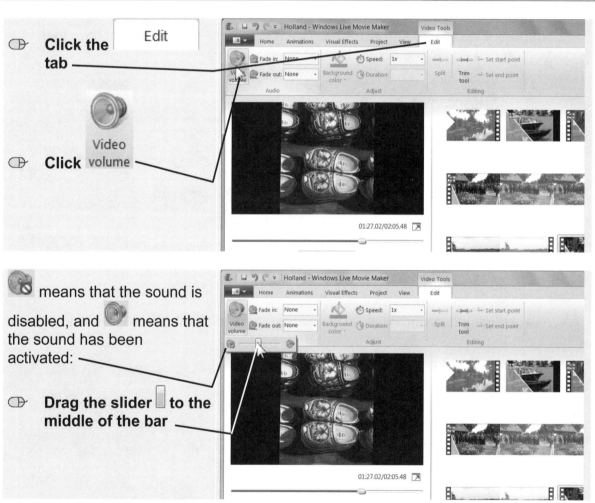

☞ **Click the Edit tab**

☞ **Click Video volume**

means that the sound is disabled, and means that the sound has been activated:

☞ **Drag the slider to the middle of the bar**

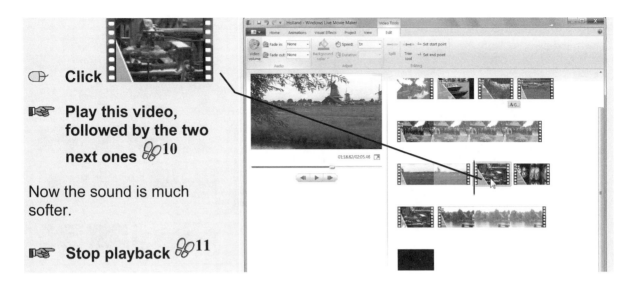

⊕ **Click**

☞ **Play this video, followed by the two next ones** 👣10

Now the sound is much softer.

☞ **Stop playback** 👣11

13.3 Adding Fade In and Fade Out Effects

If you want to prevent big differences from occurring in the sound level of consecutive videos, you can use the fade in and fade out technique. For example, you can slowly turn up the volume of the sound at the beginning of the movie. Now you are going to add a fade in:

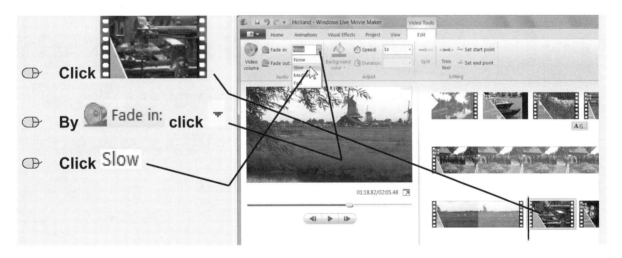

⊕ **Click**

⊕ **By** 🔊 Fade in: **click** ▾

⊕ **Click** Slow

You will hear the effect best if you play the previous video first:

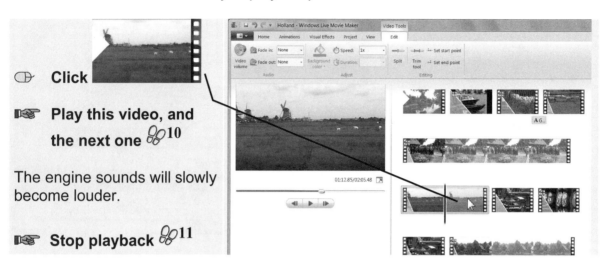

👆 **Click**

☞ **Play this video, and the next one** 👣10

The engine sounds will slowly become louder.

☞ **Stop playback** 👣11

At the end of the three videos you can add a fade out:

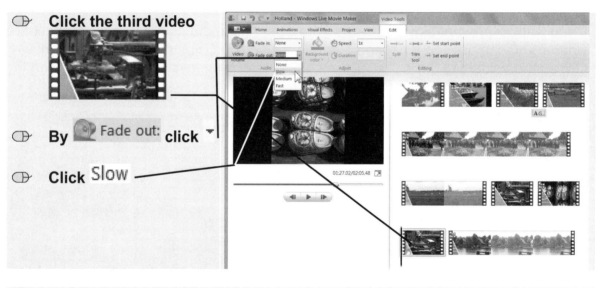

👆 **Click the third video**

👆 **By** Fade out: **click** ▾

👆 **Click Slow**

☞ **Play the video** 👣10

The sound of the engines will slowly fade away.

☞ **Stop playback** 👣11

 Tip

Loud transitions
Sometimes, you may want to use a loud sound transition to emphasize a specific, unexpected development and even startle the viewer.

13.4 Adding Background Music

Many movies use background music to create a certain atmosphere, or to make quiet or silent scenes livelier. In this step you will be adding music to the entire project:

☞ **Click the** Home **tab**

☞ **Click** ♪

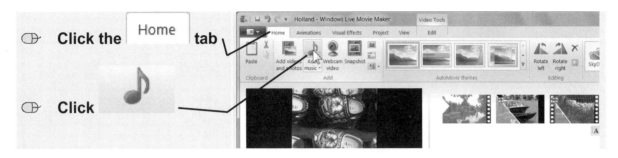

💡 Tip

Add music at a specific point
You can also add music at a specific point in the video:

☞ **Click the spot where you want the music to start**

☞ **Click** Add music ▾

☞ **Click** ♪ Add music at the curre

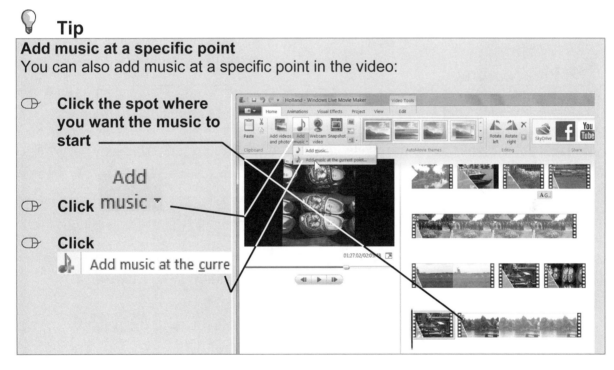

☞ **If necessary, open the practice files folder** ⑧

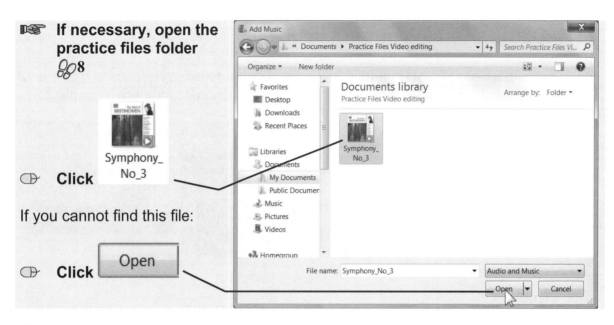

⊕ **Click** Symphony_No_3

If you cannot find this file:

⊕ **Click** | Open |

➥ **Please note:**

If you want to add music from an audio CD, DVD or MP3 player, you will need to copy this music to your computer first. Your project will contain links to the music files but not the actual files themselves. You will need to insert the disk or connect the USB stick to your computer while you are editing the project. This way, you will be able to hear the music in your project, and finalize it.

An additional music track has been added:

Track information is displayed above the video files.

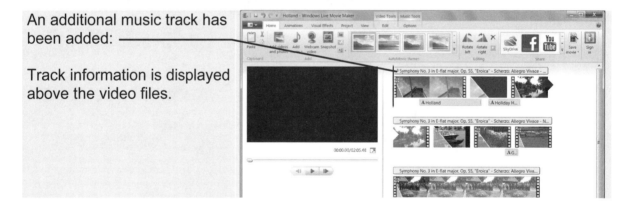

13.5 Setting the Start Time

In some parts of the movie you will want to hear the original music, in other parts you may want to hear the background music, and you might even want to hear both types of music in a few specific scenes.

☞ **Play the entire project** ⑩

You will hear the sound of the video and the background music, all mixed up together. Now you can adjust the sound, from the beginning to the end of the project. You can do this is such a way that you will clearly be able to hear the sound transitions.

In the first video you will hear the sound of the windmill, together with some background music. These sounds do go together well, but see what happens if you start playing the background music halfway through the video:

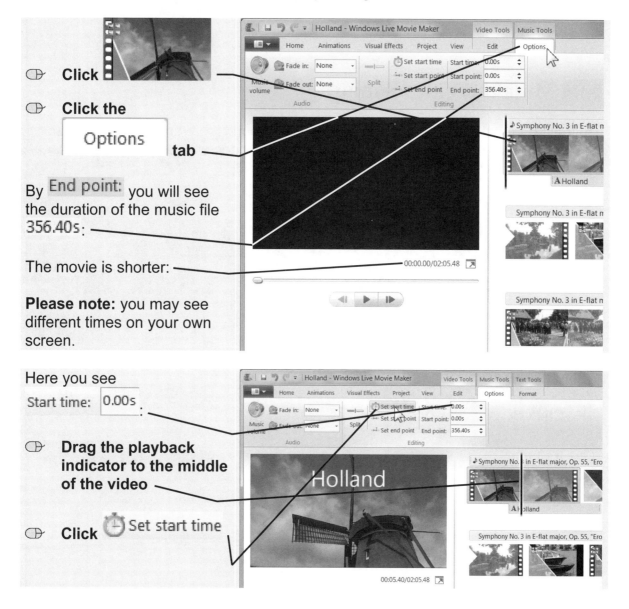

Click

Click the

Options **tab**

By End point: you will see the duration of the music file 356.40s:

The movie is shorter:

Please note: you may see different times on your own screen.

Here you see

Start time: 0.00s:

Drag the playback indicator to the middle of the video

Click Set start time

Now the start time has
changed:

The music on the sound track
has been pushed forward.
This means that the music
will only start after the first
video has been playing for a
while:

13.6 Mute the Video Sound

The next part of the project does not contain any sounds for you to save, at least, until the video of the choir starts. You can mute the video sound for that particular section, so you will only hear the music:

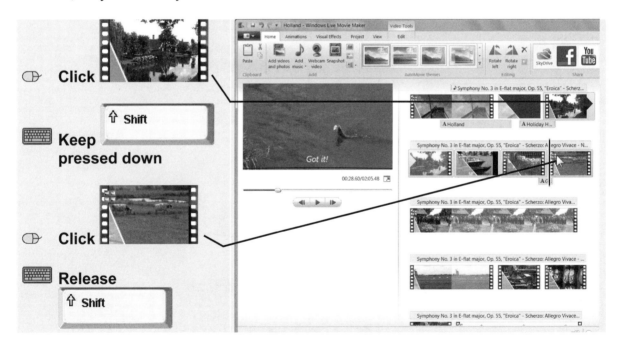

Now the videos have been selected:

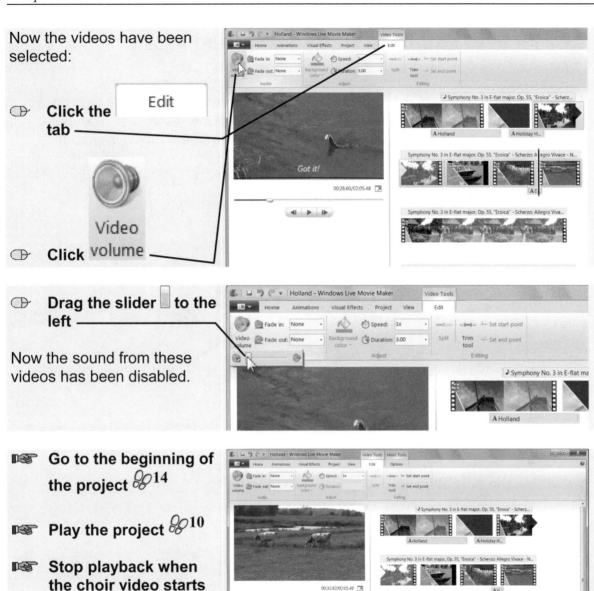

☞ **Click the** Edit **tab**

☞ **Click Video volume**

☞ **Drag the slider to the left**

Now the sound from these videos has been disabled.

☞ **Go to the beginning of the project** 🦶14

☞ **Play the project** 🦶10

☞ **Stop playback when the choir video starts to play** 🦶11

13.7 Fade In and Fade Out Background Music

The transition between the background music and the choir is very loud.
It will be nicer to fade out the background music before the choir starts singing. To fade out the music before it ends, you will need to split the music first. The music will fade out toward the splitting point, instead of at the end of the music fragment:

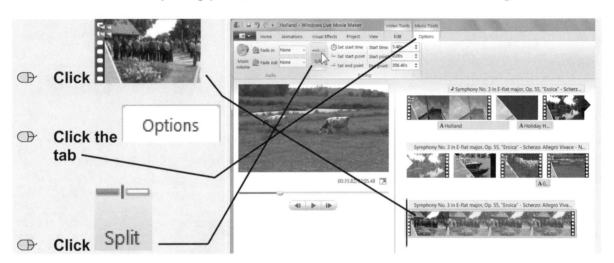

Now the music has been split. The first part will end before the choir starts. Here is how to fade out the first part:

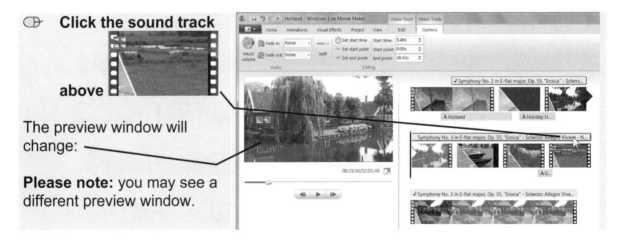

Click the sound track

above

The preview window will change:

Please note: you may see a different preview window.

 Please note:

If you want to edit the background music, you need to click the part you want to edit in the sound track. But if you want to edit the video sound, you will need to click the relevant video.

By Fade out: **click**

Click Medium

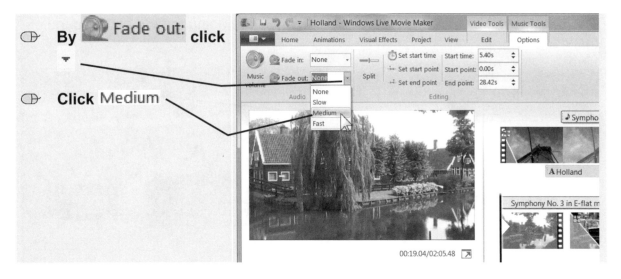

The sound of the choir is quite loud at the start. It will be less dramatic if you allow the choir to fade in slowly. First, you will need to mute the background music for the choir video, so you will only hear the video sound:

Click the sound track

above

The preview window will change again:

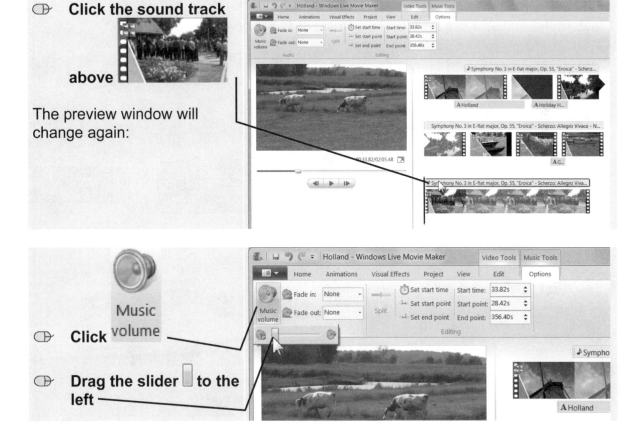

Click Music volume

Drag the slider to the left

The background music has been muted. Now you are going to fade in the sound of the video:

☞ **Click the**  **tab**

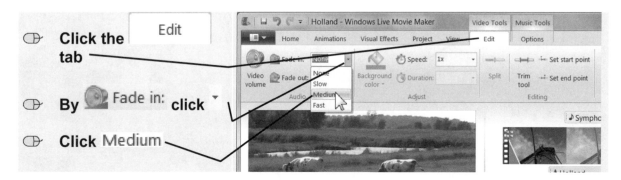

☞ **By** Fade in: **click** ▾

☞ **Click** Medium

➥ Please note:

To edit the background music, use the **Options** tab.

To edit the sound of the video, use the **Edit** tab.

Toward the end you can let the choir music fade out again:

☞ **By** Fade out: **click** ▾

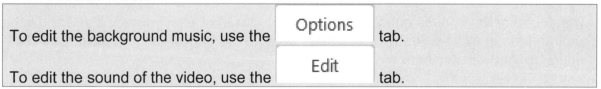

☞ **Click** Medium

☞ **Click** 🎞

☞ **Play the project** 🦶10

☞ **Stop playback after the choir has finished** 🦶11

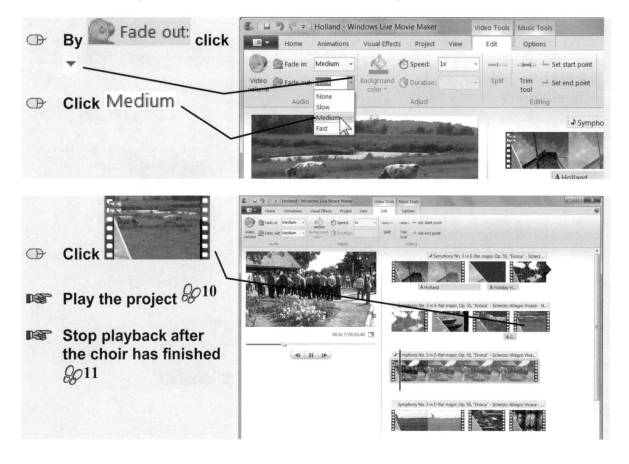

13.8 Moving Background Music

In the previous section you learned how to split the music. After you have split a music fragment, the music will continue from the point where it stopped in the first part. But since the background music has been muted, you will not be able to hear this.

If you want to play the music at a later point in the movie and continue with the music fragment previous to the split, you will need to change the start point of the second part. You can set the remainder of the music to play after the video with the clog maker:

If you do not see the end of the movie:

☞ **Drag the scroll bar downwards**

☞ **Click**

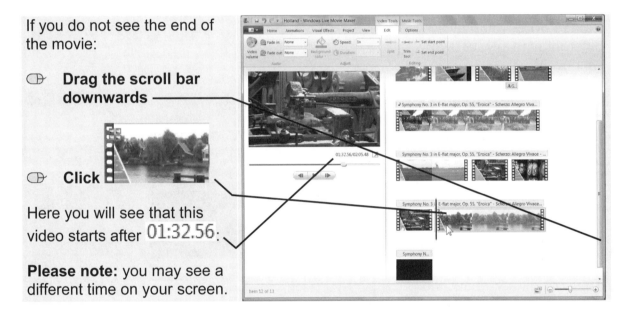

Here you will see that this video starts after `01:32.56`:

Please note: you may see a different time on your screen.

First, you are going to convert the time into seconds. In this example it is 1 minute (= 60 seconds) plus 32.56 seconds. In total 92.56 seconds. So that should be the start time for the music.

🖐 **Please note:**

Calculate your own start time with the times in your project.

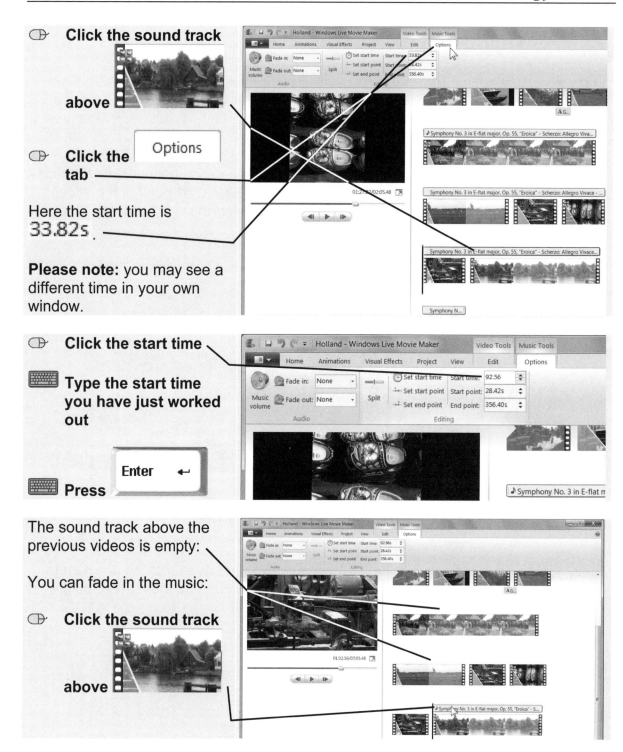

⊕ **Click the sound track**

   above

⊕ **Click the** Options
   tab

Here the start time is
33.82s .

Please note: you may see a
different time in your own
window.

⊕ **Click the start time**

⌨ **Type the start time
   you have just worked
   out**

   Enter ↵

⌨ **Press**

The sound track above the
previous videos is empty:

You can fade in the music:

⊕ **Click the sound track**

   above

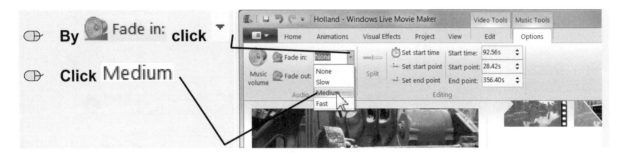

⊕ **By** Fade in: **click**

⊕ **Click Medium**

In one of the previous steps, you had muted the volume for this part of the background music. Now you can turn the volume back on:

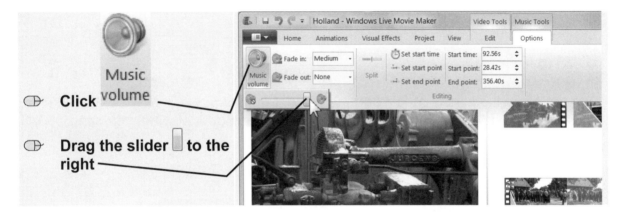

⊕ **Click** Music volume

⊕ **Drag the slider to the right**

Now you can mute the volume of the video:

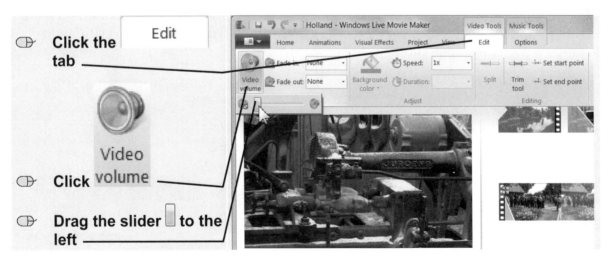

⊕ **Click the** Edit **tab**

⊕ **Click** Video volume

⊕ **Drag the slider to the left**

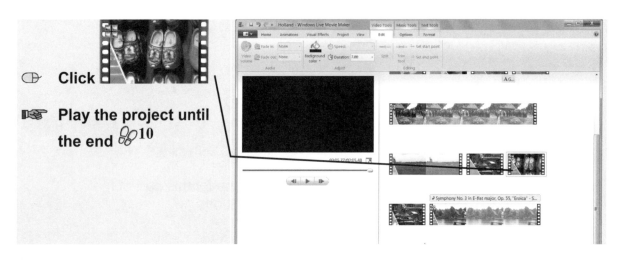

Click

☞ **Play the project until the end** ✇10

💡 **Tip**

Start background music earlier
Depending on the kind of music and the content of your video, it may be a good idea to start the music a little earlier. Before the new video starts playing, you can slowly fade in the background music.

13.9 Trim Background Sounds

The background music will stop at the end of the movie, even before the movie has finished. It seems as if the music is suddenly cut off. It will create a nicer effect if the end of the music coincides with the end of the movie. To do this, you will need to compute the times once more:

Click the Options tab

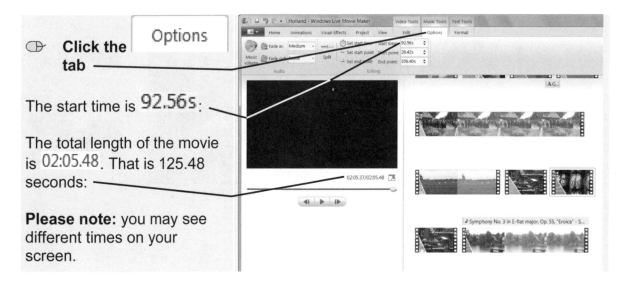

The start time is 92.56s:

The total length of the movie is 02:05.48. That is 125.48 seconds:

Please note: you may see different times on your screen.

The last music fragment takes 125.48 minus 92.56 seconds, so 32.92 seconds.

The total length of the music is 356.40s:

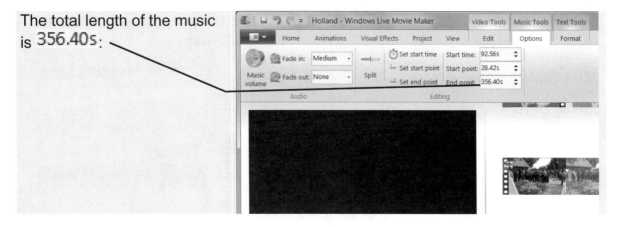

So, to end at the same time as the movie, the music needs to start 32.92 seconds before the movie ends. The music will start after 356.40 minutes and 32.91 seconds = 323.49 seconds.

 Please note:

Calculate your own start times with the times in your project.

By Start point: click the time

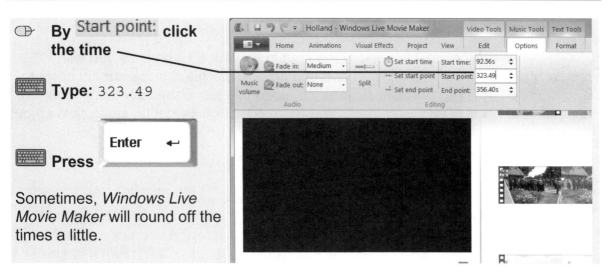

Type: 323.49

Press Enter ↵

Sometimes, *Windows Live Movie Maker* will round off the times a little.

☞ **Play the project until it finishes** ℰℰ¹⁰

You will hear the end of the music fragment, but the music will stop approximately six seconds before the end of the movie; this means the credits will not have any background music. You can move the start point forward by six seconds. Then the music will stop playing after the credits have been displayed:

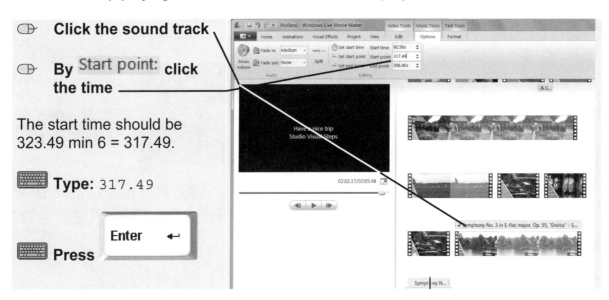

☞ **Click the sound track**

☞ **By** Start point: **click the time**

The start time should be 323.49 min 6 = 317.49.

⌨ **Type:** `317.49`

⌨ **Press** Enter ↵

☞ **Play the project until the end once more** ⚹⚹10

Now the music will stop at the end of the credits. In your own projects you will regularly need to calculate the start and end times too. This is necessary in order to synchronize the background music with the video images. Especially if you want to use different kinds of music, or play the same piece of music continuously throughout the video.

💡 **Tip**

Listen to the music first
To find the parts that are best suited to your movie, it is a good idea to listen to all the music fragments you want to use. For instance, by playing the music with the *Windows Media Player*. Write down the start and end times of the fragments you want to use. If you look at the example above, you would already have been able to tell that the music fragment would finish before the movie ended.

☞ **Save the project** ⚹⚹13

☞ **Close** *Windows Live Movie Maker* ⚹⚹6

Tip

Trimming the project
If the duration of the music fragment is longer or shorter than the project, and if the project contains photos, you can automatically fit the project to the music. This means that the movie and the music will finish at the same time.

Click the **Project** tab

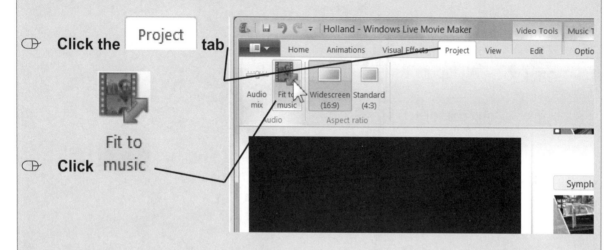

Click **Fit to music**

The display time of the photos will be shortened or prolonged as needed. The display time of videos, transitions and text items will not change.

13.10 Adding Spoken Commentary

Instead of using titles and captions, you can also record your own commentary (*voice-over*) and add it to your movie. You can use the *Windows Sound Recorder* to record the commentary:

☞ **Connect a microphone to your computer**

If you do not own a microphone, just read through this section.

 Tip

Connect the microphone
On the back of the computer case (sometimes on the front too) you will find three connection points for sound devices: a microphone, a headphone and extra speakers:
The correct connection point is indicated by a microphone icon :

Tip

Built-in microphone
Many notebooks and laptop computers have a built-in microphone. Read your
computer manual to find out if your computer has such a microphone.

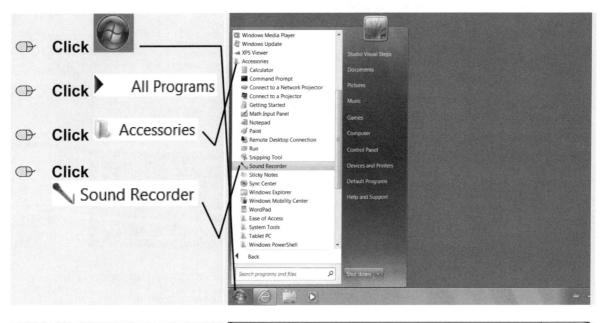

Click

Click ▶ All Programs

Click ▌ Accessories

Click
  ＼ Sound Recorder

You will see the *Sound Recorder* on your screen:

Now you are going to record your commentary:

 Tip

Take notes before you start
You will need to record the commentary smoothly and fluently. Some people might
find this difficult; it is recommended to write down your lines beforehand. It does not
need to be the entire text, a few keywords may suffice.

Click
  ● Start Recording

☞ **Record your commentary**

While you are speaking you
will see the volume indicator:

It is not necessary to record the entire message at once. To stop the recording:

⊕ **Click**

■ **Stop Recording**

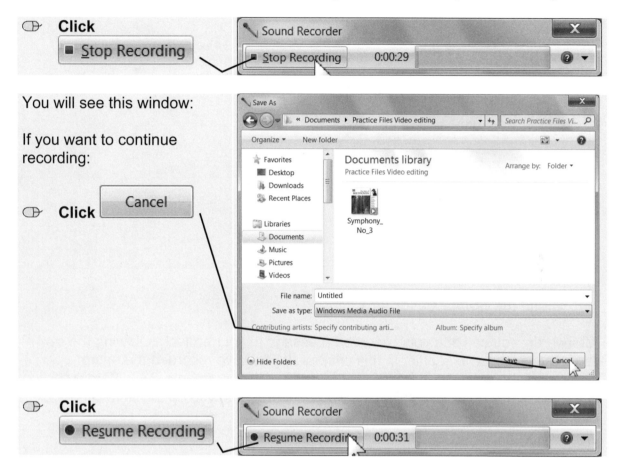

You will see this window:

If you want to continue recording:

⊕ **Click** Cancel

⊕ **Click**

● Re**s**ume Recording

After you have recorded the final message:

⊕ **Click**

■ **Stop Recording**

You are going to save the
recorded commentary:

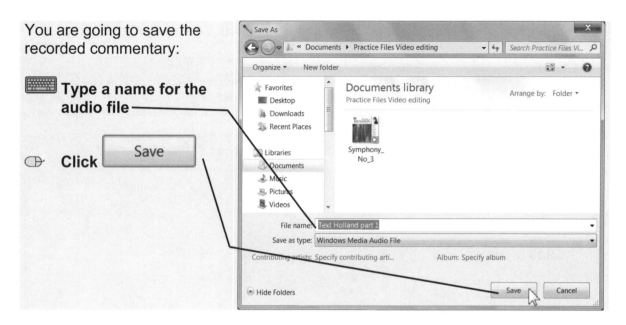

 **Type a name for the
audio file**

 Click Save

☞ **Close the** *Sound Recorder* 🐾²

Afterwards, you can add your recorded message to your project, following the same
steps that you learned earlier in this chapter. If you have recorded the entire
message at once, and you want to insert parts of the commentary in different section
of the movie, then you can split the text. You learned how to do this in *section 13.7
Fade In and Fade Out Background Music*.

💡 **Tip**

Add live commentary
To ensure that your text is synchronized with the video images, it is best to add your
commentary while you play your project. But make sure to turn down the speaker
volume, or turn the speakers off; you do not want to record the video sounds as well.

💡 **Tip**

Save text in multiple files
When you are recording your commentary, you are bound to make some mistakes.
To prevent you from having to record the entire message over and over again, you
can add the commentary in installments, and save these recordings in separate files.

13.11 Background Information

Dictionary

Mix	Synchronizing the video sound with the background sound.
Sound recorder	A program with which you can record sound via a microphone, and save the audio file to your hard disk. The *Sound Recorder* program is a standard program that is always included in *Windows*.
Sound track	The track that is displayed above the video in the edit window, where you can also see the background sound.
Voice-over	Separate recording of a spoken commentary; this is added to the movie later on.

Source: Windows Live Movie Maker Help, Wikipedia

Audio files
Windows Live Movie Maker supports the following audio file types:

Audio file types (format)	File extension
Windows Media Audio files (WMA)	.ASF, .WM and .WMA
Pulse-code Modulation files (PCM)	.AIF, .AIFF and .WAV
Advanced Audio Coding files (AAC)	.M4A
MP3 audio files	.MP3

Comments:
- Video and music files which are protected by DRM (Digital Rights Management), cannot be used in *Windows Live Movie Maker*.
- MPEG-4 video files with AAC audio can only be used if *Movie Maker* runs on a computer with *Windows 7* installed.
- Some MPEG-4 video files may be used in *Movie Maker* on a *Windows Vista* computer, but only if the necessary audio and video codecs have been installed.

Source: Windows Live Movie Maker Help

Sound

When it comes to filming videos, lots of people think it is only about images. They think sound is not as important. Although it can be fun to make a 'silent' movie, for example, a slapstick comedy, most of the time sound is an essential element in a good movie. The sound track contributes to the atmosphere of the movie and can provide additional information; it can join various scenes and movie shots together and create a coherent entity.

All digital video cameras are capable of recording sound with their built-in microphone. Usually the quality of these sound recordings is not very high; it will be just good enough for simple holiday videos. But you still need to take into account that ther might be some annoying background sounds, or the sound of the wind blowing. If you want to have a better sound quality, it is recommended to use a separate microphone. You can connect such a microphone to your video camera.

There are various microphone types:
- The lapel (lavalier) microphone is a small microphone that can be attached to your clothes. It is quite inconspicuous and is mainly used for interviewing people.
- The omnidirectional microphone will pick up sound from all directions. Sometimes, this can create the proper atmosphere. But of you are going to use this type of microphone, you need to beware of some sounds prevailing over others. For example, traffic noise will prevail over nature sounds.
- The undirectional microphone will pick up sounds from one direction only; that is, the direction to which the microphone is pointed. Often, this type of microphone will give the best results. This microphone can be handheld or fixed to the camera.

You can fit a wind protector to all of these microphones, to mute the sound of the wind a little.

- Continue reading on the next page -

When you are recording sound, always listen in with your head phones, or with a small ear microphone. This way, you will be able to hear exactly what is being recorded, and what is not. Make sure the sound is recorded continuously. For instance, if you are recording a band playing, then record the entire song, even if you intend to insert other images into the recording. If you stop filming and start recording different images, you may end up with sound gaps in your movie.

Music

Film music is nearly as old as film itself. At the very beginning, the silent movies were accompanied by live music, played in the cinema. After a couple of decades the 'talkies' appeared.

Usually, a movie consists of a number of tracks. One track is for the image, and multiple tracks are for the sound. The sounds that are part of the image, such as background sounds and people talking, are recorded on a separate sound track. You can record music on a different sound track. By attuning the movie sound and the music to each other, you can create a nice and fluent sound track for your movie.

While assembling the movie you will need to pay attention to the rhythm, the atmosphere and the volume of the music, in order to achieve the best results. If you use fast rhythms in a movie that consists of serene, quietly flowing images, the result will seem unbalanced. It might be quite hilarious to use sad, plaintive music for a wedding video, but if you want to tell a realistic story, this is not such a good idea. And if you add very loud music to your movie, people might not hear the other movie sounds.

The music needs to be added to the movie *after* the assembly phase, except in the case of a live concert recording. First, the images need to be cut into the correct length, put in the right sequence, titles and captions added and transitions or effects applied. Once this is done, you can edit the sound for your movie.

As for the choice of music, there are various options. You can make your own music, if you play some kind of instrument. In that case you can use existing songs, or your own compositions. It is usually easier to get started if you use an existing piece of music. You can select songs from a regular audio CD that you can play with your computer's CD player. Many people download music from one of the many MP3 websites on the Internet. But remember that some of these websites distribute music that is copyrighted by others and in fact, downloading these songs is illegal. It is not accepted by the rightful owners and creators of this music.

If you use music for a movie that is intended for a wider audience than just your own family and friends, you will need to take into account these music copyrights. You are compelled to pay a certain amount to the rightful owners. However, there is still a large amount of royalty-free music available on the Internet.

13.12 Tips

 Tip

Sound mixing
You can regulate the balance between the volume level of the audio/music track and the original video sound:

⊕ **Click the** Project **tab**

⊕ **Click** Audio mix

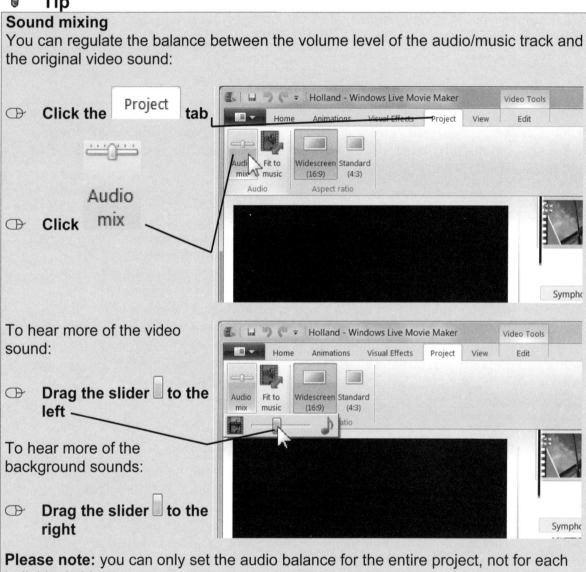

To hear more of the video sound:

⊕ **Drag the slider to the left**

To hear more of the background sounds:

⊕ **Drag the slider to the right**

Please note: you can only set the audio balance for the entire project, not for each individual video.

 Tip

Second sound track
You can only add a single sound track to your project. It is not possible to simultaneously insert background music and a voice-over in a video project. If you want to do this nevertheless, you can add a second sound track after you have finalized the movie. You can read more about this in the Tips at the back of *Chapter 14 Finalizing the Movie*.

Tip

Quick solutions

If you do not have a lot of time, and you want to make a quick movie, you can use the *AutoMovie* wizard. This wizard will help you add titles and transitions to your movie, and you can also add music. Afterwards you can finish the movie any way you want.

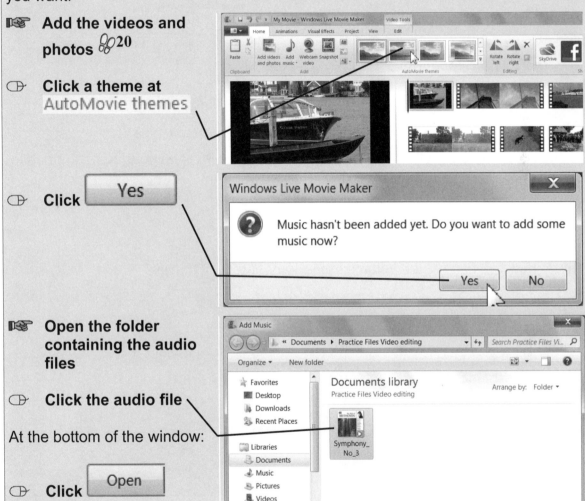

☞ **Add the videos and photos** ✄20

☞ **Click a theme at** AutoMovie themes

☞ **Click** Yes

☞ **Open the folder containing the audio files**

☞ **Click the audio file**

At the bottom of the window:

☞ **Click** Open

You will see the movie that you have created:

Afterwards, you can edit the project still further, add titles, and save the project, just like you learned in the previous chapters.

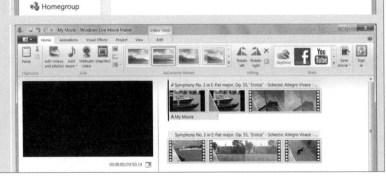

Tip

Dragging files in sound track
You can also drag the files in the sound track to a different location:

 Position the mouse pointer on the audio file

 Drag the audio file to the desired location

 Tip

Set the volume
To hear the sound of your movie properly, the volume level on your computer has to be set correctly. There are two ways of doing this:
- by using the volume knob on the computer, the keyboard, the speakers or the monitor;
- within the *Windows* program.

This is how you can set the volume in the *Windows* system tray:

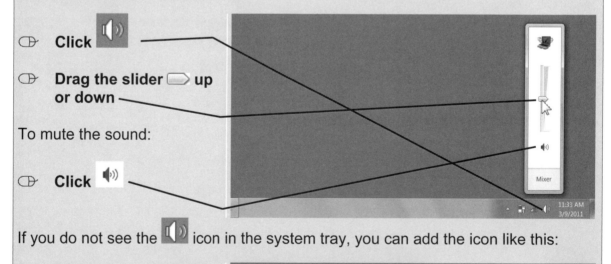

 Click

 Drag the slider ⬭ up or down

To mute the sound:

 Click

If you do not see the ⬛ icon in the system tray, you can add the icon like this:

 Right-click an empty spot on the task bar

 Click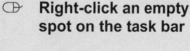

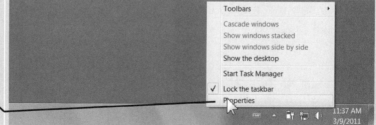

- Continue reading on the next page -

In *Windows 7*:

On the | Taskbar | tab:

☞ By Notification area,

click Customize...

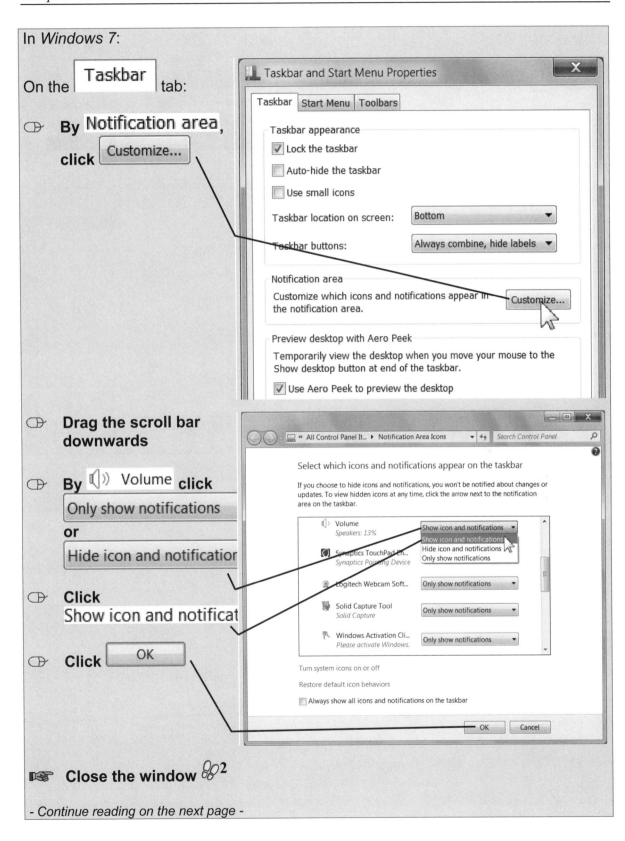

☞ **Drag the scroll bar downwards**

☞ **By** 🔊 **Volume click**

Only show notifications

or

Hide icon and notification

☞ **Click**

Show icon and notificat

☞ **Click** OK

☞ **Close the window** 👣2

- Continue reading on the next page -

In *Windows Vista*:

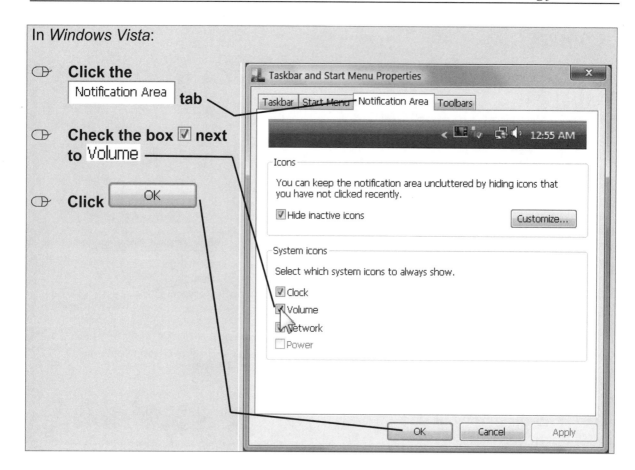

Click the Notification Area tab

Check the box ☑ next to Volume

Click OK

14. Finalizing the Movie

By this point you have edited your photos and videos and assembled them into a movie. You have added transitions and effects and created a sound track for your project. But before you can show your movie to others, you must *finalize* it first in *Windows Live Movie Maker*. You can choose among several different options for finalizing depending on how you want to use the movie and the amount of quality that will be needed. For example, you can save your movie as a file, burn it to a DVD, send it by e-mail or publish it on *YouTube*.

During the editing process you are actually using a draft copy of the movie. Once you have finalized the movie, the final version will be compiled, including all the effects, transitions and titles. This process is also called *rendering*.

This is an intensive process and requires quite a lot of computer power. All the pixels have to be assembled and recorded, image by image. Depending on the length of the movie and the capacity of your hardware it can take some time. Furthermore, the quality you choose for you movie is also relevant. A movie that is going to be shown on the Internet will have a smaller size and can be processed much faster than a video movie in HD quality.

After having finalized the movie, it is a good idea to delete all the files that you no longer need. At the end of this chapter we will explain which files to remove, and which files to keep.

In this chapter you will learn how to:

- save the movie on your computer;
- select the desired quality;
- copy your movie to a DVD;
- save multiple movies on a DVD;
- create a DVD menu;
- burn the DVD;
- send a movie by e-mail;
- publish the movie on *YouTube*;
- clean up the files.

14.1 Store a Movie on your Computer

If you want to be able to watch the movie for example, in *Windows Media Player*, the files will need to be stored on your computer. You can choose one of the following formats, depending on the quality you want:
- HD video with a resolution of 1920 x 1080 pixels
- HD video with a resolution of 1280 x 720 pixels
- Wide-screen format with a resolution of 720 x 480 pixels
- Standard format with a resolution of van 640 x 480 pixels

HD stands for *High Definition*. The higher the resolution, the higher the quality; but this also means the file size will increase as well.

🠢 Please note:

> In this section we are discussing a movie that is going to be stored onto your computer's hard drive. If you intend to use the movie for a different purpose (a DVD, e-mail, the Internet), then other factors will play a part. In later sections you will learn how save a movie in other formats.

The quality you need to choose depends on a number of things:
- If you own an HD camera and the movie is recorded in HD quality, then it is best to choose an HD resolution.
- If the movie is not recorded in HD quality, and you will be mainly watching the movie on your computer, then you can choose the wide-screen or the standard format.
- If the movie is recorded in the wide-screen format, or the standard 4:3 format, then choose the corresponding quality.

In your camera's specifications you will find the recording quality of the camera. Sometimes the camera has various options to set the recording quality. High quality recordings will produce a better image, but will take up much more space on your camera's internal memory or memory card. This means you will have less recording time. The quality level you need to use depends on the way you are going to view the movie. Not all equipment is suitable for movies in HD quality.

In the sample project you have created a wide-screen movie of standard quality. To prevent the movie from displaying black bars during playback, you can render the movie in a regular wide-screen resolution:

☞ **Start *Windows Live Movie Maker*** ⁷

☞ **Open the *Holland* project** ᡣ¹⁸

☞ **Make sure your speakers are turned on and the volume is not muted**

You will see the project:

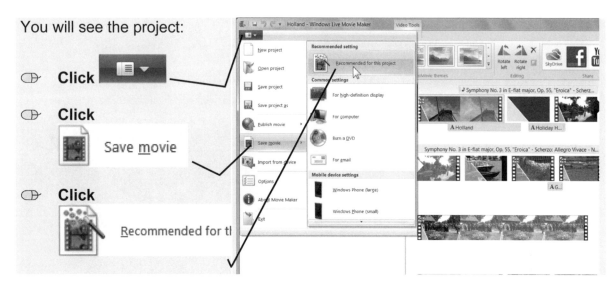

⊕ **Click**

⊕ **Click**

Save movie

⊕ **Click**

Recommended for th

In this example you will be saving the movie in the (*My*) *videos* folder:

⊕ **By** Videos **click** ▷

⊕ **Click** My Videos

In *Windows Vista* you will
need to click the folder
Videos.

☞ **If necessary, enter a**
file name by File name:

⊕ **Click** Save

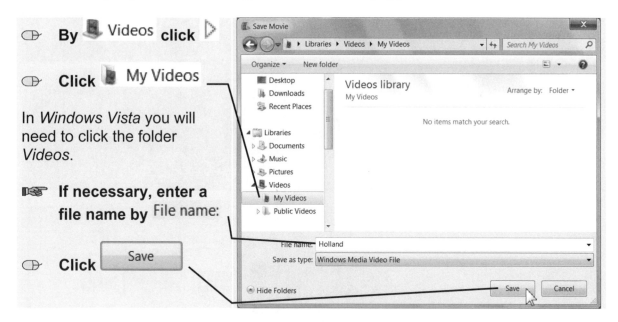

A small window appears,
indicating the progress of the
rendering (saving) process:

If the movie is long and the
quality is high, this may take
more than ten minutes.

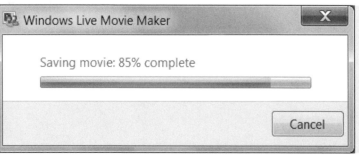

👉 **Click** [Play]

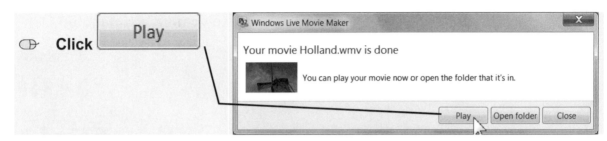

Windows Media Player will start and you will see the movie:

If you have a wide-screen monitor and have maximized the window, you will not see any black borders:

If you do not have a wide-screen monitor, then you will a black border on the top and bottom:

When the movie has finished:

👉 **Close the window** 🦶²

Now you will see the project once again:

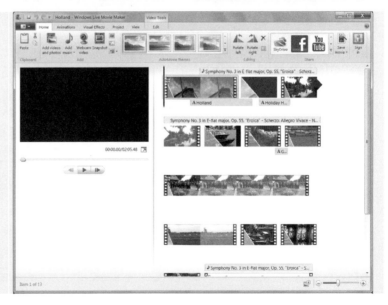

Rendering time and file size
The movie you have rendered a moment ago was just about two minutes long. If you have recorded a twenty minute movie, the rendering (saving) process will take at least ten times as long. If you have used more effects and added music, it can take even longer to render the movie.

The length of the movie will also affect the file size. Your practice movie is about 40 megabytes in size, so a 20 minute movie will take up at least 400 megabytes. If you are recording a movie in the highest HD quality, the file size for a 20 minute movie will be approximately 1 gigabyte (more than 1.000 megabytes).

14.2 Copy Your Movie to a DVD

A simple way of transporting your movie and watching it on another device is to copy it to a DVD. Then you will be able to watch it on television with the DVD player connected to your TV.

In this section you will be burning a DVD that is suited for the most common DVD players connected to television sets. *Windows Live Movie Maker* will use the regular wide-screen format of 720 x 480 pixels. You can burn the movie directly from within the program with *Windows DVD Maker*.

 Please note:

To create an HD quality movie, you will need to use a Blu-ray burner. The video images should be recorded in HD quality, to get the best results. *Windows DVD Maker* does not yet support the burning of Blu-ray disks. This means you will need to render the movie in HD quality first, following the steps performed in the previous section. Then you can use your own burning program to burn the movie to a Blu-ray disk.

 Please note:

To perform the operations in the next section, you will need to have *Windows DVD Maker* installed on your computer. This program is not included in the *Windows Vista Home Basic* and *Windows 7 Starter* editions. If you are using one of these editions, you can just read through the following section.

You will see the project:

☞ **Click** ⬚

☞ **Click**
Save movie

☞ **Click**
Burn a DVD

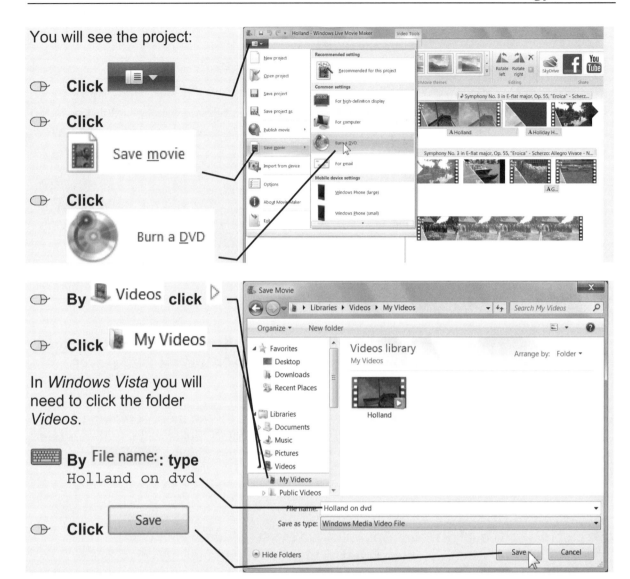

☞ **By** 📼 Videos **click** ▷

☞ **Click** 📁 My Videos

In *Windows Vista* you will need to click the folder *Videos*.

⌨ **By** File name: **type** Holland on dvd

☞ **Click** Save

A small window appears, indicating the progress of the rendering (saving) process:

For a lengthy, high quality movie, this can take quite a while.

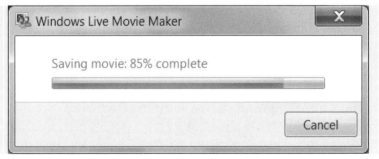

After the rendering process has finished, the *Windows DVD Maker* program will open:

If you do not see this window, then click on the task bar, or

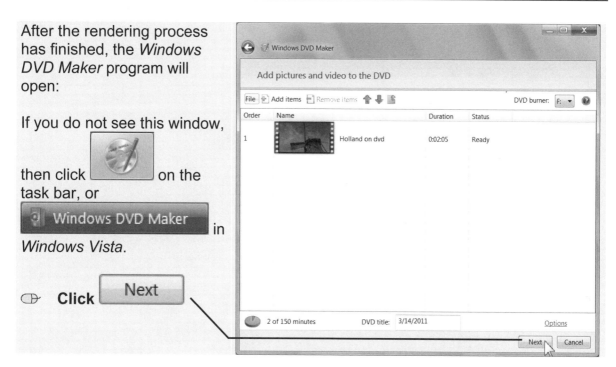

Windows DVD Maker in *Windows Vista*.

☞ **Click** Next

➜ **Please note:**

In this section we will not be discussing all of the options in *Windows DVD Maker*. Here you will only learn the essential operations for copying your movie to a DVD.

💡 **Tip**

Multiple movies on a DVD
If the DVD has a lot of free space remaining, you can add other movies to it. This is how you add a second movie:

☞ **Click** ⊞ Add items

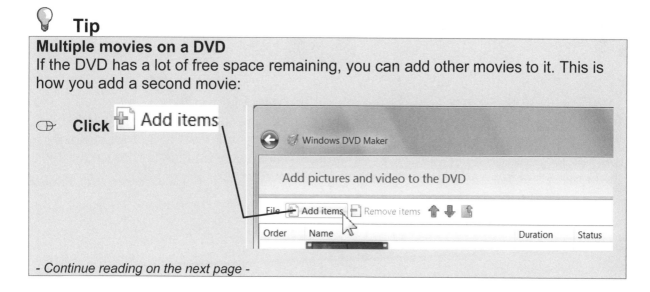

- Continue reading on the next page -

☞ **Open the folder containing the movie you want to add**

☞ **Click the movie**

☞ **Click** Add ▼

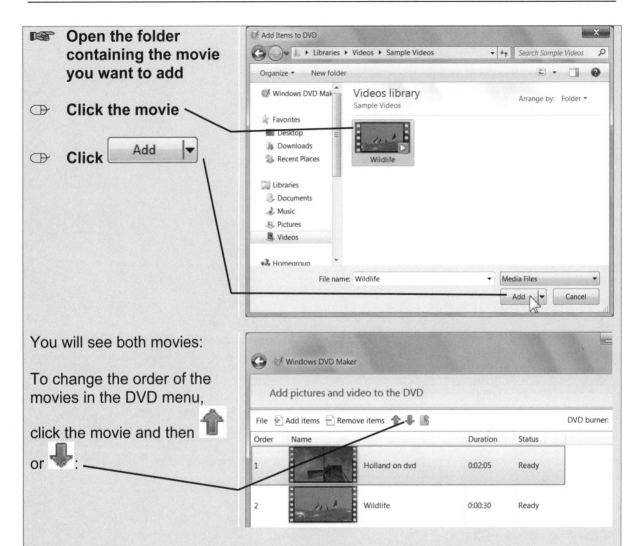

You will see both movies:

To change the order of the movies in the DVD menu,

click the movie and then ⬆

or ⬇:

Here you can see that a wide-screen movie and a regular movie will be burned to the DVD. Generally speaking, this is not recommended, because the DVD needs to be played in the same format. That is to say, in wide-screen format or in the standard 4:3 aspect ratio. In this case one of the movies will display a black border on the top and bottom of the frame or on the left and right side.

💡 Tip

Burn a DVD in wide-screen or standard size
If you already know on which type of screen the DVD will be viewed, you can take that into account when you do the burning:

In the bottom right of the window:

☞ **Click** <u>Options</u>

🖙 **Select the aspect ratio**

☞ **Click** [OK]

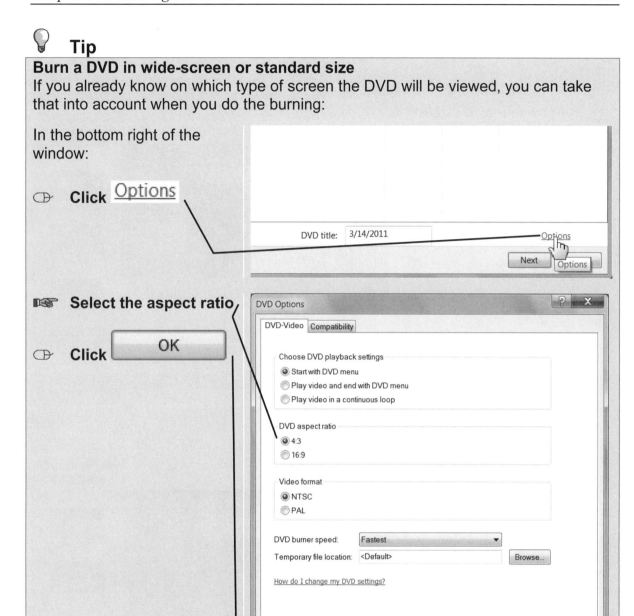

You will see a preview of the DVD menu:

You may see a different example on your own screen.

Use the scroll bar to take a look at the other menu styles:

☞ **Click a few of the other styles**

☞ **Drag the scroll bar upwards**

☞ **Click** Photographs

To replace the picture in the foreground or background by a different video or photo:

☞ **Click**
 Customize menu

In the foreground you are going to insert the boat photo, which is also used in the video:

⊕ **By** Foreground video:

click Browse...

☞ **Open the practice files folder** 𝄢8

Click IMG_0102

⊕ **Click** Add

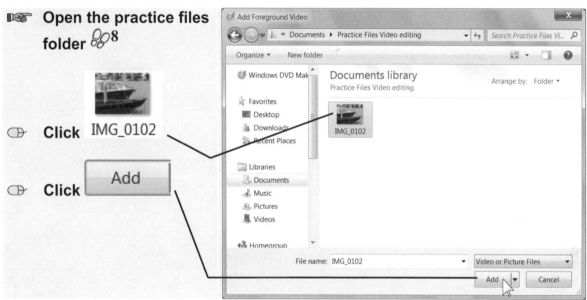

💡 **Tip**

Title photo
As shown above, you can easily set a different photo for the foreground or background, instead of a picture of the video. For example, if you have taken a picture of a sign (from a theme park, an event, or a tourist information board), you can use a photo of that in the DVD menu.

You can customize the menu further by selecting a different background video or audio (music) clip.

If you want to change the font for the menu:

☞ By Font: click ▼

You will see a list of fonts:

☞ **Drag the scroll bar upwards a little**

☞ **Click** Comic Sans MS

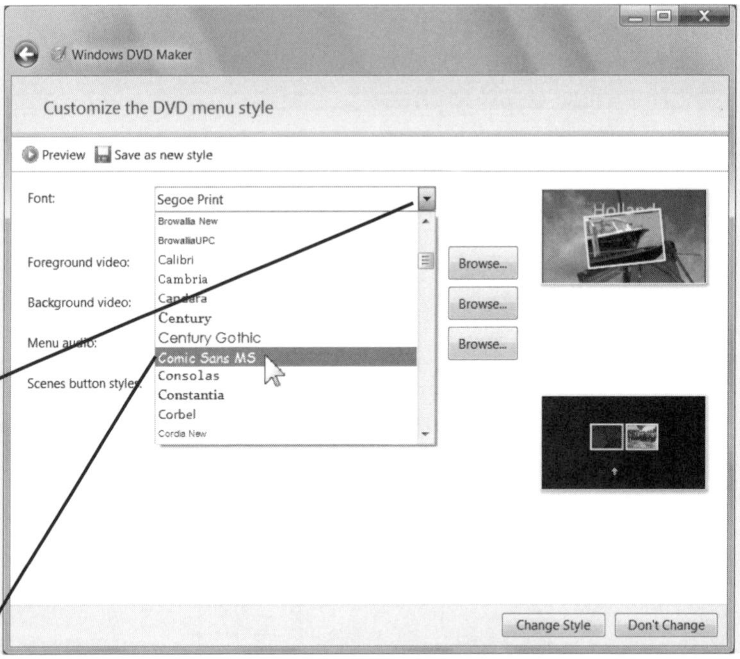

☞ **Click** ▶ Preview

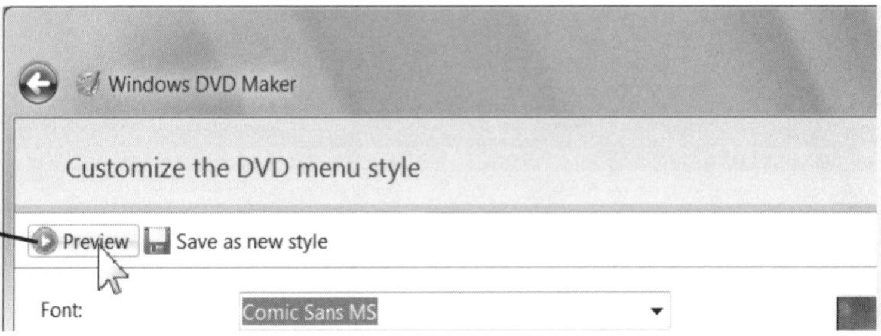

You will see a preview of the menu:

Use ▶ to play the movie:

With 🔲 Menu you return to the DVD menu:

☞ **Click** OK

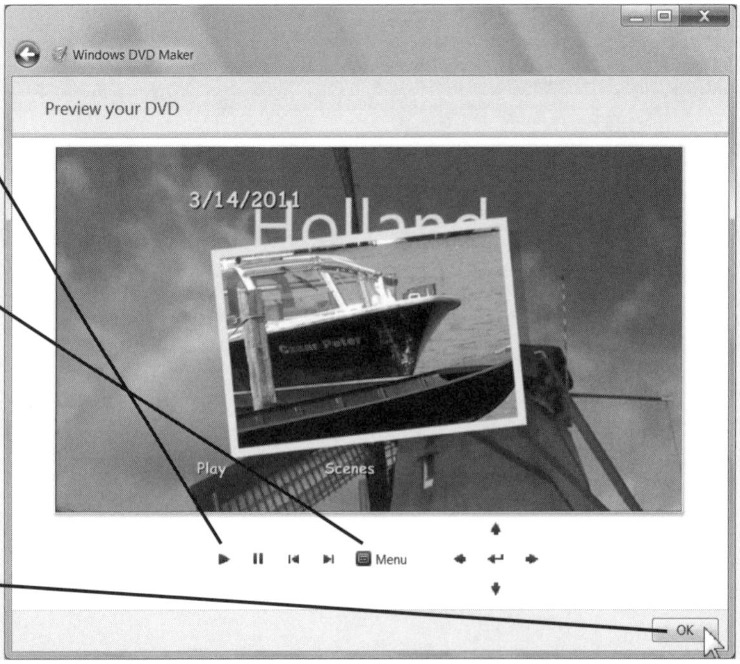

☞ **Change the menu, if you want to**

When you are satisfied:

⊕ **Click** ⟨Change Style⟩

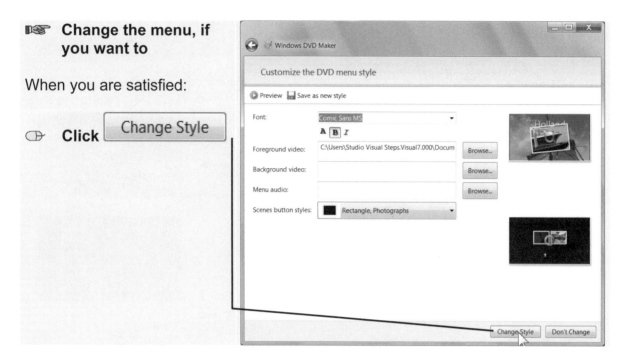

By default, the creation date will appear in the menu, in the shape of a title. You can replace this date with your own title:

⊕ **Click** 🅰 Menu text

Type: Holiday 2010

Click **Change Text**

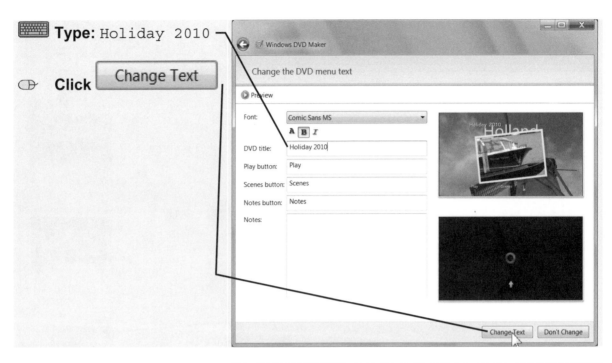

You will see the new title:

If you are completely satisfied with the result:

Click **Burn**

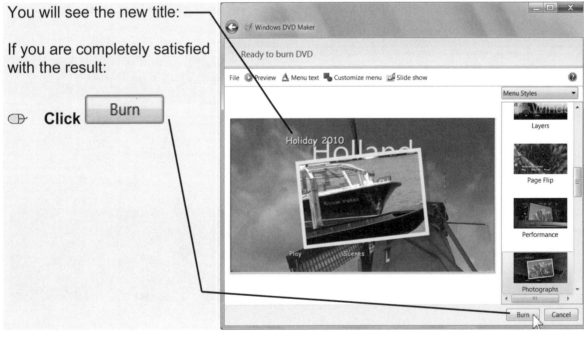

If you have not yet inserted a recordable DVD into the drive, you will see this window:

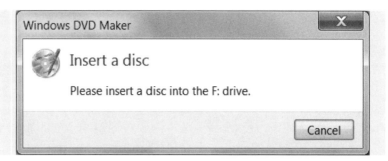

☞ **Insert a recordable DVD into the drive**

First, the movie is encoded:

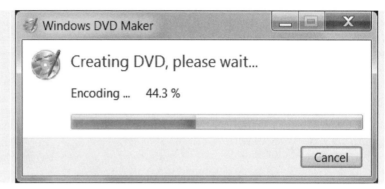

Next, the DVD will be burned:

☞ **Remove the DVD from the burner**

Now you can play this DVD in the DVD player that is connected to your television set, or in your computer's DVD player. The movie will start with the menu you have just created. If the DVD contains multiple movies, you will find these movies among the scenes in the menu.

🖑 **Click** `Close`

Tip

Scenes
The movie will start with the menu you have created. If the DVD contains multiple movies, you will find these movies among the various scenes:

☞ **Click Scenes**

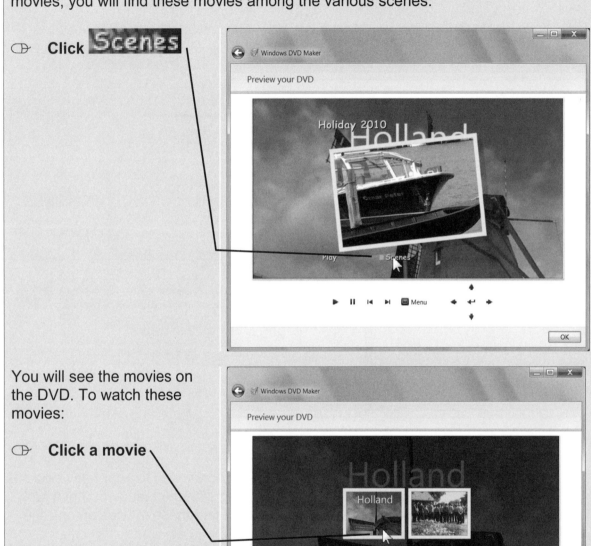

You will see the movies on the DVD. To watch these movies:

☞ **Click a movie**

Even though you may have created a single, long movie, it still can be useful to cut it up into several smaller sections. This will allow you to skip to a particular section of the movie at once. It also means your project becomes more orderly, it is easier to edit and the rendering process will take up less time.

You will see the *Windows DVD Maker* window:

☞ **Close the *Windows DVD Maker* window** 👣2

Click No

For the moment, you do not need to view the movie you just burned:

☞ **Click** Close

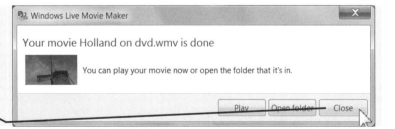

Now you will see the *Windows Live Movie Maker* window with your project:

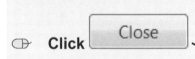

14.3 Sending the Movie by E-mail

Most movie files are usually rather large and cannot easily be sent by e-mail. Nevertheless, if you want to send the movie by e-mail, you can use *Windows Live Movie Maker* to create a special version with a lower resolution. If the movie is not too long, you will still be able to send it by e-mail.

 Tip

Send movie by e-mail or publish it on the Internet?
If you want to distribute your movie right away but maintain the quality, you can upload the movie to *YouTube* instead of sending it by e-mail. You will learn how to do that in *section 14.4 Publishing Your Movie on YouTube*.

To make the film suitable for sending by e-mail:

You will see the project:

☞ **Click**

☞ **Click** Save movie

☞ **Click** For email

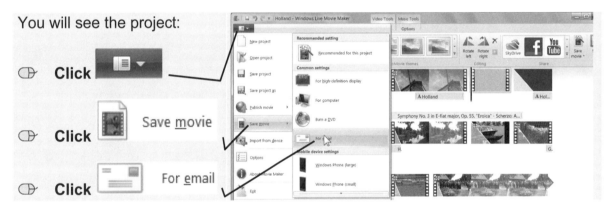

In this example you are going to save the movie in the (*My*) *Videos* folder:

☞ **By** Videos **click** ▷

☞ **Click** My Videos

In *Windows Vista* you will need to click the folder *Videos*.

⌨ **By** File name: **type:**
Holland Mail

☞ **Click** Save

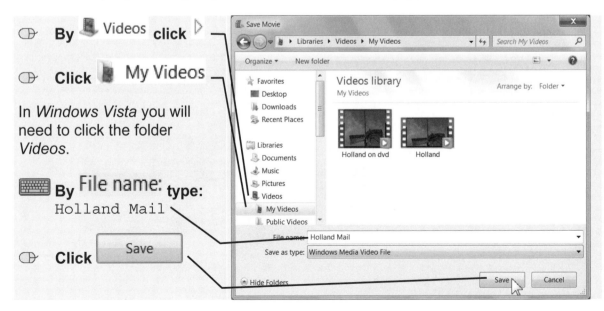

Now you will again see the rendering (saving) process:

The rendering process will not take as long, because the movie is saved in a lower quality.

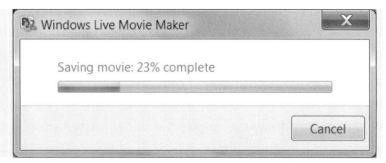

☞ **Click** Play

Windows Media Player will open and you can watch the movie:

You will see that the image is not quite as clear and also a little shaky.

☞ **Stop playback** ⌨11

☞ **Close the window** ⌨2

Now you can send this version of the movie as an attachment to an e-mail message.

 Please note:

The size of this sample movie is about 4.5 megabytes. That is roughly 10% of the size of a regular wide-screen movie. A slightly lengthier movie will often be still too large to send it by e-mail.

Tip

Save a version for mobile devices

More and more mobile devices, such as cell phones, are capable of playing movies. *Windows Live Movie Maker* can also create a special version for use on a mobile device:

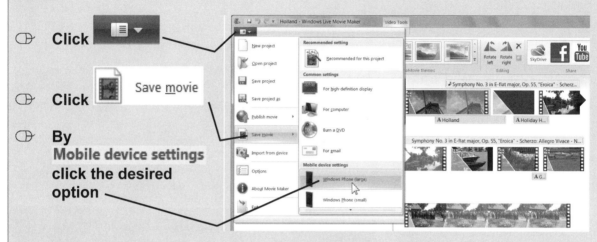

☞ **Click**

☞ **Click**

☞ **By Mobile device settings click the desired option**

The resolution will be just as low as the e-mail version, but the image will be more stable.

14.4 Publishing Your Movie on YouTube

A simple way of presenting your movie to your audience is by uploading it to *YouTube*. Nowadays more and more households have a broadband Internet connection, which makes viewing movies on the Internet with a service such as *YouTube* a very tangible option.

The movie will be saved and published on *YouTube* in the format corresponding to the aspect ratio of your movie. If the project has the standard aspect ratio (4:3), the movie will be published on *YouTube* with the same aspect ratio and a resolution of 640x480 pixels. If the project is saved in the wide-screen format (16:9), the movie will be published on *YouTube* as a HD video with the same aspect ratio and a resolution of 1280x720 pixels. It will take longer to publish a movie in HD format.

 Please note:

Of you want to publish your movie on *YouTube* you will need to have a *YouTube* account. If you do not have such an account, or if you do not want to publish the movie on *YouTube*, then just read through this section. If, after reading this section, you decide to publish your movie on *YouTube*, you can create an account for free. In *Appendix B. Create a YouTube Account* you can read how to create such an account.

This is how to publish your movie on *YouTube*:

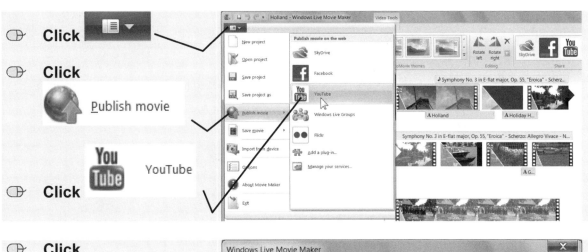

Click

Click
Publish movie

Click YouTube

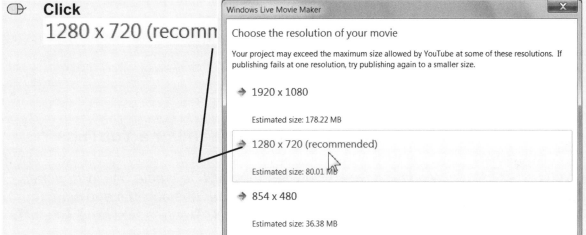

Click 1280 x 720 (recomn

You will need to sign in to *Windows Live*:

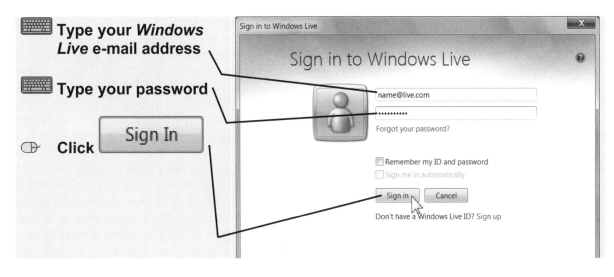

Type your *Windows Live* e-mail address

Type your password

Click Sign In

Now you are going to sign in to *YouTube*:

 Type your *YouTube* user name ——

 Type your password ——

Click **Sign In**

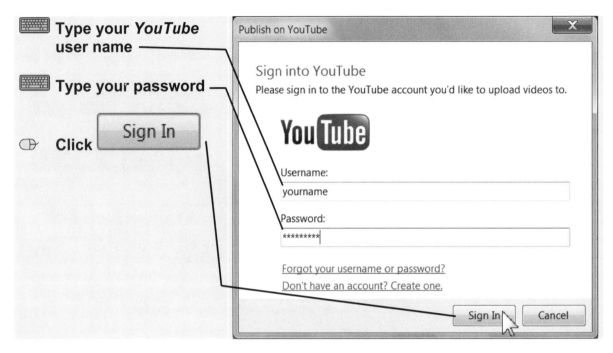

HELP! I do not have a Windows Live ID and/or a YouTube account.

If you do not have a *Windows Live ID,* you can read how to create one in *Appendix C. Create a Windows Live ID.* If you do not have a *YouTube* account and want to create one, you can read how to do this in *Appendix B. Create a YouTube Account.*

☞ **Change the title, if you want to** ——

 By Description: type:
practice film
Windows Live Movie
Maker ——

By Tags: **type:**
Holland, wind
mills

These are the keywords
people can use when
searching for the movie on
YouTube.

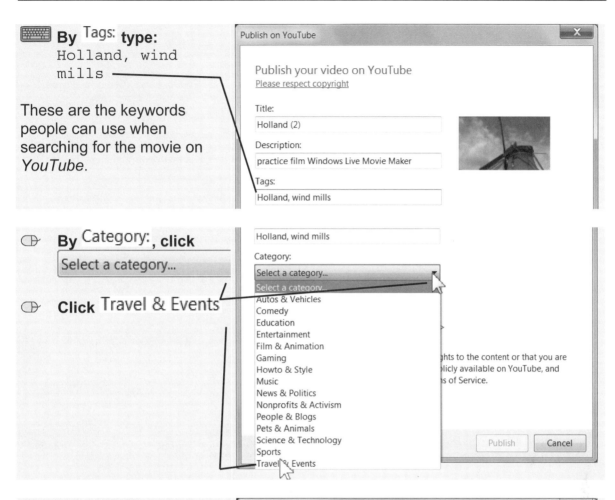

By Category: **, click**

Select a category...

Click Travel & Events

If you want to allow anyone to
be able to watch your movie,
then do not change the
Public permission by
Permission::

Select the Private option to
publish a video that is only
available to your friends.

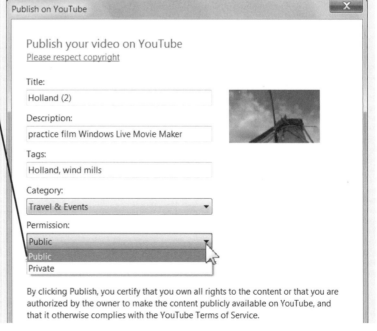

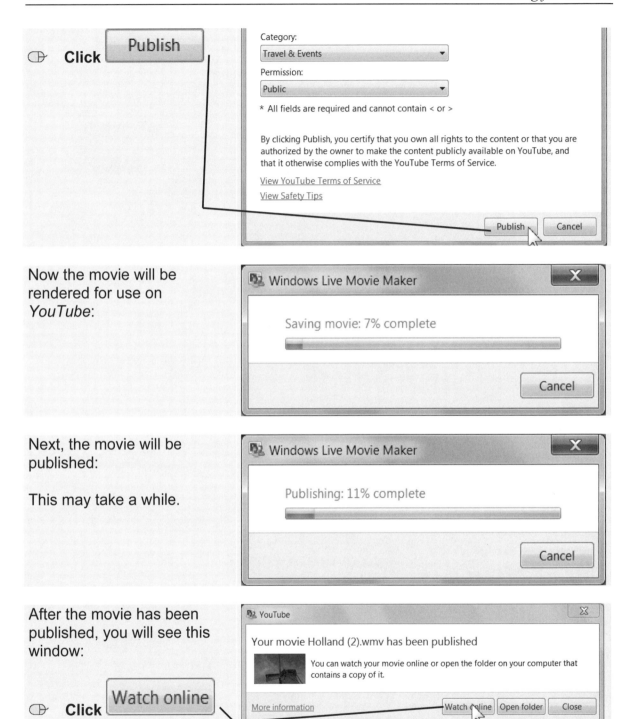

Click **Publish**

Category:
Travel & Events

Permission:
Public

* All fields are required and cannot contain < or >

By clicking Publish, you certify that you own all rights to the content or that you are authorized by the owner to make the content publicly available on YouTube, and that it otherwise complies with the YouTube Terms of Service.

View YouTube Terms of Service
View Safety Tips

Publish   Cancel

Now the movie will be rendered for use on *YouTube*:

Windows Live Movie Maker

Saving movie: 7% complete

Cancel

Next, the movie will be published:

This may take a while.

Windows Live Movie Maker

Publishing: 11% complete

Cancel

After the movie has been published, you will see this window:

Click **Watch online**

YouTube

Your movie Holland (2).wmv has been published

You can watch your movie online or open the folder on your computer that contains a copy of it.

More information   Watch online   Open folder   Close

Sometimes, the movie will not be available on *YouTube* straight away. Then you will see: ——

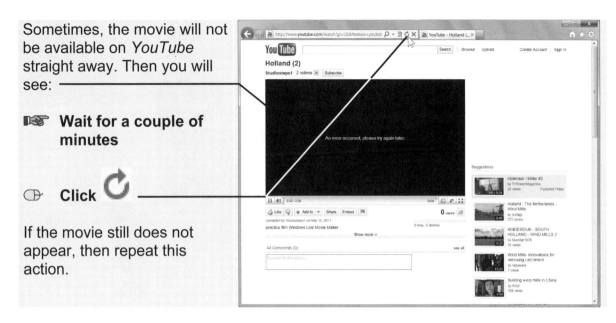

☞ **Wait for a couple of minutes**

 Click ⟳ ——————————

If the movie still does not appear, then repeat this action.

Now the movie will be played:

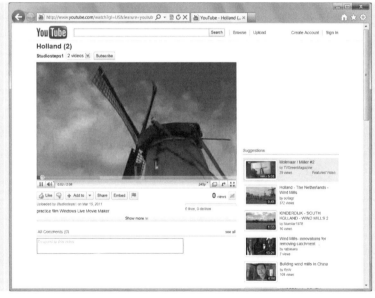

HELP! The quality of the movie is poor.

It may take a while before the movie is available in high resolution. Until that moment you will be watching the movie in a lower resolution, so the quality will be lower.

When the movie has finished playing, you will see a number of similar movies on the right-hand side of the window.

Please note: you will see different movies on your own screen.

☞ **Close the window** ❨❩²

Now the movie has been published on *YouTube*; if you have made the movie available to the public, anyone can watch this movie, even people who do not have a *YouTube* account.

💡 **Tip**

Add a hyperlink to the movie
Do you want to let your friends know that your movie can be viewed on *YouTube*?
Send them an e-mail message with a hyperlink to the movie:

⊕ **Right-click the address bar**

⊕ **Click Copy**

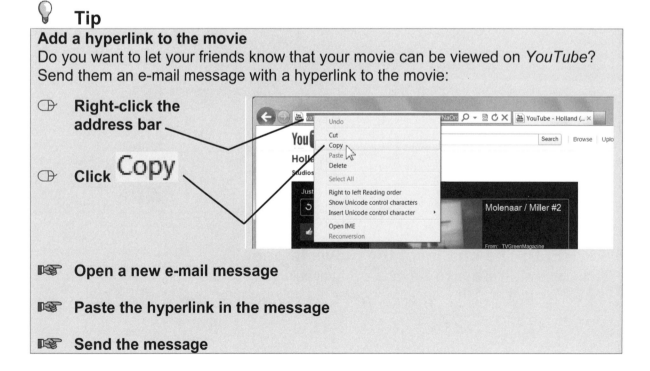

☞ **Open a new e-mail message**

☞ **Paste the hyperlink in the message**

☞ **Send the message**

Tip

Share your movie (1)
To save, publish or send your movie by e-mail you can also use the buttons on the

Home tab:

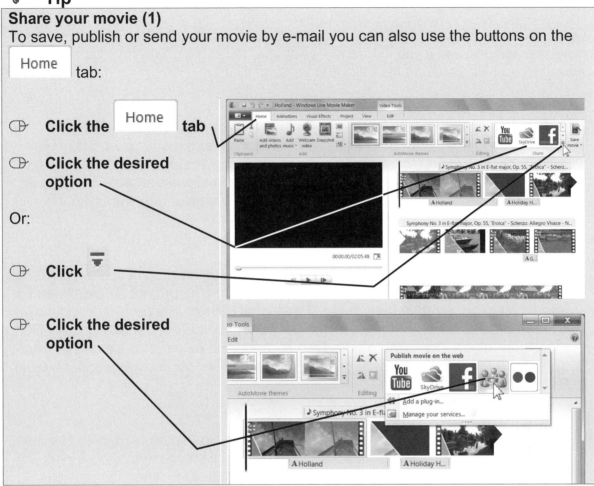

⊕ **Click the** Home **tab**

⊕ **Click the desired option**

Or:

⊕ **Click** ☰

⊕ **Click the desired option**

 Tip

Share your movie (2)
In this chapter you have learned how to upload your movie to *YouTube*. If you have a *Facebook*, *SkyDrive*, *Windows Live Groups* and/or *Flickr* account, you can also publish your movie on one of those services.

⊕ **Click the relevant button**

☞ **Follow the instructions in the next few windows**

14.5 Cleaning Up Files

Once you have finalized a project, it is always good practice to look at the files you have created and see if you can remove some of these files. When you are creating a project, you will be using the following types of files:

1. **Your videos, photos and audio files**
   You cannot delete, move, or rename these files while you are still editing the project. If you try to perform one of the operations mentioned above, the project will not be able to find these files anymore. As a consequence, you will need to add (and edit) them all over again. After you have finalized the project and have saved or published the movie, you are free to do whatever you want with these files.

2. **Project file**
   You can recognize a project file by its file type .WMLP. A project contains links to all the videos, photos and audio files that are used in the project. The edits and effects are also stored in the project. If a file that is used in a project, is moved, deleted or renamed, the link will no longer work and you will need to add the file to the project again. Once you have saved a project file as a movie file and you are sure that you will never want to change the project file, you can delete the project file, if you want.

3. **Movie file**
   In the end, a project will result in a movie. A movie file can be recognized by the file type .WMV. Here, all the videos, photos and audio files have been joined together along with their edits and effects into a single file. When the movie is played, the original files are no longer used. In a movie file you cannot edit the separate elements, or their effects, unless you add the movie to a new project.

Now you are going to take a look at the movies you have made and delete the movies you no longer need:

You will see your movies:

If you do not see the movies:

☞ **Open the folder in which you have stored your movies**

If you have worked through all the exercises in this book, your movies will have been saved in the (*My*) *Videos* folder.

In this case, you can delete the movie that you have sent by e-mail:

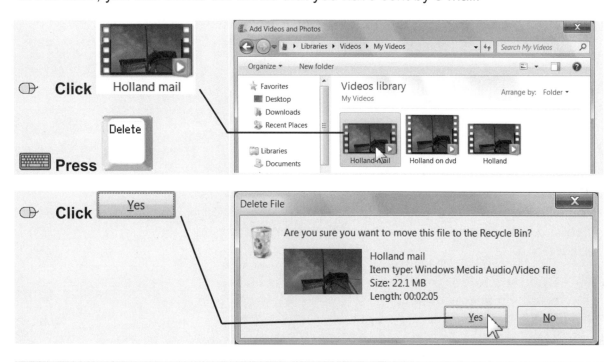

☞ **Click** Holland mail

☞ **Press** Delete

☞ **Click** Yes

☞ **If you want, you can also delete the other movies you no longer need**

➣ Please note:

Always save a copy of the movie in the best possible quality, in case you need to edit the movie at a later stage. The best quality is not necessarily the highest quality. If your movie has not been recorded in HD quality, a lesser quality might be more useful.

☞ **Close the *Add Photos and Videos* window** **2**

If you are sure you do not ever want to change the project, then you can also delete the project files. First, you need to close the current project:

☞ **Save the project** ⏾¹³

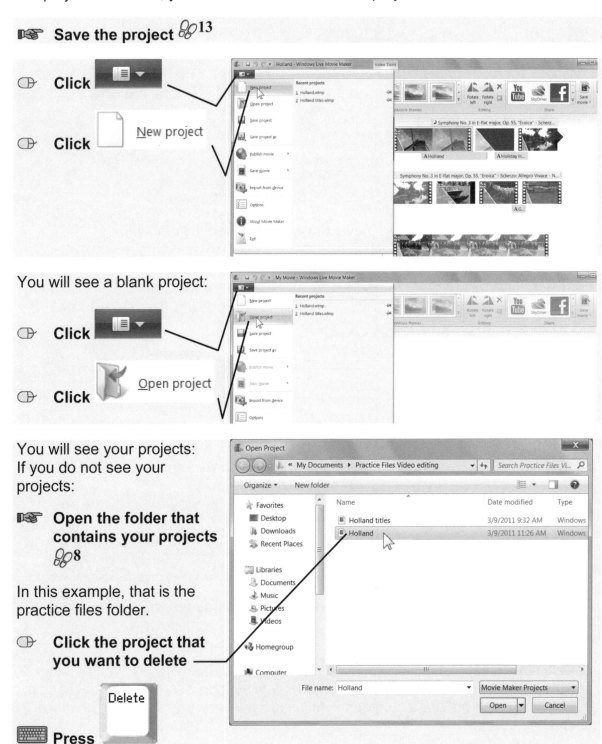

Click

Click ☐ New project

You will see a blank project:

Click

Click 📂 Open project

You will see your projects:
If you do not see your projects:

☞ **Open the folder that contains your projects** ⏾8

In this example, that is the practice files folder.

⊕ **Click the project that you want to delete**

⌨ **Press** Delete

Tip

Save projects
Project files do not take up a lot of space. So it will not really be necessary to delete these files to create extra space. But it will help you maintain a good overview of your files, if you delete the older projects once in a while, especially if the files used in a project have been moved or deleted. In that case, it is really unnecessary to save the project file.

Click **Yes**

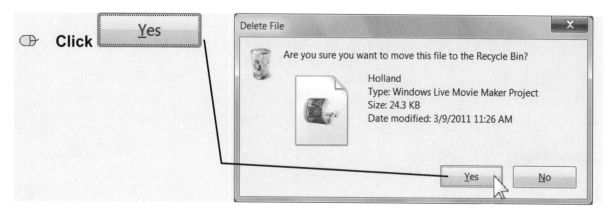

☞ **Close the window** ⚕²

You have turned your project into a movie and you have published it. This has concluded the project. In the last chapter of this book you will learn how to import your own recordings from your video camera to *Windows Live Movie Maker*.

☞ **Close** *Windows Live Movie Maker* ⚕²

14.6 Background Information

Dictionary	
Blu-ray	Blu-ray is a movie format that is used for saving movies in HD quality; it is intended to be the successor of the DVD.
Facebook	Social media site. You can create a profile and link your profile to that of other people within the site.
HD video	HD stands for High Definition. This is a standard format for recording, saving and playing high quality videos.
Movie file	The final result of a project is a movie. A movie file is defined by the .WMV file type.
Project file	A project is defined by the .WMLP file type and contains links to the videos, photos and audio files that are used in the project. The edits and effects are stored there as well.
Rendering	Assembling a movie. In this process, the actual video images are created, including the titles, sounds and transitions. This is the stage that follows the editing stage. Rendering requires a lot of computing power and can take up a lot of time.
Scene	Parts of a movie that belong together. Often a single event.
Windows Live SkyDrive	A *Windows Live* service that lets you store files on the Internet.
YouTube	*YouTube* is a website where you can upload, view, and share videos for free; all the videos are created by the users.

Source: Windows Live Movie Maker Help and Wikipedia

DVD standards

Currently, there exist two DVD standards: -r and –rw, and +r and +rw. Both types are supported by a different group of manufacturers. *Pioneer* and *Apple* support DVD-r and DVD-rw. Dvd+r and +rw were developed by *Sony* and *Philips*.

The advantage of -r and –rw, is that these disks can be played on every DVD player. Also on the player connected to your television set.
A disadvantage is that the +r and +rw disk are sometimes not recognized by older DVD players (connected to your TV).

Some of the older DVD burners are only able to burn disks of one of these two standard types. The current generation of DVD burners is able to burn disks of both types.

DVD-r

DVD -rw

DVD +r

DVD +rw

Burners

When the DVD burner was first introduced, there were huge differences among these burners. Some of the burners were only capable of burning DVD minus disks (-r and -rw), others could only burn DVD plus disks (+r and +rw). The current generation of DVD burners is capable of burning both types of disks.

If you own an older DVD burner, then you need to check your burner's manual to find out which type of disks it can burn.

In the DVD burners' specifications you can usually find the types of CDs and DVDs that the burner can handle:

Modes supported:

- DVD-ROM, DVD-R, DVD-RW, DVD+R, DVD+RW, DVD-Video, CD-ROM, CD-ROM XA, CD-Audio, CD Extra, CD Text, CD-I Ready, CD-Bridge, Photo-CD, Video CD, Hybrid CD

The latest development in the field of DVD burning is the Blu-ray burner. Compared to a regular DVD burner, this type of burner is still quite expensive.

With a Blu-ray burner you can burn the special Blu-ray disks, also called BD disks.

To make the introduction of Blu-ray more acceptable to the public, the Blu-ray burner has been adapted, so it can also burn regular CD-r-, DVD-r and DVD-rw disks and dual layer DVDs.

14.7 Tips

 Tip

Extra sound track
Previously, you have seen that voice recordings can only be added to the sound track in places where there is no music. If you want to add both music and voice recordings to your movie, then this is a useful trick:

☞ **Assemble the entire movie, including effects, transitions, titles and music**

Make sure that the movie is completely 'finished', and that you do not need to change anything later on.
The voice recording should be the only missing element.

☞ **Publish the movie and give the movie a name** 👣**26**
☞ **Just to be on the safe side, save the project that you have just published** 👣**13**

Now you are going to open a new project:

👉 **Click**

👉 **Click** New project

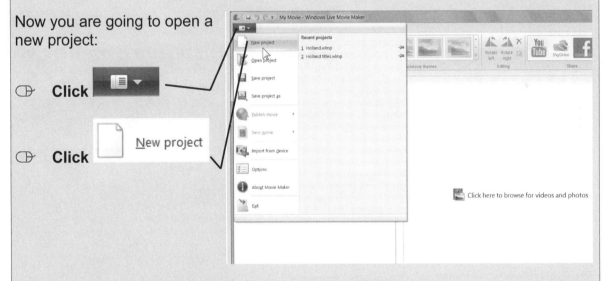

☞ **Add the movie that you have just created** 👣**20**

- Continue reading on the next page -

Now the movie has been imported as a new project. The music and the other sounds are part of the video and you will be able to add a new sound track:

You will see the movie as a single video:

☞ **Start the *Sound Recorder* 𝒷𝒷22**

☞ **Play the movie 𝒷𝒷10**

☞ **Record the spoken text, one part at a time 𝒷𝒷23**

☞ **Save the text 𝒷𝒷24**

⊕ **Position the playback indicator at the start point of the spoken text**

⊕ **Click Add music ▾**

⊕ **Click**
    🎵 Add music at the current p

⊕ **Click the commentary file**

In the bottom of the window:

⊕ **Click Open**

In the new sound track you will see the file which contains the commentary:

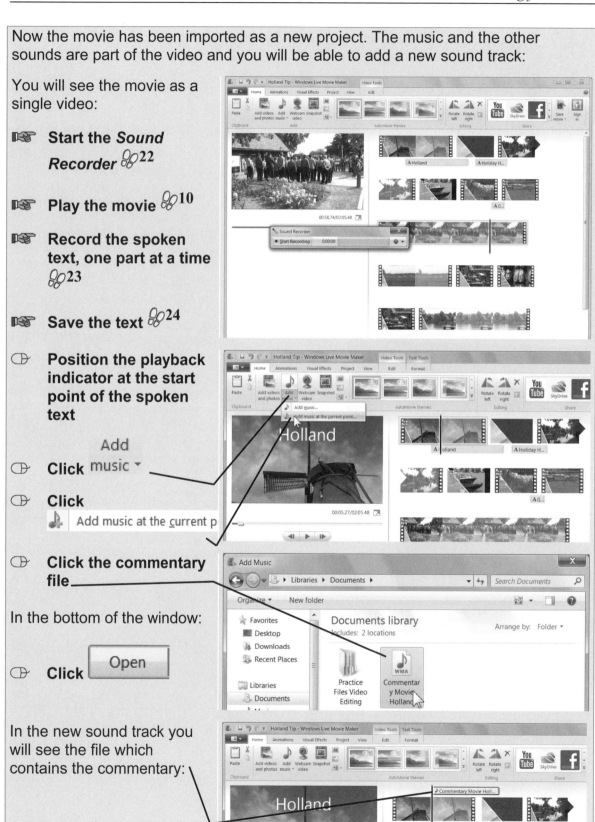

15. Importing Your Own Files

Up until now, you have used the practice files while working through the exercises in this book. At this point, you may feel you are ready to start a project using your own material. If you have never learned how to import (or transfer) the files from your camera, or cell phone then this is just the chapter for you! Here you will learn various methods for importing files from a camera or cell phone directly to your computer.

The method used for transferring depends on the type of video or photo camera you own. Most modern digital cameras and cell phones can be connected to a computer by means of a USB or Firewire cable; or the files can be transferred directly from the memory card. The computer will recognize the camera or cell phone as a separate disk drive. If your camera is not recognized by your computer, then it may be necessary to install the manufacturer's driver software first. You can find the driver program on the CD or DVD that was included in the package when you purchased your camera, or on the manufacturer's website.

If you own an older type of camera, it may be necessary to buy a special cable and/or a video capture card. Such a card converts analog data to digital data, so that it can be edited and saved on a computer. You can read more about this topic in the *Background Information* at the end of this chapter.

Once you have transferred your photos and videos to your computer, you can start a new project, assemble, edit, and add captions, titles, transitions and effects by using the techniques learned in the previous chapters.

In this chapter you will learn how to:

- transfer photo and video files from an SD card;
- transfer photo and video files by using a USB cable;
- import all the images, or only import new images;
- transfer photo and video files by using a Firewire cable;
- import individual scenes from a video file;
- import the entire video file.

 Please note:

In this chapter you will only need to read the sections that correspond with the type of camera you are using.

Please note:

Do not remove photos and videos from your digital camera, cell phone or SD card with *Windows* but only with the device itself. The camera uses its own index and if you delete files from within *Windows*, the content will not correspond to the camera's index anymore. The internal memory will need to be formatted all over again and you will lose your recordings.

15.1 Copying From an SD Card

Modern video cameras, such as *camcorders* and mobile phones, often store their recordings on an SD card. If you own a card reader, you can insert the card into the reader and import the files to *Windows Live Movie Maker*.

A Secure Digital card (SD card) is a memory card that can be used in portable electronic devices, such as digital cameras and cell phones. You can buy special cards with a higher *write* speed, for use in digital video and photo cameras.

 Please note:

In order to use this method, your computer needs to have a built-in card reader (or an external card reader connected to the computer) that is suited for SD cards.

☞ **Start *Windows Live Movie Maker*** [7]

☞ **Insert the card into the card reader**

☞ **If necessary, close the**
AutoPlay window ⌘²

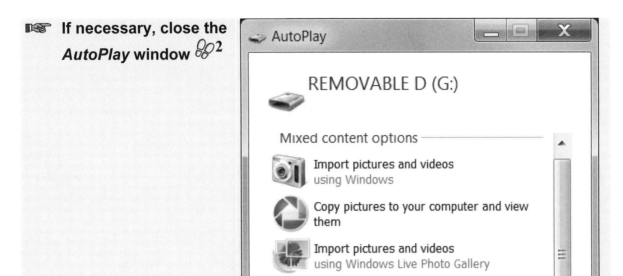

⊕ **Click**

⊕ **Click** Import from <u>device</u>

You will see the following
window:

⊕ **Click** OK

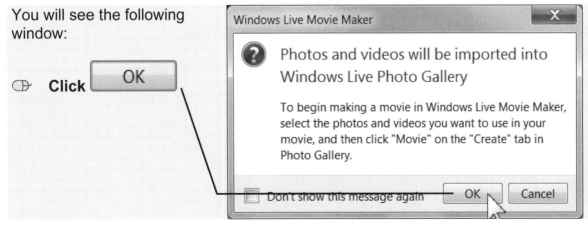

On this computer, the SD card has been assigned the drive letter G: ——————

Sometimes you will also see the camera's brand, for

example, 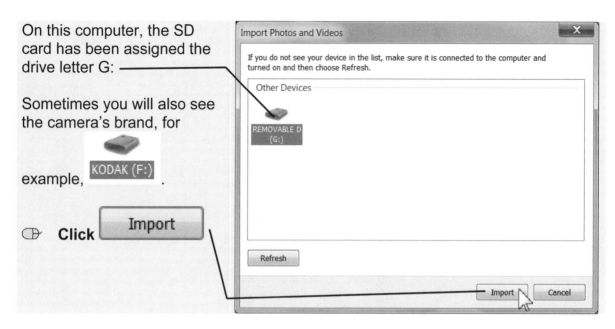 .

⊕ **Click** Import

Please note:

The screenshots in this chapter have been taken on a computer running *Windows* 7. In *Windows Vista* you may see slightly different windows, once in a while. However, the tasks you will be performing are the same.

The program will search for files containing photos and videos:

You will see the number of new photos and videos that have been found: ——————

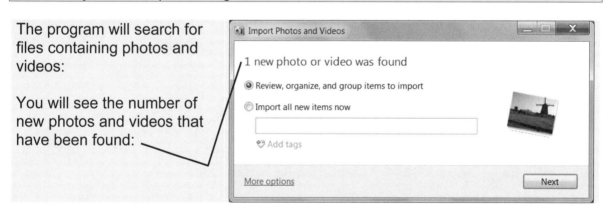

☞ **Continue with** *Section 15.3 Checking the Settings*

15.2 Copying With a USB Cable

If your computer does not have a card reader, or your camera does not use an SD card, then you can often connect the camera or mobile phone to your computer by using a USB cable. Here is how to copy the files to your computer with a USB cable:

☞ **Open *Windows Live Movie Maker* ❦⁷**

☞ **Make sure the camera has been turned off**

☞ **Connect the camera to the power supply**

☞ **Connect the camera to your computer, with the USB cable**

☞ **Turn the camera on**

 Please note:

It is possible that your camera needs to be connected to the computer in a different way. In that case, please consult the manual that came with the camera.

☞ **If necessary, close the *AutoPlay* window ❦²**

👆 **Click**

👆 **Click** Import from **d**evice

You will see this window:

⊕ **Click** OK

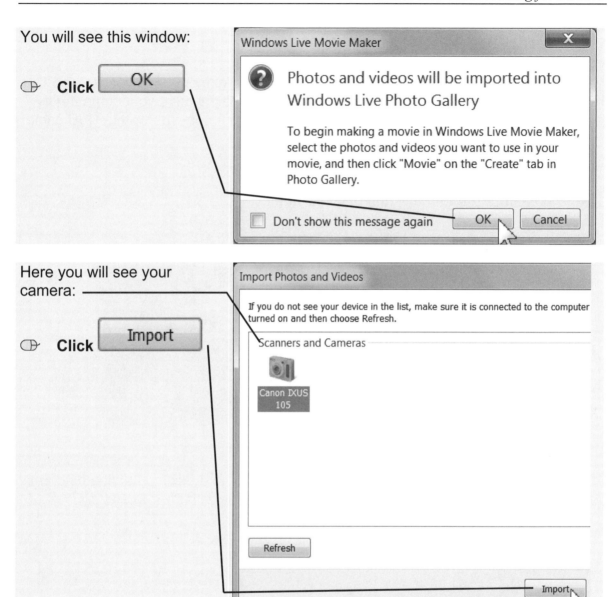

Windows Live Movie Maker

? **Photos and videos will be imported into Windows Live Photo Gallery**

To begin making a movie in Windows Live Movie Maker, select the photos and videos you want to use in your movie, and then click "Movie" on the "Create" tab in Photo Gallery.

☐ Don't show this message again   OK   Cancel

Here you will see your camera:

⊕ **Click** Import

Import Photos and Videos

If you do not see your device in the list, make sure it is connected to the computer turned on and then choose Refresh.

Scanners and Cameras

Canon IXUS 105

Refresh

Import

HELP! The camera cannot be found.

If the computer does not recognize the camera, you will see the following window:

Sometimes it takes a while for your computer to find the camera:

 **Wait a few minutes**

☞ **Click**  Refresh

If your camera still is not found, this may be caused by the following reasons:
- Your digital video camera is turned off.
- Your digital video camera is in stand-by mode. With some cameras, the stand-by mode is activated while the camera is in recording mode (*Camera* mode) and while the camera contains a tape, but no video or audio data is being transferred.

You can try a number of things:
- Check if your digital video camera is connected correctly to the computer.
- Check if your camera has been turned on and in *Play* mode.
- Turn your camera off and then turn it on again in *Play* mode (also called *Player* or *VCR* mode).

☞ **Click** Refresh

Source: Windows Help and Support

The program will look for files that contain photos and videos:

You will see the number of new photos and videos that have been found:

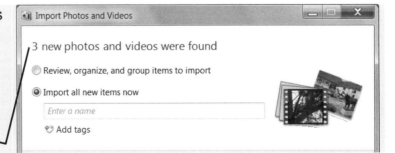

15.3 Checking the Settings

Before you start importing files, you need to check the program settings:

Click <u>More options</u>

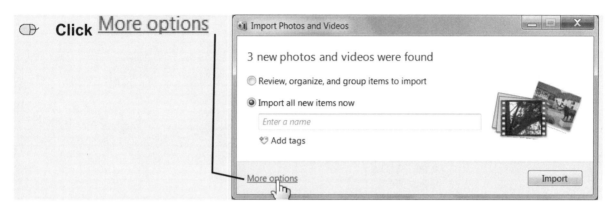

The videos and photos that you import are stored in a single folder. In this case the videos are more important, so it is a good idea to store the files in the (*My*) *Videos* folder:

By **Import to:** click

My Pictures

Click 🎬 My Videos

In *Windows Vista* you will need to click the folder *Videos*.

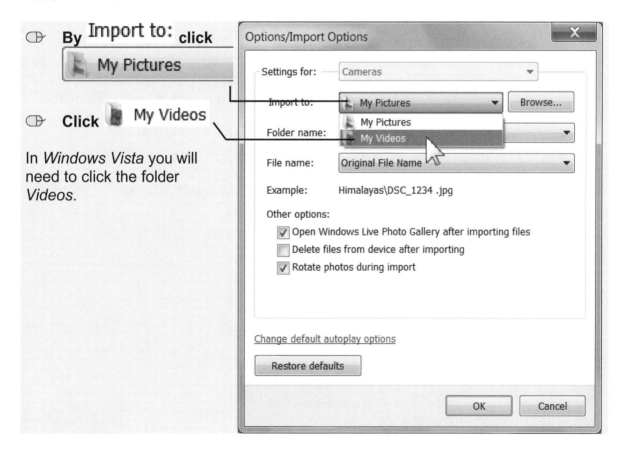

Tip

Store photos and videos together in one project

Did you take pictures *and* record videos from a recent event or a trip? Do you want to use both of these file types in the same project? Then you can store all the files together in a new folder:

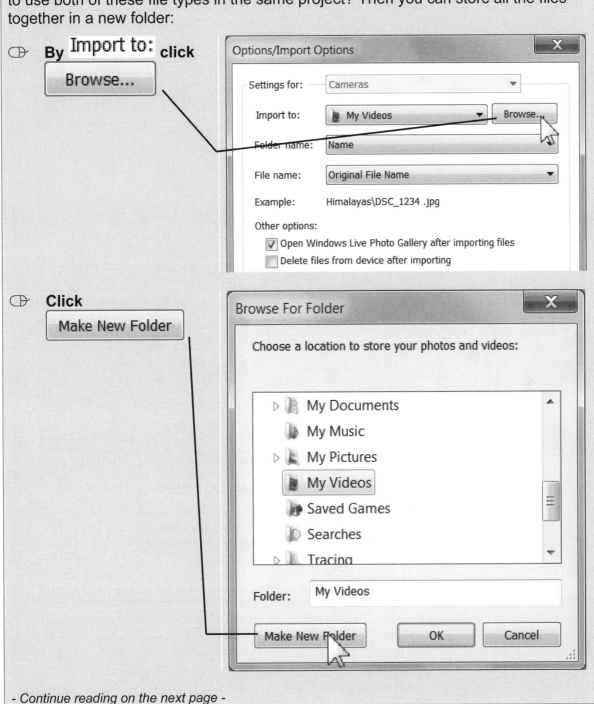

- Continue reading on the next page -

You will see a new folder:

⌨ **Enter a name for the folder** ——

👆 **Click** [OK]

It is recommended to begin with the year or date, when you enter a name for the folder. This way, all the folders containing recordings for a specific year will automatically be grouped together.

The folder name has been entered:

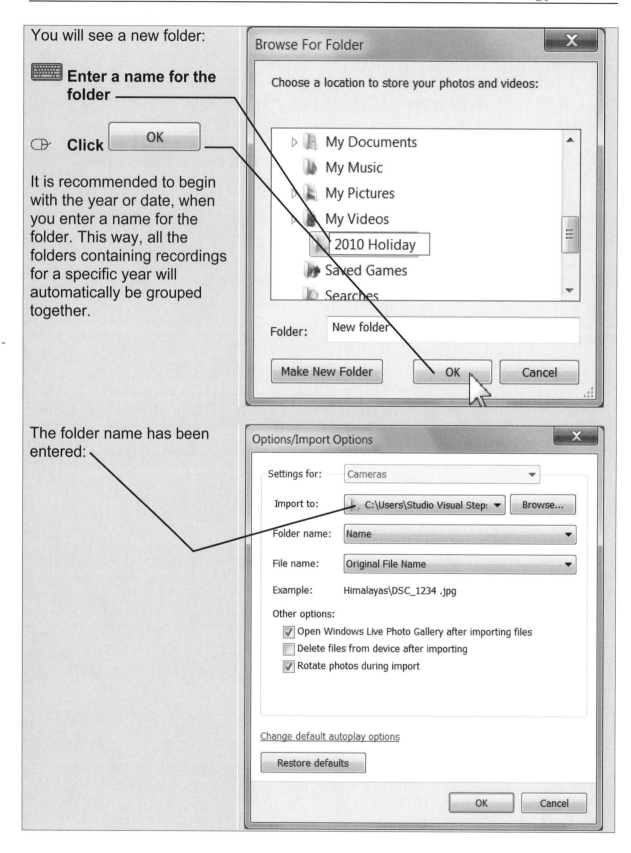

Browse For Folder

Choose a location to store your photos and videos:

▷ 🗐 My Documents
　 🎵 My Music
▷ 🖼 My Pictures
▷ 🎬 My Videos
　　 2010 Holiday
　 ▶ Saved Games
　 🔍 Searches

Folder: New folder

[Make New Folder]　[OK]　[Cancel]

Options/Import Options

Settings for: Cameras ▼

Import to: 　C:\Users\Studio Visual Step: ▼　[Browse...]

Folder name: Name ▼

File name: Original File Name ▼

Example: Himalayas\DSC_1234 .jpg

Other options:
☑ Open Windows Live Photo Gallery after importing files
☐ Delete files from device after importing
☑ Rotate photos during import

Change default autoplay options

[Restore defaults]

[OK]　[Cancel]

The file name starts with the date on which the file has been transferred to the computer. Usually, this is a different date from the recording date. You can also use the recording date in the file name, but if the images are recorded on different dates (for instance, during a trip) the files will be scattered among different folders. It is better to move all recordings from the same period to the same folder:

☞ **By** Folder name: **click**

Name

☞ **Click**
Date Taken Range + N

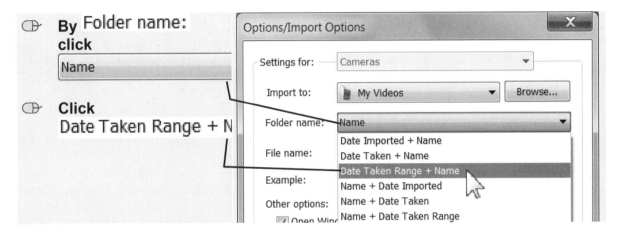

The day the recording was taken will be entered, starting with the earliest date.

Instead of using the original file name, you can enter a new file name yourself:

☞ **By** File name: **click**

Original File Name

If you select
Original File Name (Prese
the original folders will be copied from the camera as well.

Often, the original folder and file names on the camera are not very practical, and it is easier not to use them.

☞ **Click** Name

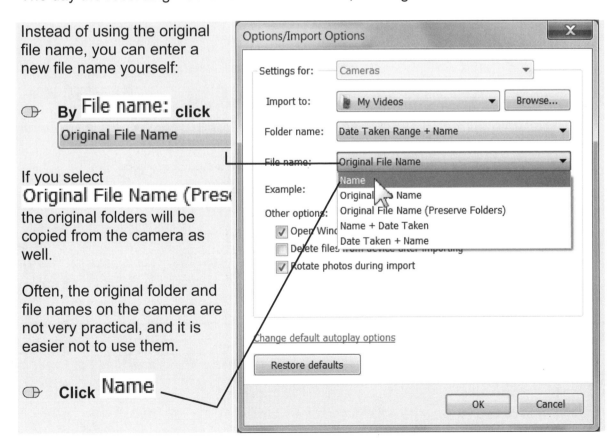

Tip

Revert to default settings
Did you change the settings and have you forgotten what the original settings were? Then you can restore the default settings:

In the bottom of the window:

Click

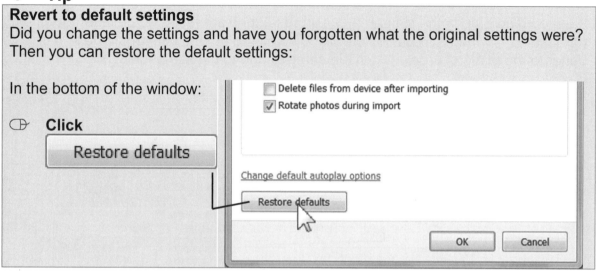

In the bottom of the window:

Click

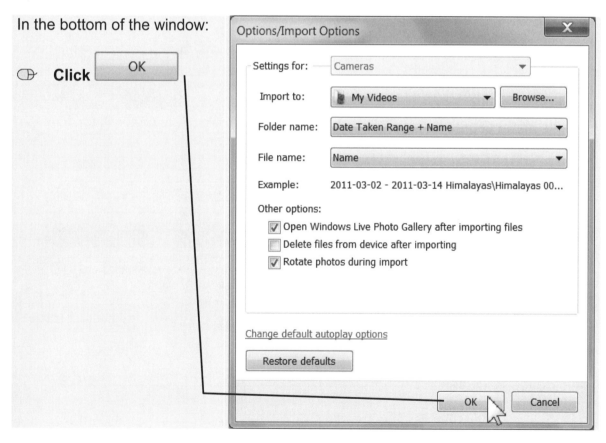

15.4 Importing All New Files

You can decide whether to import all new files, or make a selection yourself and import only the selected files. To import all new files:

 Please note:

If you do not want to import all the files, but just a selection, then you can continue with *Section 15.5 Importing selected files*.

 Tip

Import everything, or only selected files?
In most cases it is wiser to import all the files at once, and then decide later which files to keep. In the first place, you will have a clearer image of the video or photo on your computer screen. You can decide on the spot if you want to save all the images or delete some of them. This will also free up more space on your device for new recordings.

☞ **Click the radio button** ⦿ **by**
Import all new items now

⌨ **Type a name**

☞ **Click** [**Import**]

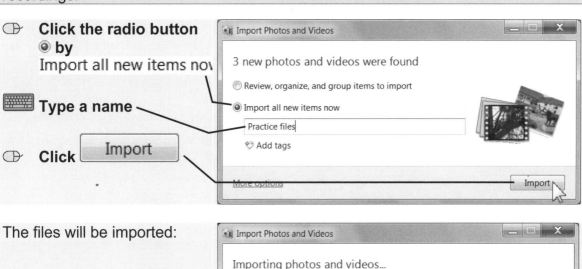

The files will be imported:

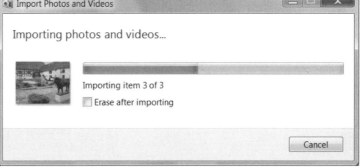

You will see the imported videos and photos (if any), in *Windows Live Photo Gallery*:

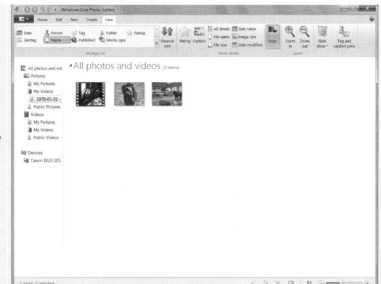

☞ **Close the window** 🐾²

When the import has finished, you can add the files to *Windows Live Movie Maker*. In *Section 9.2 Adding Video Files* you can read how to do this.

HELP! I see a different window.

If *Windows Live Photo Gallery* is not your default program for viewing photos, you will see this window:

☞ **Check the box** ☑ **by** Don't show me this again

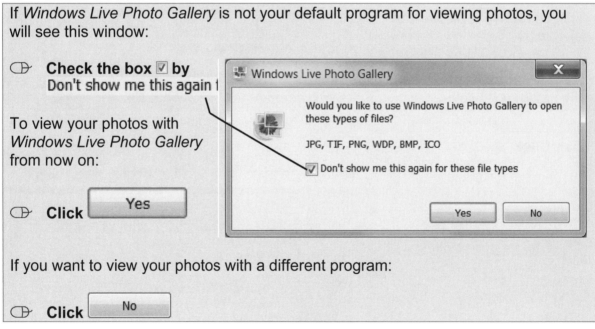

To view your photos with *Windows Live Photo Gallery* from now on:

☞ **Click** Yes

If you want to view your photos with a different program:

☞ **Click** No

15.5 Importing Selected Files

If you do not want to import all of the files, you can select only the files you want:

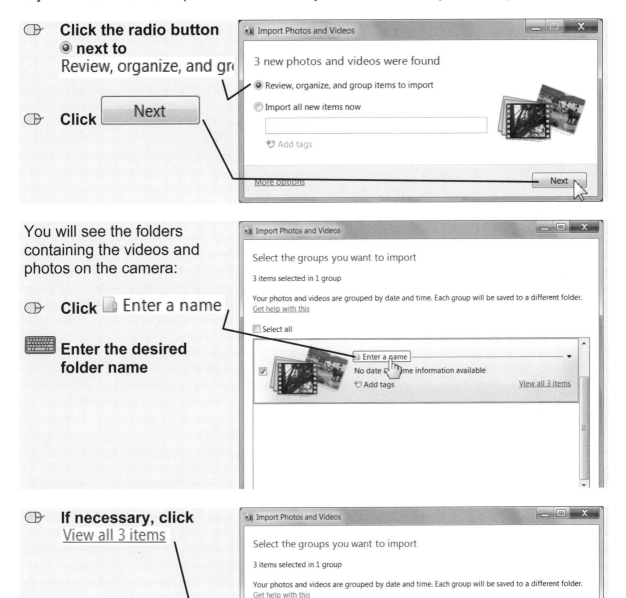

⊕ **Click the radio button**
⊙ next to
Review, organize, and gr⊙

⊕ **Click** [Next]

You will see the folders
containing the videos and
photos on the camera:

⊕ **Click** 📁 Enter a name

⌨ **Enter the desired**
folder name

⊕ **If necessary, click**
View all 3 items

☞ **Check the box ☑ next to the files you want to import**

You can choose one of these options:
- all the files on the camera
- all the files in a specific folder
- specific files

☞ **Click** Import

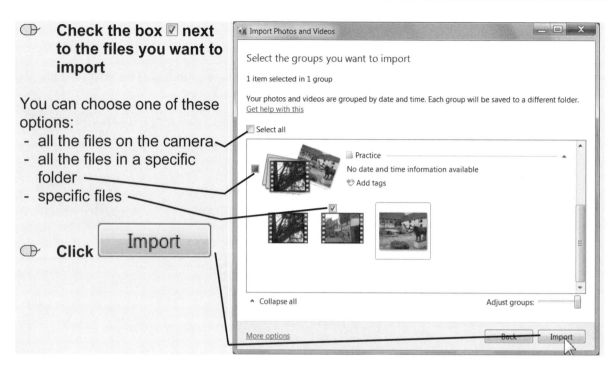

The files will be imported:

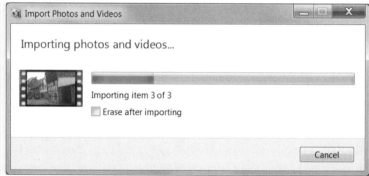

You will see the imported files in *Windows Live Photo Gallery*:

☞ **Close the window** 𝒫²

Afterwards, you can add these files to *Windows Live Movie Maker*. In *Section 9.2 Adding Video Files* you can read how to do this.

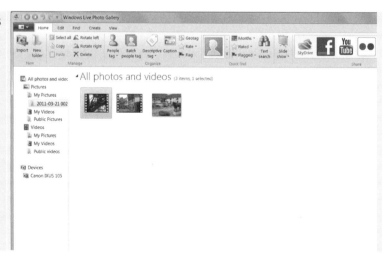

HELP! I see a different window.

If *Windows Live Photo Gallery* is not your default program for viewing photos, you will see this window:

☞ **Check the box** ☑ **at** Don't show me this again

To view your photos with *Windows Live Photo Gallery* from now on:

☞ **Click** ⟨ Yes ⟩

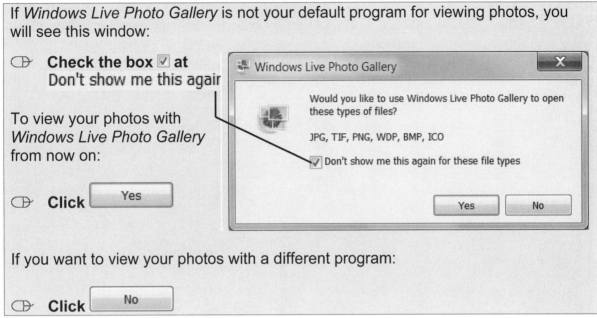

If you want to view your photos with a different program:

☞ **Click** ⟨ No ⟩

15.6 A Firewire Connection

You can connect your video recorder with a Firewire cable in the same way as a USB connection. First, you connect your digital video camera to your computer. You can do this by using the so-called Firewire, IEEE 1394 or i-link connection. This will only work on a computer that has this type of connection port built-in.

Your camera package will have included a small cable. Connect the smallest plug on this cable to your camera's DV OUT/ IN connector(or simply called DV):

The other end with the larger 6-pin plug is connected to the computer's Firewire connector:

Please note:

Some computers are equipped with a small Firewire connector. In that case, you will need to use a different cable, with a 4-pin plug on both ends. If necessary, check your camera and computer manual.

Next, turn the camera on, in *Play* mode (also called *Player* or *VCR* mode).

☞ **Close the *AutoPlay* window** 𝄇𝄇2

☞ **Start *Windows Live Movie Maker*** 𝄇𝄇7

You will see this window:

☞ **Click** [icon]

☞ **Click**

[camera icon] Import from devi

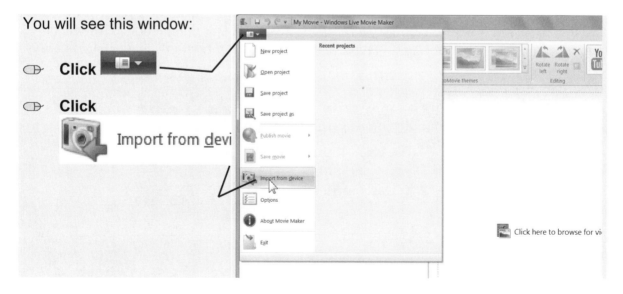

Click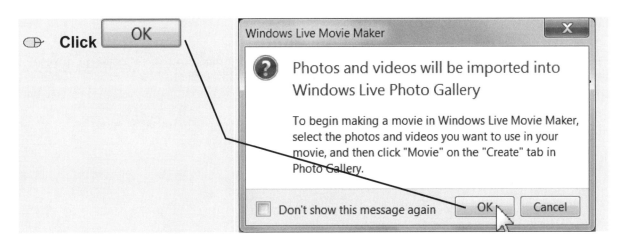

☞ **Connect the camera to the computer**

☞ **Turn the camera on**

Click the camera icon

Click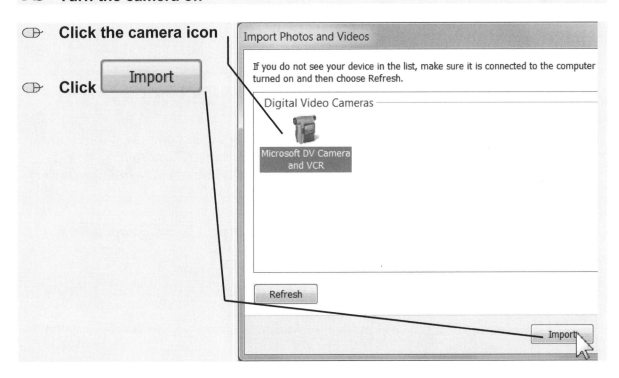

HELP! The camera cannot be found.

If your computer does not recognize your camera, you will see the following window:

Sometimes it takes a while
before the camera is
recognized:

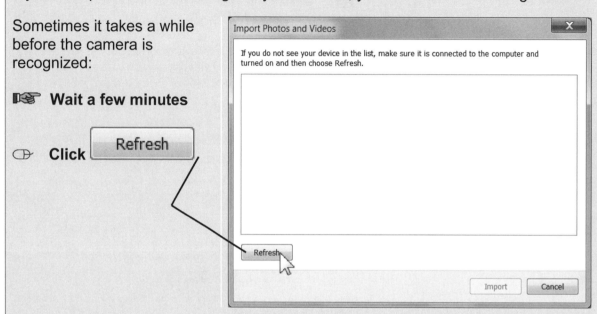

☞ **Wait a few minutes**

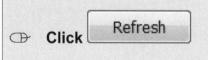 **Click** Refresh

If your camera still is not found, this may be caused by the following reasons:
- Your digital video camera is turned off.
- Your digital video camera is in stand-by mode. With some cameras, the stand-by mode is activated while the camera is in recording mode (*Camera* mode) and while the camera contains a tape, but no video or audio data is being transferred.

You can try a number of things:
- Check if your digital video camera is connected correctly to the computer, via a Firewire, IEE1394 or i-link connection.
- Check if your camera has been turned on and in *Play* mode.
- Turn your camera off and then turn it on again in *Play* mode (also called *Player* or *VCR* mode).

☞ **Click** Refresh

Source: Windows Help and Support

You will see this window:

⊕ **Click** More options

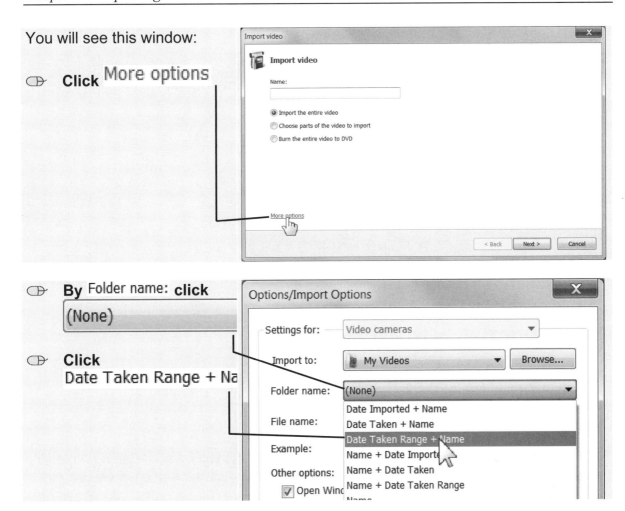

⊕ **By** Folder name: **click**
(None)

⊕ **Click**
Date Taken Range + Na

The day the recording was taken will be entered, starting with the earliest date.

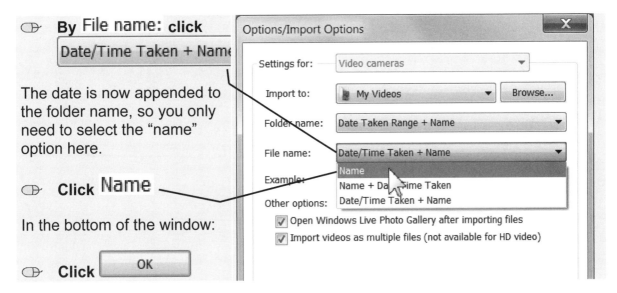

⊕ **By** File name: **click**
Date/Time Taken + Name

The date is now appended to the folder name, so you only need to select the "name" option here.

⊕ **Click** Name

In the bottom of the window:

⊕ **Click** OK

Tip

Revert to the default settings
Did you change the settings and have you forgotten what the original settings were?
Then you can restore the default settings:

In the bottom of the window:

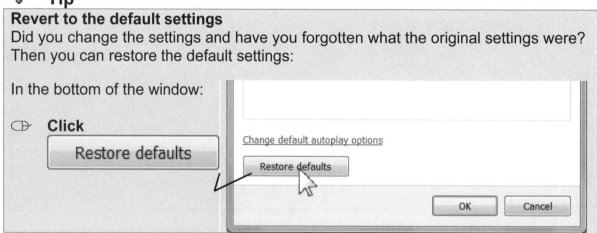

☞ **Click** Restore defaults

15.7 Importing Selected Parts

If you do not want to import the entire video, you can play the parts you want to
import and have them transferred to your computer simultaneously.

Please note:

If you select parts of a video yourself, the selected parts will be saved in a single file.
You will then need to split the file later in *Windows Live Movie Maker*. If you import
the entire video at once, the program will automatically split the video into separate
scenes. In *Section 15.8 Importing an Entire Video* you can read how to do this.

You will see this window:

 Enter a name for this
video

☞ **Click the radio button**
◉ by
Choose parts of the video t

☞ **Click** Next >

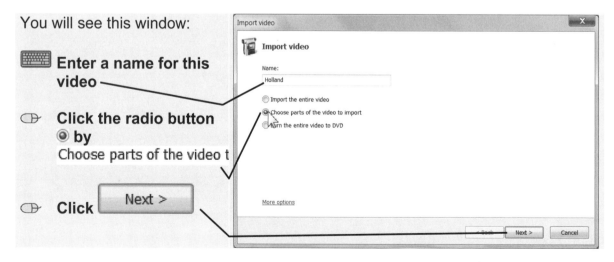

If your camera has recorded the scenes in wide-screen format:

⬤➤ **Check the box ☑ by**
Show widescreen preview

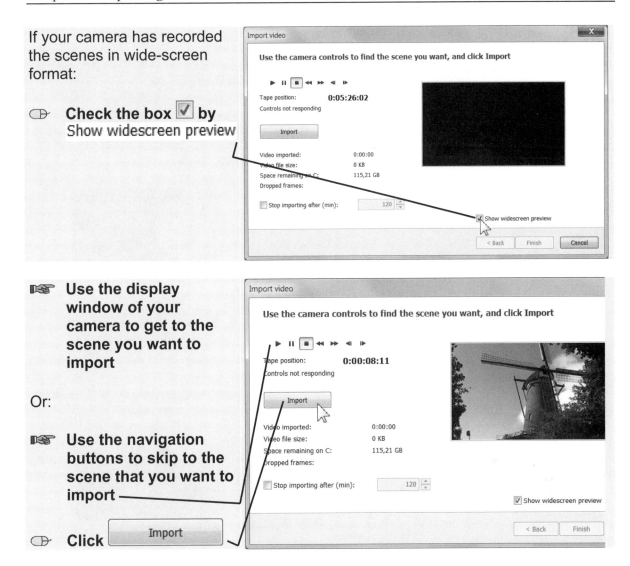

☞ **Use the display window of your camera to get to the scene you want to import**

Or:

☞ **Use the navigation buttons to skip to the scene that you want to import**

⬤➤ **Click** [Import]

You will see the images appear in the preview window, as they are imported.

To stop importing images:

⬤➤ **Click** [Stop]

☞ **Repeat these actions for each scene you want to import**

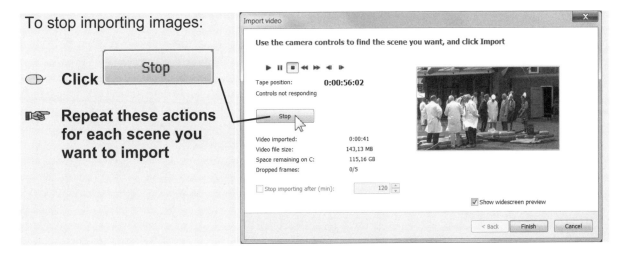

Tip

How large is the file that you have imported?
This window also shows you how large the segment is and how long it will take to play:

The duration of the imported scenes: ———————

The file size: ———————

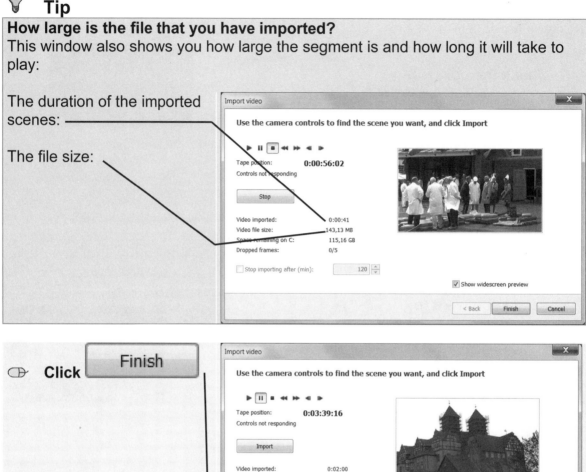

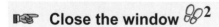 **Click** [**Finish**]

You will see the imported video:

☞ **Close the window** ⧉ ²

HELP! I see a different window.

If *Windows Live Photo Gallery* is not your default program for viewing photos, you will see the following window:

⬤ **Check the box ☑ by**
Don't show me this again for th

To view your photos with
Windows Live Photo Gallery
from now on:

⬤ **Click** [Yes]

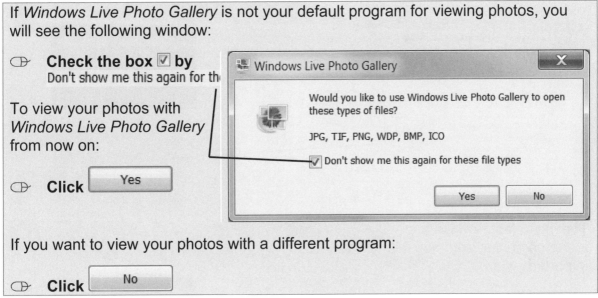

If you want to view your photos with a different program:

⬤ **Click** [No]

When the import has finished, you can add the files to your project. In *section 9.2 Adding Video Files* you can read how to do this.

15.8 Importing an Entire Video

You can also import the entire video at once. The video will automatically be split into separate scenes by *Windows Live Movie Maker*. The division will coincide with the recording times. If two scenes in a video are more than 30 seconds apart, they will be saved as separate scenes.

➤ **Please note:**

By **More options**, adjust the settings for the folder and file names, just like you did in *Section 15.6 A Firewire Connection*.

 Enter a name for this video

⬤ **Click the radio button ⬤ next to**
Import the entire video

In the bottom of the window:

⬤ **Click** [Next >]

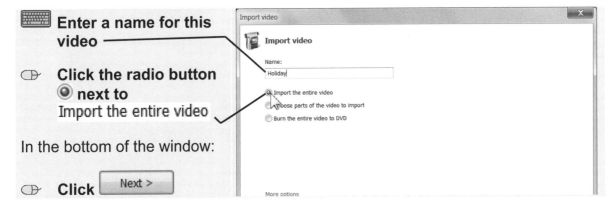

If your camera is recording in wide-screen mode:

☞ **Check the box ☑ by** Show widescreen preview

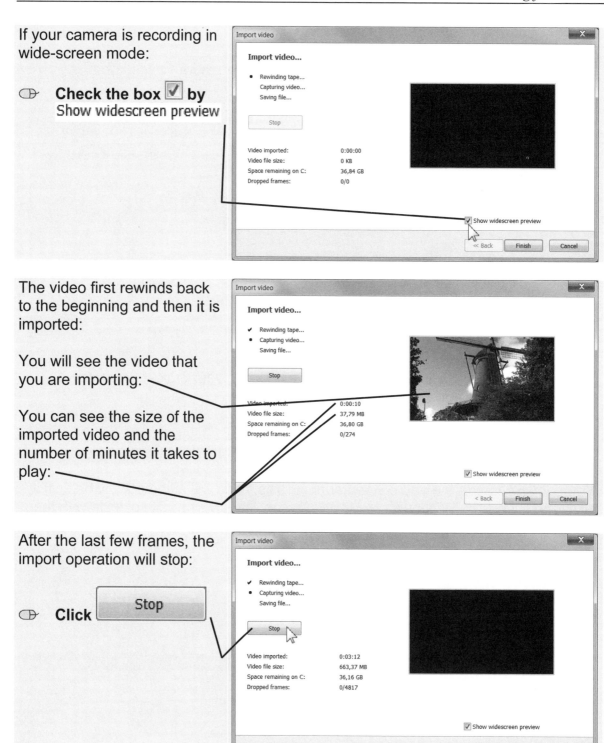

The video first rewinds back to the beginning and then it is imported:

You will see the video that you are importing:

You can see the size of the imported video and the number of minutes it takes to play:

After the last few frames, the import operation will stop:

☞ **Click** Stop

⊙ **Click** Yes

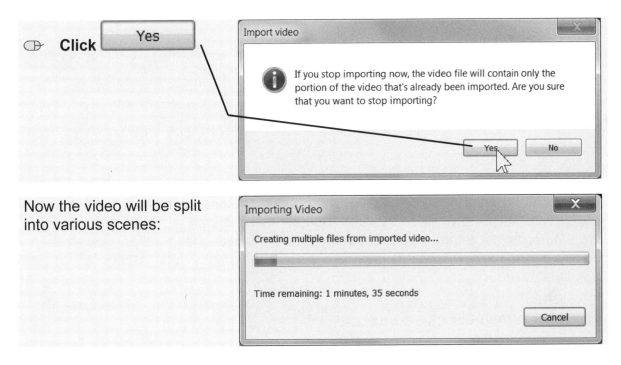

Now the video will be split into various scenes:

You will see that the imported video has been split into separate scenes. These scenes will be stored as individual files.

☞ **Close the window** ²

HELP! I see a different window.

If *Windows Live Photo Gallery* is not your default program for viewing photos, you will see the following window:

⊙ **Check the box** ☑ **by**
Don't show me this again

To view your photos with *Windows Live Photo Gallery* from now on:

⊙ **Click** Yes

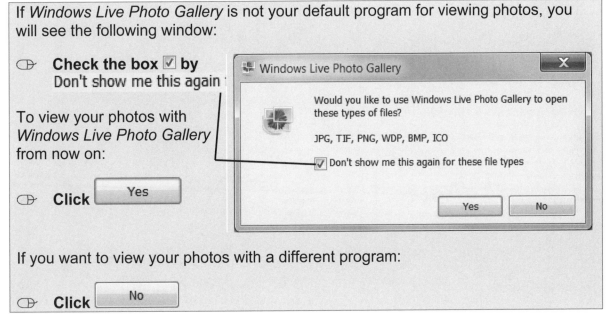

If you want to view your photos with a different program:

⊙ **Click** No

Please note:

The videos that you see in this *Windows Live Photo Gallery* window are the original files themselves. They do not contain *links* to the original files, like the project files you see in *Windows Live Movie Maker*.

You can now add the files to your project. In *Section 9.2 Adding Video Files* you can read how to do this.

In the previous chapters you have used the practice files to become acquainted with the various features in *Windows Live Movie Maker*. In this chapter you have learned how to import your own video material. So now you can start with your first real project. Do not forget to make a copy of your original video files, before you start editing them. These recordings may be precious and unique. You cannot record them a second time.

☞ **Close *Windows Live Movie Maker*** &8 ^{2}

15.9 Visual Steps Website and Newsletter

You may have noticed that the Visual Steps method is a great way to gather knowledge quickly and efficiently. All the books published by Visual Steps have been written using this same method. There are books available in a wide range of subject areas. For instance, there are books about *Windows*, photo editing and about free software applications, such as *Windows Live Essentials, Google Earth, Google Maps, Picasa* and *Skype*.

Book + software
One of the Visual Steps books includes a CD with the program that is discussed. The full version of this high quality, easy-to-use software is included. You can recognize this Visual Steps book with an enclosed CD by this logo on the book cover:

Website
Use the blue *Catalog* button on the **www.visualsteps.com** website to read an extensive description of all available Visual Steps titles, including the full table of contents and a sample chapter (as a PDF file). In this way you can find out if the book is what you expected.

This instructive website also contains:
- free computer booklets and informative guides (PDF files) on a range of subjects;
- free computer tips, that are described using the Visual Steps method;
- a large number of frequently asked questions and their answers;
- information on the free Computer certificate you can obtain on the online test website **www.ccforseniors.com**;
- free 'Notify me' e-mail service: receive an e-mail when a new book is published.

Visual Steps Newsletter
Do you want to keep yourself informed of all Visual Steps publications? Then you can subscribe (with no strings attached) to the free Visual Steps Newsletter, sent out at regular intervals by e-mail.

This Newsletter provides you with information on:
- the latest titles, as well as older books;
- special offers and discounts;
- new, free computer booklets and guides.

As a subscriber to the Visual Steps Newsletter you have direct access to the free booklets and guides, on the webpage **www.visualsteps.com/info_downloads**

15.10 Background Information

Dictionary

Firewire Firewire is a fast connection between the computer and an external device, such as an external hard drive or a camera. Firewire is also known as IEEE 1394, or IEEE 1394b. A Firewire connection is indicated by this symbol: .

Importing Transferring digital media files to *Windows Live Movie Maker*, so you can use these files in various projects.

SD card A Secure Digital card (SD card) is a memory card that can be used in portable electronic devices, such as digital cameras and mobile phones. You can buy special cards with a higher *write* speed and use them with your digital video and photo camera

USB USB connections (Universal Serial Bus) are often used for connecting external devices to your computer, for example a mouse, keyboard, scanner, printer, webcam, digital camera, mobile phone or an external hard drive. You can recognize a USB connection by the symbol that is usually printed on the

connector: .

Source: Windows Help and Support, Wikipedia

The history of the video camera

Video is not that old yet. The first video recorders that could record in black and white did not appear until the end of the sixties. They were soon followed by the color video recorders. The first video devices did not use tapes, but reels or spools.

The first video recorders that could use cassette tapes emerged at the beginning of the seventies. Various manufacturers developed their own systems. Philips had its V2000, Sony had Betamax and JVC developed the well-known VHS system. Eventually, the last system (VHS) was the one that prevailed.

Very soon after the first video recorders became available to the greater public, the first video cameras were released. If you wanted to use one of these cameras, you had to drag along quite a lot of equipment. The camera was a separate device, connected to the recorder by a cable. This recorder had to be carried separately and was rather heavy.

Within a few years, the video manufacturers developed lighter systems which could use smaller video cassettes. This is how the Video 8 and C(ompact) VHS systems emerged. They could use cassettes of the same size as the average audio cassette.

The newer compact systems did not need to use separate video recorders anymore, which was an advantage. The video recorder could be combined with the camera: the so-called *camcorder*. Earlier on, there had already been camcorders for the older, larger cassettes of the VHS and Betamax type, but they were too heavy and too sluggish to carry. To be able to manage these cameras, a lot of functions had to be eliminated, such as the fast forward and fast backward options. This was something you had to do on a regular video recorder. The more compact systems had no need to eliminate these types of functions, so these systems survived for a long time.

By the end of the nineties, the first digital video cameras were launched. These were Sony's Digital 8 system and the more popular DV system. This meant a greater technical change for the field of video recording because from this point on, images could be digitally recorded and edited. Not only was there a significant improvement in quality, it also became possible to import and edit video files directly on the computer.

- Continue reading on the next page -

The latest development is the High Definition (HD) video camera. The image format which these video cameras can record is about four times sharper than that of a traditional digital video camera. The results are spectacular. The tiniest details become visible, which renders the image much clearer and more sparkling. This is caused by the higher resolution of the HD recordings. A regular digital video camera composes the image of 576 image lines, while an HD camera uses 1080 lines.

However, this higher resolution results in much larger video files. If you want to edit these files in a video editing program, you will need to have a computer with lots of computing power and storage space.

Please note: when you are going to play your HD video movies on your television set, you will not see any difference on your regular TV. You will only be able to see how clear the images are, if you view them on a TV that is suitable for displaying HD images.

Nowadays, all major digital video camera manufacturers produce at least one type of HD camera.

Different kinds of video cameras

If you want to record videos, you can choose from a wide variety of cameras. Each has their own advantages and drawbacks:

Analog cameras
This is the original video system that has been used for many years. The most famous system is the Video 8 system. Advantage: currently this type of camera is relatively cheap.
Drawback: the quality of this camera is now inferior to the digital systems.

- Continue reading on the next page -

Digital8

The digital video system that is exclusively used by Sony. It is based on the analog Video 8 system. Advantage: the camera can also play older Video 8 tapes and is cheaper than a MiniDV.
Drawback: the camera is bigger and inferior to MiniDV. There is also a smaller selection of cameras available.

MiniDV

The other digital video system. MiniDV is not just a Sony product. All well-known video manufacturers sell MiniDV cameras, which record the video material on tape.
Advantage: apart from HD, it offers the best quality, it is compact and there is a wide variety of models. After the release of the HD video camera, this type of camera has become less expensive.

8 cm DVD

In this type of camera the tape has been replaced by a mini DVD disk that records the images. Advantage: you can immediately view the DVD disk on your television. Drawback: the image quality is less than that of a tape. This is a result of the image compression.

- Continue reading on the next page -

Hard disk recorder

In this type of recorder, no removable storage medium is used (such as a tape or a DVD). Instead, the recorder has a built-in hard drive to record the images.
Drawback: the image quality is not quite as good as the tape recordings, due to the compression factor.

HD DVD recorder

The latest generation of video cameras offers you a choice between cameras that use a tape, a built-in hard drive, an 8 cm DVD or a memory stick/card.

Different manufacturers use different image formats:

AVCHD (very strong compression) and MPEG2 (larger files, but better quality).
Advantage: excellent image quality.
Drawback: currently quite expensive, large video files.

- Continue reading on the next page -

Camcorder

In the last few years, the sales figures for digital camcorders have greatly increased. These cameras record digital images on a digital storage medium, such as a flash memory card, a hard drive or a tape. After recording, you can transfer the video images directly to the computer with a Firewire or USB cable.

With the release of flash memory cards with a larger capacity, for instance the 32 GB SDHC cards, it has become possible to record several hours of video material in HD quality. Camcorders that use flash memory exclusively are lighter and smaller, and do not contain any mechanical storage components, which makes them less prone to malfunction. In time, we expect these types of flash memory cards to replace all other storage media. Also, digital photo cameras and mobile phones will eventually take over some of the tasks of the traditional camcorders.

Advantage: cameras and memory cards are less expensive.
Drawback: limited storage capacity, lower video quality due to compression.

How does a digital video camera work?

The digital video camera uses a CCD chip to transfer the image to digital information. CCD stands for Charged Coupled Device. A CCD chip is a light-sensitive chip. The light enters the camera through the lens.
The CCD chip converts the light to digital information. Next, this digital information is transferred to the video cassette.

Eventually, the number of pixels and the size of the CCD chip will determine the quality of the recorded image. Most consumer cameras use a single CCD chip. But there also exist cameras with three CCD chips: one for each basic color (red, green, blue). These cameras deliver high quality images, but are much more expensive. Such cameras are almost exclusively used for professional purposes.

Advantages and drawbacks of various storage media
If you want to buy a traditional digital video camera, you can choose between cameras that record images on a tape, on a mini DVD (8 cm) or a built-in hard drive. The newest generation of HD video cameras has added memory sticks and memory cards to this selection.

Each storage medium has its own, specific advantages and drawbacks. We have made an overview for you:

Tape **Advantages:**
- easily obtainable;
- inexpensive;
- long recording time;
- better recording quality than other storage media;
- tape is great as an archive for your images.

Drawbacks:
- difficult to retrieve specific sections of the movie;
- risky, the images can be deleted by accident;
- transferring the images to the computer takes a lot of time.

8 cm mini DVD **Advantages:**
- easily obtainable;
- can be copied directly to the computer;
- disk can be played on latest DVD players right away.

Drawbacks:
- limited recording capacity (twenty minutes max);
- image quality not as good as tapes, due to compression.

Built-in hard disk **Advantages:**
- large recording capacity (hours);
- no risk of overwriting older recordings;
- quick transfer to computer;
- specific sections of the movie can quickly be found.

Drawbacks:
- full is full; when the disk is full, the images need to be transferred to the computer;
- lower image quality, due to compression;
- high power consumption.

- Continue reading on the next page -

Memory card/ memory stick	**Advantages:** • quick transfer to computer; • low power consumption; • small, light, silent. **Drawbacks:** • limited recording capacity; • image quality not as good as tapes, due to compression.

Analog video cameras

Before the digital video cameras appeared on the scene, the market had been cornered by the analog video cameras. The difference between digital and analog lies in the way the information is recorded. A digital camera stores the information in separate bits, where each bit can take only two values: 0 or 1. The analog camera stores the information in the form of a single, lengthy, uninterrupted signal. You can also look at it this way: when you send a message by telegraph, the message is conveyed in the shape of dots and dashes, while talking to somebody on the phone relays the message by means of sound waves.

Digital recording has several advantages over analog recording:

- the image and sound quality is better;
- copying and assembling the images will not result in loss of quality;
- the images and sound can be stored for a much longer period;
- the images and sounds can be edited directly on a computer.

You might still have some recordings that you have made with your analog video camera. You can use your computer to convert these recordings to digital versions and then burn them to a CD or a DVD. This conversion process is called *capturing*. If necessary, you can even enhance the images on your computer by using video editing software. Afterwards, you will have produced a recording that will last much longer.

To be able to transfer the images from an analog camera to a computer, the computer needs to be equipped with a video capture card; such a card will transfer the analog information into digital information. You can connect the video camera with a coax cable, a scart cable, or an S video cable. You can use the software that comes packaged with the video capture card to transfer the information to the computer. Make sure you have enough storage space available, because a video can take up to 30 MB per second of storage capacity.

- Continue reading on the next page -

While you are converting the images, you can select various settings to enhance the quality of the video. For example, you can make the image brighter, or remove ragged borders. You can also compress the images, without loss of quality; this way, they will take up less space on your computer.

When you are satisfied with the final result of the analog to digital conversion, you can burn the movie to a CD or a DVD. If you select the correct settings, you can even play such a CD on a DVD player as a video CD or DVD.

Video capture card and Firewire card

If you want to transfer video images and sounds from your digital video camera to your computer, but your camera does not have a USB connection, you will need a video capture card or a Firewire card. Your computer also needs to have the required slots built-in. You can connect a special cable to such a card (usually included in the package of the camera, or the card).

A video capture card performs two important actions. The first function is only relevant if you own an old-fashioned analog camera. You can edit the images you have made with this camera on your computer, but first you will need to convert the analog information to digital information. A computer can only process digital information. A video capture card converts analog images to digital images, so the computer will be able to process them.

The second function of a video capture card is to compress the images. Video images take up a good deal of space. A single minute of video footing can result in a 1 GB file. If you would transfer these images directly from a MiniDV camera to the computer, in a matter of minutes your hard drive would be completely full. In such a case it would not be possible to assemble the images on the computer. To prevent this from happening, the video images need to be compressed. A video capture card will do this for you.

To transfer analog images to your computer, you need to have an analog-digital video capture card. To capture digital images you can use a digital-digital video capture card. Video recordings that have been made with a camera that uses a hard drive, DVD or memory card are already compressed; that is why these images do not need to be compressed when they are transferred to the computer.

Video capture card

Firewire, i-link or IEEE 1394 card

- Continue reading on the next page -

You can also use a so-called Firewire card to transfer images from a digital camera to your computer. A Firewire card transfers information to the computer very fast. This card is not a specific video card, so you can use it for other purposes as well. For instance, for quickly copying information from an external hard drive to your computer. Another advantage of a Firewire card is that it is relatively inexpensive.

Please note: ask your retailer for professional advice on the type of card you need. You can buy several types of cards with varying read and write speeds. Which card is best suited for your purpose, depends on your hardware and your specific demands.

15.11 Tips

 Tip

Adding files from Windows Live Photo Gallery
If you want to add files to your *Windows Live Movie Maker* project, immediately after you have imported them, you can do that directly from *Windows Live Photo Gallery*:

☞ **Select the video(s) you want to edit**

☞ **Click the Create tab**

☞ **Click Movie**

Windows Live Movie Maker will be opened:

Now the selected videos have been added.

You can start assembling your movie.

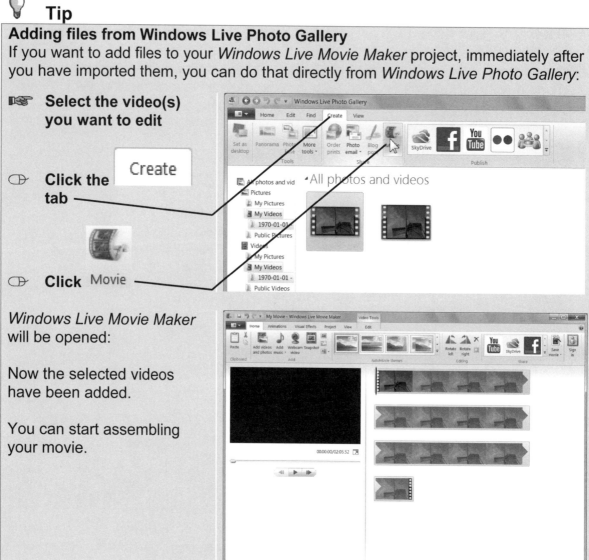

Tip

Present your own movie, use a webcam

Does your computer have a webcam? Then you can record yourself while you are adding your commentary to the movie. You can save these recordings and add them to your video later on. This will provide a nice interlude, and add a personal touch to your movie.

☞ **Position the playback indicator on the spot where you want to insert the recording**

⊕ **Click the** Home **tab**

⊕ **Click** Webcam video

You will see the image recorded by the webcam:

⊕ **Click** Record

When you have finished:

⊕ **Click** Stop

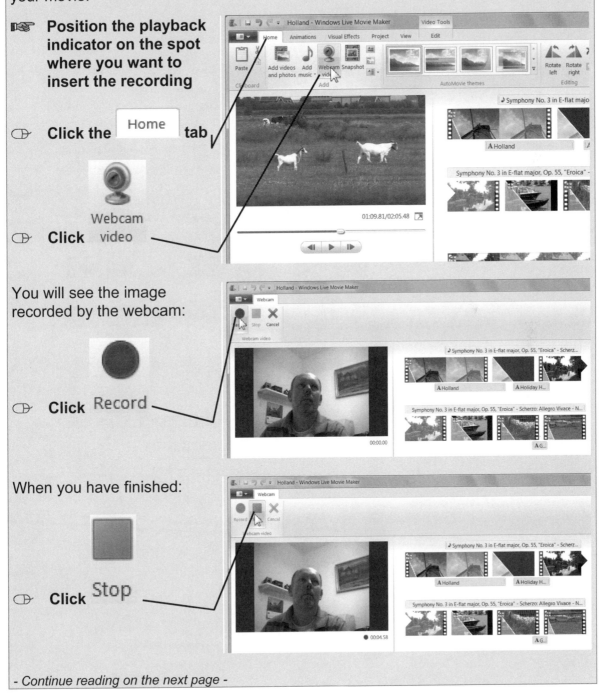

- *Continue reading on the next page -*

☞ **Change the file name, if you want**

⊙ **Click** Save

The recording has been inserted:

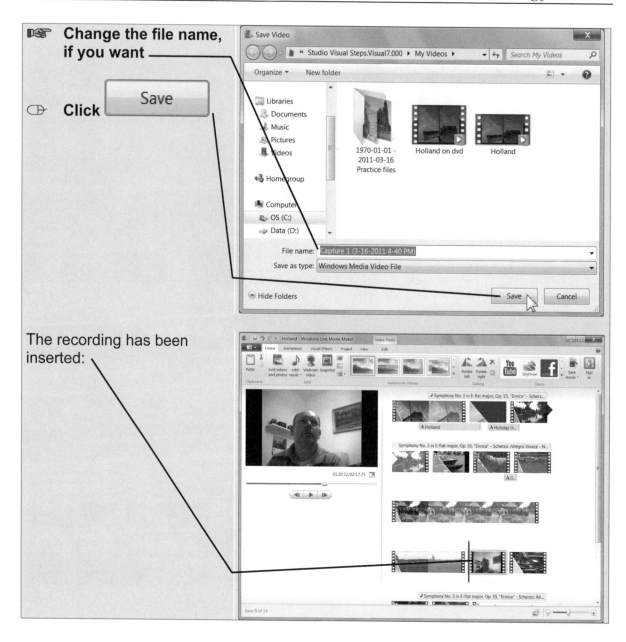

Appendix A. How Do I Do That Again?

In this book you will find many instructions and exercises that are marked with footsteps: 1 Find the corresponding number in the appendix below to see how to perform a specific action.

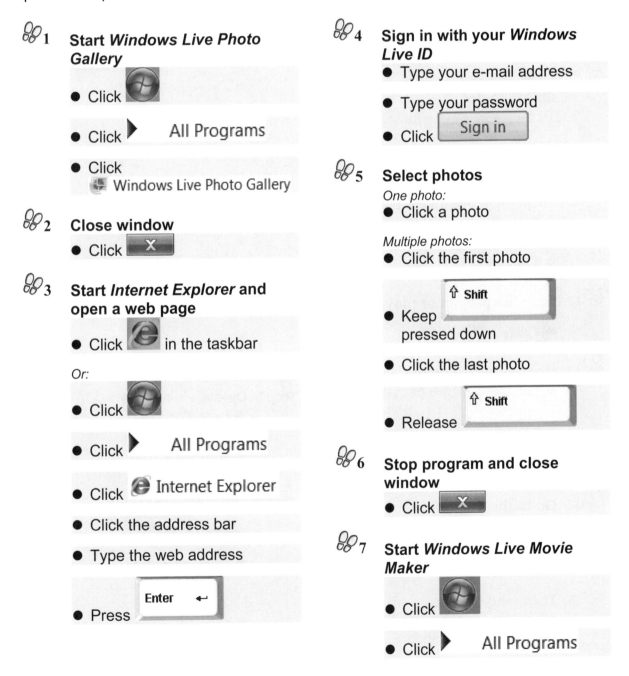

1 Start *Windows Live Photo Gallery*

● Click

● Click All Programs

● Click
   Windows Live Photo Gallery

2 Close window

● Click X

3 Start *Internet Explorer* and open a web page

● Click in the taskbar

Or:

● Click

● Click All Programs

● Click Internet Explorer

● Click the address bar

● Type the web address

● Press Enter

4 Sign in with your *Windows Live ID*

● Type your e-mail address

● Type your password

● Click Sign in

5 Select photos

One photo:
● Click a photo

Multiple photos:
● Click the first photo

● Keep ⇧ Shift pressed down

● Click the last photo

● Release ⇧ Shift

6 Stop program and close window

● Click X

7 Start *Windows Live Movie Maker*

● Click

● Click All Programs

- Click
  Windows Live Movie Maker

₰₰ 8 Open the *Practice Files* folder

- Click Documents

- Click Practice Files Photo editing

  or Practice Files Video editing

₰₰ 9 Open the *Documents* library/folder

- Click Documents

₰₰ 10 Play project or movie

- Click the place in the project where you want the playback to start.

- Click ▶

₰₰ 11 Stop the project or movie

- Click ⏸

₰₰ 12 Open photo in editing window

- Double-click the photo

₰₰ 13 Save the project

- Click 💾

₰₰ 14 Go to the beginning

- Press Home

₰₰ 15 Trimming a video

- Drag the playback indicator to the desired location

- Click the tab
- Click ⊢ Set end point

Or:

- Click ⊢ Set start point

₰₰ 16 Move video files

- Click the file

- Drag the file to the desired location

Or:

- Click the file

- Click ✂

- Click the video clip that comes before the new video clip

- Click Paste

₰₰ 17 Delete video files

- Click the file

- Click ✕

₰₰ 18 Open a project

- Click

- Click the project

Or:

- Click

- Click  Open project

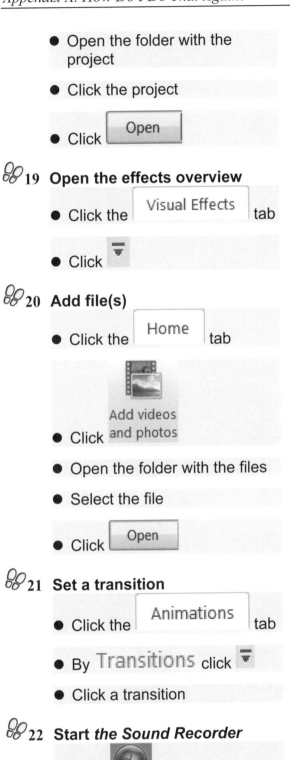

- Open the folder with the project

- Click the project

- Click ⬚ Open

19 Open the effects overview

- Click the ⬚ Visual Effects ⬚ tab

- Click ⬚

20 Add file(s)

- Click the ⬚ Home ⬚ tab

- Click ⬚ Add videos and photos

- Open the folder with the files

- Select the file

- Click ⬚ Open

21 Set a transition

- Click the ⬚ Animations ⬚ tab

- By Transitions click ⬚

- Click a transition

22 Start *the Sound Recorder*

- Click ⬚

- Click ▶ All Programs

- Click ⬚ Accessories

- Click ⬚ Sound Recorder

23 Start recording

- Click ⬚ ● Start Recording

24 Save recording

- Click ⬚ ■ Stop Recording

- Type a name for the audio file

- Click ⬚ Save

25 Adding background music

- Click ⬚ Add music ▾

To add music from the beginning:

- Click ⬚ Add music...

To add music at a specific point in the video:

- Click ⬚ Add music at the current point.

- Open the folder with the music

- Click the audio file

- Click ⬚ Open

26 Publish the movie

- Click ⬚

- Click ⬚ Publish movie

- Click one of the options

27 **Select text**

- Position the mouse pointer at the beginning of the first word

- Press the mouse button and keep it pressed in

- Drag over the text you want to select

- Release the mouse button

Appendix B. Create a YouTube Account

If you want to upload your movies to *YouTube*, you will need to have an account. This is how you create one:

☞ **Open the web page www.youtube.com** 🦶3

In the top right of your window:

☞ **Click**
   Create Account

By **Email Address**:

⌨ **Type an e-mail address**

By **Username**:

⌨ **Type a user name**

☞ **Click**
   Check Availability

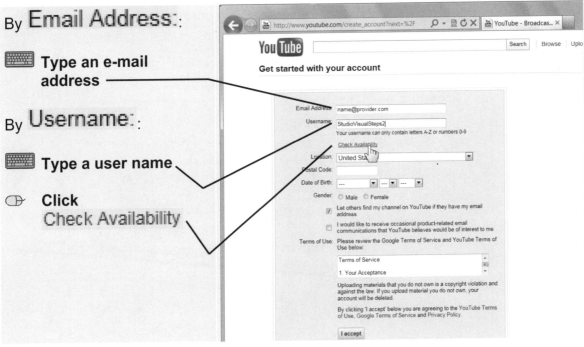

If the name you entered is not available, or not valid, try a different name.

If the name is valid, you will see **Username available!**:

☞ **Enter the remaining information**

◑ **If necessary, drag the scroll bar downwards**

◑ **Click** I accept

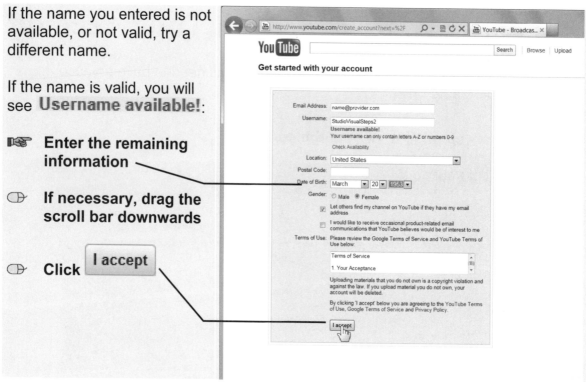

If you already have a *Google* account, you will see this window:

◑ **Click** Link accounts

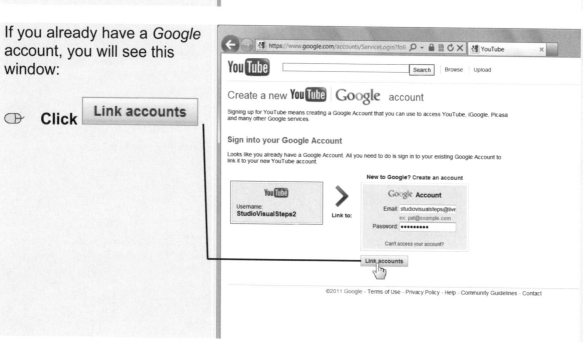

If you don't have a *Google* account, you will see this window:

Type your e-mail address

Type a password

Retype the password

Type the letters in this image

Please note: you will see different letters on your own screen.

☞ **Click**

Create my new ac

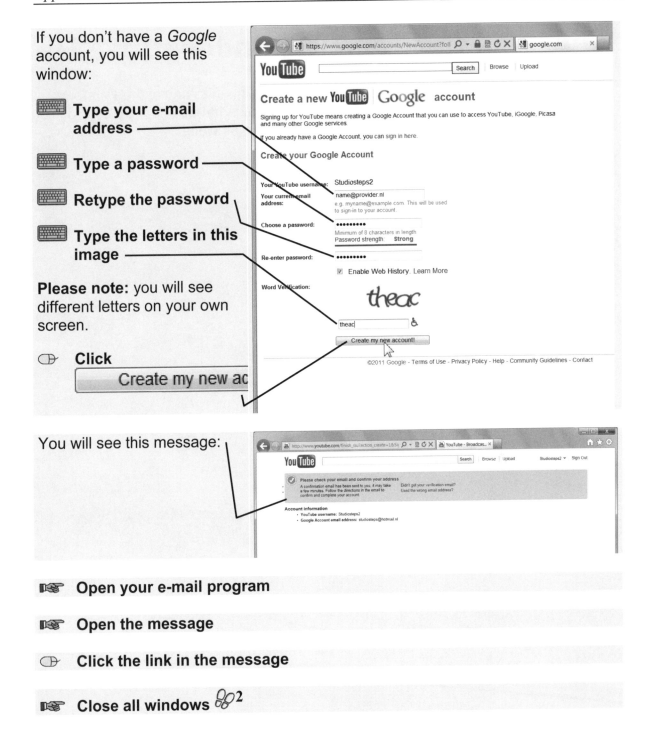

You will see this message:

☞ **Open your e-mail program**

☞ **Open the message**

☞ **Click the link in the message**

☞ **Close all windows** 🦶²

Appendix C. Create a Windows Live ID

You will need to have a *Windows Live ID* in order to sign in to any of the *Windows Live* products or services. This ID consists of an e-mail address and a password. You will also be asked to enter some additional information as well.

☞ **Open the web page home.live.com** ✇³

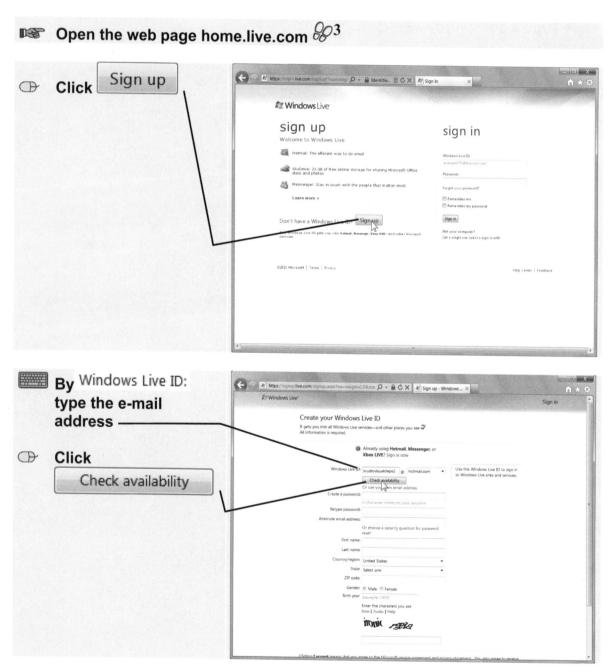

⊕ **Click** Sign up

⌨ **By** Windows Live ID:
type the e-mail
address

⊕ **Click**
Check availability

If the name you entered is not
available, or not valid, try a
different name.

By
Create a password:
type a password

By Retype password:
**retype the same
password**

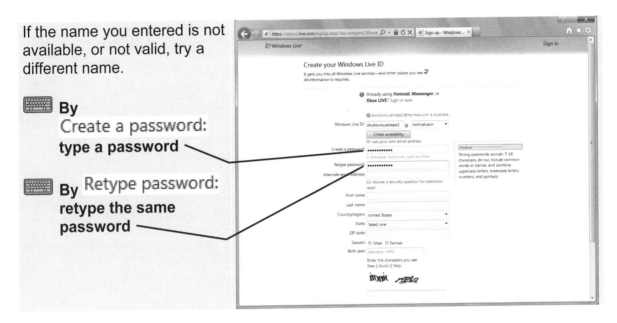

In case you forget your password, you can enter an alternative e-mail address. You
can also choose a secret question that will help you reset your password in the
future.

Click
Or choose a security ques
reset

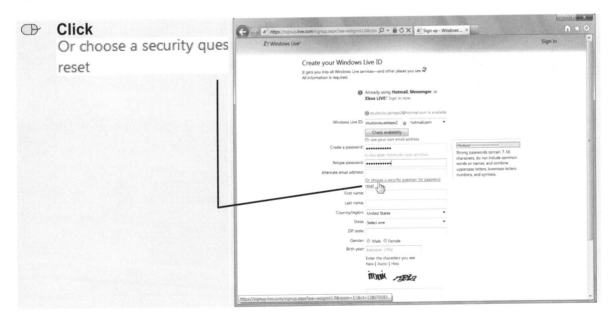

☞ By Select one select
a question ⎯⎯⎯

⌨ By Secret answer:
type your answer

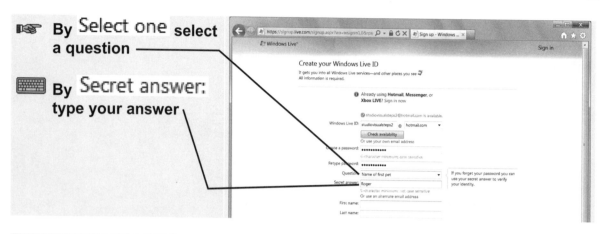

⊕ Drag the scroll bar
downwards ⎯⎯⎯

⌨ Type the remaining
information

You will see an image with a
number of characters for you
to copy.

⌨ Type the characters
from the image ⎯⎯

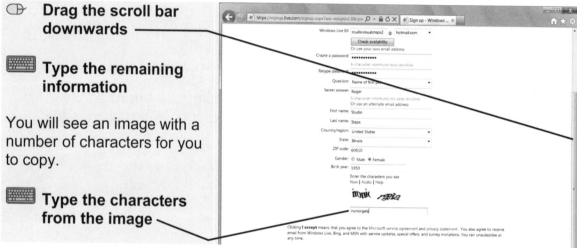

At the bottom of the window:

⊕ Click [I accept]

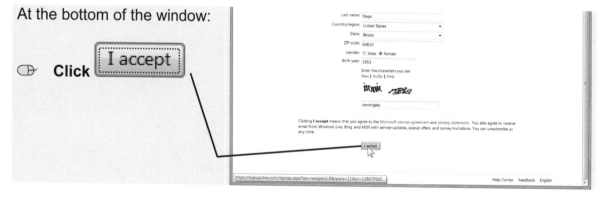

Now you will see your *Inbox*.
You can close this page:

⊕ Click [X]

Appendix D. Index

Z

Windows Live Essentials for SENIORS

Windows Live Essentials for SENIORS
Get acquainted with free Windows Live Essentials applications

Author: Studio Visual Steps
ISBN: 978 90 5905 356 4
Book type: Paperback
Number of pages: 280 pages
Accompanying website:
www.visualsteps.com/windowslive

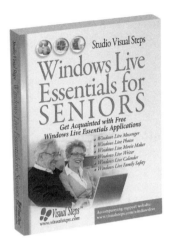

Are you already taking advantage of the free Windows Live Essentials programs that Microsoft has to offer? The Windows Live Essentials package includes lots of useful software, part of which will be installed to your computer, while other programs are accessible on the Internet. For example, from any place in the world you can use the Internet to access your e-mail messages, your calendar, and your address book.
Do you take a lot of pictures, and do you want to share them with friends? With just a few mouse clicks you can convert your own Windows Live web space into a beautiful photo album. Also, you can edit video files en change them into online movies, or conduct a video conversation and have a live chat with your friends. Furthermore, you will get 25 GB online storage space for your personal files on the Windows Live servers – this comes in useful if you want to use these files on different computers. And the free Windows Live Essentials software also contains lots of other features.
In this book you will learn how to use all the program elements in an efficient and effective way, step by step and for various applications. With Windows Live Essentials you have access to the latest developments in the field of computing!

Learn how to:
- have a video chat with Windows Live Messenger
- create an online photo album with Windows Live photos
- make movies with Windows Live Movie Maker
- create a blog with Windows Live Writer
- share files with Windows Live Groups
- maintain a digital calendar with Windows Live Calendar
- set parental controls with Windows Live Family Safety

This book is suitable for:
- Windows 7
- Windows Vista

Microsoft Office 2010 and 2007 for SENIORS

Microsoft Office 2010 and 2007 for SENIORS
Practical applications for everyday usage

Author: Studio Visual Steps
ISBN: 978 90 5905 177 5
Book type: Paperback
Nr of pages: 440 pages
Accompanying website:
www.visualsteps.com/officeseniors

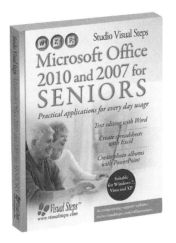

This practical book will help you accomplish everyday tasks more quickly and efficiently. You will learn how to work with the most essential features in Word, Excel and PowerPoint. Create professional looking documents in Word by using Quick Styles and document themes. Use Artistic Effects to apply a wide range of special effects to images inserted into your documents. Choose from a variety of templates to create your own custom greeting cards or booklets.
In Excel you will learn how to keep track of your family finances by creating a budget spreadsheet. Choose from a variety of built-in formulas to automatically calculate and analyze columns of data. You can also use Excel as a database to maintain lists of your CD/DVD collection, your books or your stamp collection.
In PowerPoint you will learn how to create a beautiful slideshow highlighting pictures from a recent vacation. You can liven up your presentations by adding text, illustrations, audio clips, video clips and voice messages to your slides. You can then share your presentation with family or friends by sending it in an e-mail, burning it to a CD, or copying it to a USB stick.

Please note: You will need to have Office 2010 or Office 2007 already installed on your computer in order to work with this book.

Learn how to:
- create letters, greeting cards and brochures in Word
- create a budget spreadsheet, manage, store and filter information in Excel
- create a photo album with audio, video and transition effects in PowerPoint

Suitable for:
- Word, Excel and PowerPoint version 2010 and 2007
- Windows 7, Vista and XP